Human
Rights &
SOCIAL
TECHNOLOGY

THE NEW WAR ON
DISCRIMINATION

Human
Rights &
SOCIAL
TECHNOLOGY

THE NEW WAR ON DISCRIMINATION

Rainer Knopff
With Thomas Flanagan

Carleton University Press
Ottawa, Canada
1990

©Carleton University Press Inc. 1989

ISBN   0-88629-088-0   (paperback)
        0-88629-097-X   (casebound)

Printed and bound in Canada
Reprinted 1990
Carleton Library Series #156

Canadian Cataloguing in Publication Data

Knopff, Rainer, 1948-
    Human rights and social technology

(The Carleton library; 156)
Includes index.
ISBN 0-88629-097-X (bound) —
ISBN 0-88629-088-0 (pbk.)

    1. Human rights—Government policy—Canada.
    2. Discrimination—Government policy—Canada.
    I. Title. II. Series.

    KE4395.K66 1989   323.4'0971   C89-090143-0

Distributed by: Oxford University Press Canada
                   70 Wynford Drive,
                   Don Mills, Ontario.
                   Canada. M3C 1J9
                   (416) 441-2941

Cover Design: Robert Chitty

Acknowledgements

Carleton University Press gratefully acknowledges the support extended to its publishing programme by the Canada Council and the Ontario Arts Council.

This book is published with the help of a grant from the Social Science Federation of Canada, using funds provided by the Social Sciences and Humanities Research Council of Canada.

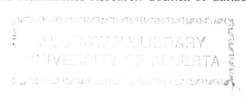

For
K. H. K.
and
R. J. K.

Table of Contents

PREFACE

The evolution of political language makes a fascinating study. History is strewn with words of political rhetoric that begin with one meaning and end with quite another. In North America, for example, today's conservatives are yesterday's liberals, while yesterday's conservatives are nowhere to be found. This transformation of meaning is often driven by the rhetorical needs of those who oppose successful political parties or programs. The word liberalism is a prominent modern example. So successful was classical liberalism that its opponents on the left have often found that they could best succeed by stealing the label, forcing classical liberals to define themselves as "conservatives," something the latter often do reluctantly and with a bad conscience, knowing full well they are not really conservatives and thus insisting on the prefix "neo."

The fate of liberalism as such is shared by its central concepts, particularly the idea of "rights." Virtually every regime in the world claims the term as its own, even marxist regimes, whose theoretical founder considered the notion a bourgeois relic. Nor does Jeremy Bentham's disdainful dismissal of rights as "nonsense upon stilts" find much public resonance in liberal democracies. All parties and political schools claim to have the proper understanding of rights and the policies best suited to protecting or promoting them. In this book I am concerned with how the language of human rights has been successfully appropriated by the partisans of a novel form of anti-discrimination policy, one in which the term discrimination has itself been linguistically transformed, meaning something today that its earlier opponents would not have recognized. More traditional liberal rights now tend to march under the banner of "fundamental freedoms."

An inevitable by-product of such stretching of political language is a decline in conceptual clarity. Turning old words to new purposes is rhetorically attractive because it allows people to think that new goods can be pursued without abandoning old ones, that hard choices need not be made. This is rarely the case. This book is about the illiberal (using the term now in its early modern sense) aspects of recent or emerging developments in "human rights" policy. It considers these developments mainly in the Canadian context, but the same trends are evident in all of the Western liberal democracies and the analysis is thus of wider significance.

The book focuses on three interrelated "equality rights" initiatives: 1) anti-discrimination legislation enforced by human rights commissions, 2) the constitutional prohibition of discrimination in section 15 of the new *Canadian Charter of Rights and Freedoms*, and 3) affirmative action programs. This list of contemporary anti-discrimination policies is not exhaustive—it does not, for example, include the burgeoning policy of "equal pay for work of equal value" (known in the United States as "comparable worth")—but it is sufficient for my purpose, which is not to write a textbook but to make an argument.

The battle against discrimination embodied in these policies has undergone two interrelated transformations since its initial flowering in the period after World War II. First is the shift from an attack on direct discrimination based on irrational prejudice or bigotry to a broader attack on prospective decision making and the generalizations underlying it. This change is, in part, the fulfillment of the rhetoric of individualized treatment so often used to justify anti-discrimination policy; its most obvious manifestation is the steady proliferation in the number and kinds of prohibited grounds of discrimination. Early anti-discrimination legislation protected mainly racial, ethnic, and religious groups; today Canadian legislation contains thirty prohibited grounds of discrimination, including such traits as age, mental disability, and sexual preference.

Second is the increasing tendency to define discrimination not as the *act* of differential treatment arising out of some form of mistaken categorical thinking but as the effect of a non-discriminatory *behaviour* on one of the protected groups, a development reflecting the current emphasis on the achievement of equality of group results rather than mere formal equality of

10

opportunity for individuals. For example, educational qualifications for employment have been challenged not only because they are unwarranted generalizations but also because of their contribution to the overall inequality of "undereducated" racial and ethnic groups.

My central argument is that this "new war on discrimination" promotes social equality at the cost of undermining private liberty and the democratic political process, and that it implies an exercise in "social technology" which, despite its rhetoric of human rights, actually deprives the idea of rights of any solid foundation.

An overview of this argument is sketched in the introduction. Chapter two outlines the historical development in Canada of the three policy areas I have chosen to emphasize and chapter three describes and classifies the ever-expanding list of protected groups. Chapters four through eight probe the theoretical underpinnings of the most prominent formulations of the new war on discrimination, unearthing inarticulate premises, teasing out hidden implications, and taking arguments to their logical conclusions.

Spinning out the logic of ideas in this way often takes them further than many of their current proponents would wish to go. At their logical extreme ideas tend toward practical implications that transcend the practices they currently justify. Thus the book is less about the current practice of anti-discrimination policy than about the full development of the logic underlying that practice and its justifying rhetoric. This is an important exercise because ideas are powerful; they have a way of working themselves pure and of taking policy in the direction of corollaries that may not be apparent at the outset. The more extreme corollaries of the ideas explored in this book are not always accepted by human rights practitioners, and the institutional implications of these corollaries are not always fully in place. Nevertheless, once an idea is established in public discourse it becomes a rhetorical resource in the pursuit of its further implications—implications that may not have been evident to those who originally legitimized the idea. As Thomas Sowell argues, while the corollaries implicit in a vision may go unnoticed or even be explicitly repudiated by the early proponents of the vision, they may in the long run prove "to be more decisive than the positions taken by the" originators of the vision. "Visions have a momentum of their own," he says, "and those who accept their assumptions have entailed their corollaries, however surprised they may be when these corollaries emerge historically."[1]

Whether the logical momentum of a vision is actually fulfilled, of course, depends on many contextual factors, such as institutional inertia, practical moderation, and the presence and power of countervailing ideas and traditions. If countervailing forces are sufficiently powerful, the fulfillment of a vision may be not only delayed but actually arrested or reversed, and there have been examples of this in the Canadian development of the new war on discrimination. Still, the vision remains influential and there have been no decisive reversals; it continues to press in the direction of its logical end, and it is worth clarifying the trend it promotes by understanding it in light of this end.

This study is best described as an essay that takes sides in an important contemporary debate. We have constitutionalized this debate in section 15 of the *Charter,* and it will be with us for a long time. The issues composing it are subtle, many-faceted and complicated, and cannot all be addressed in a single essay. It is enough to map out certain prominent features of the terrain and attempt to make them clear. This essay is a foray into the debate, an attempt to contribute to the discussion by clarifying its terms. It will certainly not settle the controversy.

I could not have written this book without the help of many friends and colleagues. I owe the greatest debt to Thomas Flanagan, who first encouraged me to undertake the project and whose own work in the area has influenced my thinking. Although he played no direct role in drafting the book, he has generously permitted me to incorporate parts of two papers he wrote for other purposes. Chapter three reproduces much of his article, "The Manufacture of Minorities"; in chapter four I have revised and expanded his unpublished essay, "On Treating People as Individuals."

I learned much of relevance to this study from Barry Cooper and F.L. Morton. The days we shared afield hunting grouse or pheasants were often also spent in pursuit of intellectual game. The fruits of those expeditions did not always end up on the dinner table; some of them found their way into these pages.

As I wrote the book, I frequently discussed its themes and arguments with Leslie A. Pal. His penetrating observations always helped me to clarify and organize my thoughts.

All of the aforementioned read drafts of the entire manuscript with great care, substantially improving both my prose and my arguments. Significant improvements were also suggested by the anonymous readers who assessed the manuscript for Carleton University Press and for the publication subsidy program of the Social Science Federation of Canada. I am grateful for the spirit of constructive criticism they brought to their task. Much of the book was also read (more than once) by Judi Powell, who, while providing welcome help at the keyboard, often spotted problems that had eluded me. I alone, of course, am responsible for any errors and infelicities that remain.

This book has been published with the help of a grant from the Social Science Federation of Canada, using funds provided by the Social Sciences and Humanities Research Council of Canada. The SSHRCC also funded the research. This support allowed me to retain the research assistance of Thomas Bateman, Merrill Cooper, and Thomas Heilke at various times in the life of the project. Their contributions were substantial. I am particularly happy to acknowledge my reliance in chapter four on material reported and discussed in Bateman's 1988 M.A. thesis, "The Law and Politics of Human Rights in British Columbia, 1983-1984."

My work on this book began during a sabbatical leave, part of which I spent at the Human Rights Research and Education Centre of the University of Ottawa. All of those associated with the Centre helped to make my time there both pleasant and productive. The book was substantially completed while on a partial leave funded by the Calgary Institute for the Humanities. The C.I.H. provided me not only with the time but also with a congenial setting in which to complete the writing.

Flanagan's "The Manufacture of Minorities" originally appeared in *Minorities and the Canadian State*, edited by Neil Nevitte and Allan Kornberg and published by Mosaic Press. I am grateful to the editors and publisher for allowing me to reprint parts of this article. I am equally grateful for permission to draw on several previously published articles of my own, including one that also appeared in *Minorities and the Canadian State*.[2] The others were published in the *Canadian Journal of Political Science*,[3] the *Saskatchewan Law Review*,[4] *Canadian Public Policy*,[5] and the *Canadian Human Rights Yearbook*.[6] None of these articles has been appropriated in its entirety as a chapter or major section of the book; the material I have drawn from them has been extensively reworked and redistributed to fit the plan of the book—it is found mainly in chapters two, six, and seven.

I save the best for last in thanking my wife and sons for sharing in my pleasure when things were going well and patiently enduring me when they were not. Only those who do not write, or who have no family on which to inflict the process of authorship, will see this as a ritual incantation.

Notes

[1] Thomas Sowell, *Civil Rights: Rhetoric or Reality?* (New York: William Morrow, 1984), 38.

[2] "The Statistical Protection of Minorities: Affirmative Action Policy in Canada."

[3] "What Do Constitutional Equality Rights Protect Canadians Against?" 20:2(1987).

[4] "Prohibiting Systemic Discrimination: Policy Development or Discontinuity?" 50(1985-86).

[5] On Proving Discrimination: Statistical Methods and Unfolding Policy Logics" 12:4(1986).

[6] "Unfairness to Individuals vs. Group Representation: A Policy Dilemma in the Legal Prohibition of Systemic Discrimination" (1984-85).

I

INTRODUCTION

Liberal Democracy vs. Guardian Democracy

The new war on discrimination is far different from anything that could have been envisioned by the classical liberal mind. Classical liberalism emphasizes individual freedom, while contemporary anti-discrimination policy is oriented above all to social equality. This does not mean that equality played no role in traditional liberal theory. To the contrary, liberal theorists saw equality and liberty as intimately, though ambiguously, interconnected. However, they were concerned with political rather than social equality. It was because all people were politically equal, because no one had a natural or divine right to rule, that all individuals were naturally free.[1] This meant that the natural condition of man was apolitical—the famous "state of nature" of Hobbes and Locke. Because of the inconveniences of absolute freedom, government proved to be necessary, but political equality made consent its only legitimate foundation.[2] Furthermore free individuals would give their consent to government only better to secure their freedom, not to provide themselves with moral preceptors who would determine how, in a positive sense, they should exercise that freedom. In brief, government was thought to exist in order to protect and secure a private domain of individual liberty.[3]

In this private realm inequality was expected to flourish. To say that people were politically equal did not mean that they were equal in all respects, only that undeniable inequalities—of strength, intelligence or ambition, for example—were politically irrelevant. The natural elite had no right to rule politically, but it was expected to predominate socially and economically, to the benefit not only of itself but of society as a whole.[4] "The first object of government," said James Madison, echoing Locke, is "the protection of different and unequal faculties of acquiring property."[5] Furthermore, because reproduction is not cloning, the inequality generated by natural differences would be confounded with a conventional social inequality that does not correspond to the natural meritocracy. The children of the naturally gifted do not always inherit those gifts but nevertheless benefit from the status attained by their parents. Similarly, the gifted children of lower-class parents suffer many disadvantages. For liberalism, however, as long as the avenues of mobility were not closed—as long as the gifted and determined could find their natural level—this conventional distortion of the natural hierarchy had to be tolerated in order to maintain freedom itself.[6] The unacceptable alternative was spelled out in Plato's Republic, in which a perfectly just meritocracy was shown to require the rule of philosopher kings, supplemented by a "guardian" elite. To ensure that children would be placed in their natural rather than conventional classes, the natural preference of parents for their own children had to be overcome.[7] Ultimately this meant taking children from their parents at birth and raising them in common, taking every precaution to prevent those related by blood from recognizing each other.[8] In other words, the perfect achievement of the natural meritocracy requires extreme political inequality and the complete destruction of the private realm.[9]

Discrimination on the basis of such group traits as religion or race has always posed a serious theoretical and practical dilemma for liberal democracy. Such discrimination often implies the inherent inferiority of some groups and the right of others to dominate or rule them. In short, it denies the politically relevant equality on which liberalism is based. In a liberal *democratic* context such discrimination and the beliefs on which it is grounded will eventually express themselves in public policy if they are allowed to flourish in the private realm. Thus liberal democracies cannot ignore private discrimination that embodies notions of political inferiority. On the other hand, classical liberal theory leads one to expect the persistence of some degree of inegalitarian prejudice and thus of discrimination. For the classical liberals human beings are naturally rather nasty and anti-social, though reasonable, creatures, who require and consent to government primarily to protect themselves from each other. In this account vanity, pride, and selfishness are considered ineradicable aspects of human nature that will always tempt people to formulate their political opinions in terms of irrational claims to rule. If this view is correct, it will be impossible to expunge discrimination altogether except by undermining the individual freedom that permits it to flourish.[10] From the perspective of classical liberalism, then, discrimination poses a permanent and insoluble dilemma or tension and is thus a perennial object of liberal democratic statesmanship.[11] The early forms of anti-discrimination policy were appropriate expressions of such statesmanship and this book does not challenge them. However, these legitimate confrontations with discrimination have long since given way to "the new war on discrimination."

The new war on discrimination reverses the terms of the classical liberal equation. In the name of social equality it is willing to restrict individual freedom and to whittle away the private domain in favour of increased public authority. Within the public sphere it fosters the growth of relatively unaccountable administrative, judicial, and quasi-judicial agencies, and encourages a shift in power from more accountable institutions to these agencies. These undemocratic agencies are designed to emphasize rationality over interest or passion and are thus particularly open to the influence of intellectuals. In short, they provide knowledge with an avenue to power. Although the new war on discrimination is waged rhetorically in traditional liberal terms, it actually points in the direction of Plato's unification of power and knowledge in an elite class of rulers. If it does not exactly lead to the rule of philosopher kings, it certainly fosters a "guardian" rather than a "liberal" democracy.[12]

The "guardian ethic" is fed by a stream of modern thought rooted in Rousseau's critique of the classical liberalism of Hobbes and Locke. Believing men to be inherently good rather than naturally anti-social, this perspective adds "fraternity" to the traditional liberal concepts of political equality and individual freedom. Not considering human nastiness to be natural, proponents of this school can envision what would be unthinkable to classical liberals, namely, "a social state in which men would wish to benefit themselves only in ways that are beneficial or at least not harmful to others, [a state in which] men's perfect integration into the community would be indistinguishable from their perfect freedom to do as they please."[13] In this view human nastiness is the product not of "nature" but of "society" or the "system." Whereas classical liberalism "supposes that there is a development from man's asociality to his property," the Rousseauan stream of modernity "believes the development is from his property to his asociality."[14]

The Rousseauan stream of modernity tends toward what F.A. Hayek has called "constructivism."[15] This is the view that society can be reconstructed in light of such intellectually derived criteria as "equality of result" or "individual treatment," using the coercive power of the state if necessary. Constructivists are confident that such transformatory projects can succeed because they attribute man's unpleasant characteristics to the effects of a "system" that is within man's power to alter and control. They no longer seriously entertain the hypothesis that man's selfish attributes are a part of his nature or are rooted in patterns of social interaction that are not within the power of anyone to change. At the extreme this orientation can become a form of "political messianism," believing that state action can solve all problems by making society over according to the abstract image of the social theorist. More moderately it engenders confidence that society can be indefinitely improved through a continuing series of state-sponsored reforms.

The constructivist confidence that society can be refashioned in accordance with a rational plan is often supported rhetorically by the claim that present structures were themselves deliberately constructed, that what was consciously made can be similarly remade. This has been called the "animistic fallacy." In the final analysis constructivists are forced to concede that it is indeed a fallacy, that the "designs" they oppose and wish to replace are often those of amorphous social or "systemic" processes rather than the result of anyone's conscious intention. Constructivism thus rests, ultimately, on the technological faith that deliberate human planning can overcome and replace the unconscious forces of "society." Nevertheless, constructivism continues to find it useful to use animist rhetoric, as when it uses the word "discrimination," which has traditionally connoted intention, as a label for systemic and societal forces. What this does is to personify "society."

Leaving aside the matter of animist rhetoric, constructivism in the social sphere mirrors the technological approach to physical problems. Technology is the peculiarly modern unification of making and knowing in which knowledge is oriented not to contemplation of what is, including permanent tensions or dilemmas, but to the overcoming of the "is" in the name of the humanly willed "ought."[16] In the physical realm this requires understanding the forces of nature in order to be able to control them. Similarly, social technology assumes that it is possible to know the societal or "systemic" determinants of human "behaviour" in a way that permits them to be manipulated and controlled. The new war on discrimination embodies this constructivist or social technological perspective. The older view—that discrimination constitutes a permanent dilemma and a matter for statesmanship—still persists. It is present, for example, in that part of anti-discrimination legislation that emphasizes education and the conciliation of individual conflicts. Increasingly, however, discrimination is understood not as a matter of inegalitarian prejudice manifested and implemented by individuals but as the reflection of "societal" or "systemic" forces that can be overcome through social engineering. Discrimination is seen as a much broader or more pervasive problem, but not one that we must learn to live with; in principle it is amenable to technical solution and does not require ongoing statesmanship.

The technological marriage of knowing and making, or knowledge and power, gives new influence to the possessors of knowledge. In the case of "social technology" it requires the predominance of institutions responsive to transformatory knowledge rather than to the human objects of transformation. Unlike the liberal democratic statesman, the social technologist cannot concede anything to prejudiced opinion. Far from being the manifestation of a permanent tension, such opinion constitutes the problem to be overcome. The technological approach to discrimination thus augments the power of administrative and judicial agencies at the expense of more democratically accountable institutions. It also transfers decision-making power from the private realm to these institutions.

This suppression of both private freedom and government by consent is inherent in projects of social engineering. If the point is to remake man by changing the social environment, then those who were molded by the old environment cannot be permitted the freedom and power to perpetuate it. The consequent decline of private freedom is considered acceptable because the very notion of a "voluntary" private sphere is untenable. Individual motivations are strictly speaking the product of the environment. To respect the "voluntary" and "private," therefore, is to acquiesce in the self-perpetuation of the unacceptable "system."

If human beings really are the product of their social environment, and if it is possible successfully to remake them by reconstructing their environment, this suppression of freedom can be seen as a temporary expedient in the historical march to a greater and more comprehensive freedom. Once men have been transformed so that their "perfect integration into the community would be indistinguishable from their perfect freedom to do as they please," it might even be possible to hope for the "withering away of the state." If, on the other hand, anti-social tendencies are rooted in nature, as both ancient and early modern political philosophy agreed (and as I believe), such projects in social engineering are fundamentally misconceived and the suppression of freedom they require will be permanent, not temporary.

It is ironic that technology and liberalism should come into conflict in this way, for they were originally allies in the modern project. The technological conquest of non-human nature was thought to support liberal freedom, just as freedom would benefit technological science.[17] That human nature should itself be subject to technological conquest, and that this should be done in part through a social technology that undermines the private sphere was apparently not considered. Yet this is what is now emerging.

In an important sense liberalism's attempt to save a part of human nature from its more general orientation to the conquest of nature was theoretically doomed from the outset. As I shall argue at greater length in chapter eight, once liberalism had set in motion the non-teleological view of nature on which technology is based, it had difficulty sustaining the idea of the natural permanence of even the anti-social passions. Hobbes and Locke were vulnerable to Rousseau's claim that they were trying to have their cake and eat it too, that if man was not naturally *social* neither could he be naturally *anti*-social, for both sets of traits presupposed society. Following their own logic, Rousseau successfully accused Hobbes and Locke of not pursuing it to the true state of nature, a state in which human traits as we know them, including

22

anti-social traits, scarcely exist. The assumption on which social technology rests—that man is the product not of nature but of society—thus represents the logical fulfillment of central assumptions in classical liberal theory.

The reader will no doubt understand that if this is true it poses difficulties for those, such as myself, who are sympathetic to classical liberal practice and who wish to oppose the practical consequences of subsequent "waves of modernity,"[18] which themselves represent the unfolding of classical liberal premises. On what theoretical ground does one stand to defend practical orientations when the theory out of which those orientations emerged succeeded only in digging its own grave? A full answer to this question is impossible in the present context. It must suffice to indicate that I follow George Grant in thinking that much of what is good in liberal practice can be defended (and has been practically sustained) on the grounds of pre-liberal theory as well as on the basis of classical liberalism itself.[19] This is certainly true of the liberal orientations I am concerned to defend in this book, especially the view that there are permanent dilemmas, rooted in nature, which more appropriately evoke statesmanship than technical solution.

The constructivist or social technological approach to discrimination is manifest in and promoted by both sides of the new war on discrimination: the intransigent pursuit of individual treatment and the emphasis on equality of group results. In certain practical respects these two orientations are at odds with each other—individual treatment, for example, requires the ignoring of group traits that must be emphasized in order to achieve equal results—but they can be reconciled in a deeper theoretical unity. If social traits and patterns are "constructed," then the present inequality of results among groups must have been caused by past discrimination—i.e., by former violations of individual treatment. Had members of the currently disadvantaged groups always been treated as individuals, their groups would not now be disadvantaged. In short, true individual treatment leads to equality of group results. Of course individual treatment *now,* in the aftermath of a pervasive history of discrimination, cannot achieve equality of result because discrimination has deprived minorities of a fair start in life's competition. Thus individual treatment may have to be temporarily set aside in favour of group preferences until minorities are restored to the position they would have held in the absence of discrimination, and until the tendency to discriminate has been rooted out. The purpose of this temporary violation of individual treatment, however, is to achieve true individual treatment in the future, a future in which individual treatment will be as perfectly compatible with equal group results as it would have been all along but for the "original sin" of discrimination.

The apparent tensions between the individual-treatment and equality-of-result orientations are also overwhelmed by their common tendency to augment the power of "guardian democracy." In this book I shall emphasize what the two approaches have in common rather than what sets them apart. The idea of "individual treatment" is analysed in chapter four; "equality of results" is the subject of chapters five through seven. The rest of this introduction provides a brief overview of these two orientations.

Individual Treatment and the Proliferation of Protected Groups

Anti-discrimination policy was originally directed against actions rooted in the irrational dislike of a limited number of groups defined by characteristics such as race, colour, ethnic origin, and religion. Inegalitarian claims to rule on the basis of these traits had been the principal source of the kind of civil strife (including civil war) that liberalism was intended to overcome. The attack on this kind of discrimination was justified in part by an appeal to the principle of individual treatment. People should be judged as individuals on their merits, it was argued, rather than prejudged in terms of group traits. This appeal to individualism is powerful in liberal democratic regimes, and it was a useful rhetoric with which to oppose discrimination based on traits that were almost always irrelevant to the decision at hand. But it also clouded the issues. In addition to serving as a convenient rhetoric with which to oppose prejudice and bigotry, the logic of individual treatment implied a new way of understanding discrimination. Individualized treatment turned out to require much more than the cessation of acts based on prejudice against racial, ethnic, and religious groups; differential treatment based on many new and different group characteristics had to be eschewed as well. The result was a radical expansion of the prohibited grounds of discrimination.

In most circumstances, to judge someone on his "merits" rather than in terms of his possession of ethnic or religious characteristics is to treat him as an individual only in a very loose manner of speaking. If one puts aside prejudice and hires a member of a racial minority who can present evidence of the requisite qualifications—say, a degree in law or engineering—is one treating that person as an individual or as a member of the group of the qualified? Is one not still discriminating on the basis of group characteristics—in this case against the "unqualified" and in favour of degree holders? And may this not also violate the principle of individual treatment? After all, John Marshall, generally acknowledged as one of the greatest judges to serve on the United States Supreme Court, had very little legal training and would thus have been excluded from consideration under present standards of qualification. Similarly, most universities now grant tenure only to academics who hold a Ph.D., although it is still possible to point to older scholars who have established solid reputations without the degree—indeed, without ever having entered a doctoral program.[20]

In its early form anti-discrimination policy was clearly directed not at categorization as such but only at categorization based on a limited number of group traits. The rhetoric of individual treatment through which the policy often expressed itself was thus a way of demanding a finer sorting of groups. Treating people as individuals meant substituting relevant for irrelevant group traits as the basis for judgment. As the above examples show, however, when taken seriously in its own terms the rhetoric of individualism entails a logic that calls into question the very idea of "relevant" group traits, especially when they are used for prospective decision making. The closest approximation to treating someone on his individual merits is to judge retrospectively on the basis of actual performance. In the employment sphere this would mean hiring on a first-come, first-served basis and retaining only those who demonstrated on-the-job competence during a probationary period. But most policy, both public and private, is based on prospective prediction. An employer cannot afford the luxury of a completely retrospective hiring process and endeavours to find traits that are good proxies for actual performance. Thus it is not unreasonable for a university to assume that those who have managed to complete a Ph.D. are more likely to be good scholars than those who have not. By the same token, those who have to appoint judges are not altogether mistaken in thinking that a law degree is a helpful prerequisite. However, from the point of view of the individual exceptions to the rules, such prospective screening devices fail to catch their true individual merit; these devices therefore fail to meet the requirements of individual treatment. The problem is that prospective planning is always based on statistical categories, to which there are always individual exceptions. When its logic is probed to the core, the rhetoric of individual treatment reveals itself to be hostile to statistical categories and prospective decision making as such.

Recent changes in anti-discrimination policy can be understood in terms of a serious dedication to the logic of individual treatment. Prospective decision making cannot be outlawed altogether, but an ever expanding number of group traits has been added to the list of prohibited grounds. Many of the new grounds—such as age, sex, marital status, pregnancy, and handicap—do not share the fatal defects of the original traits as the basis of decision making. They are often better statistical predictors of performance, and discrimination based on them is rarely associated with dislike of the group they define. Their incorporation in anti-discrimination laws must be understood as reflecting a more generalized attack on statistical or categorical prediction as such.

In addition to expanding the number and kinds of prohibited grounds of discrimination, the rhetoric of individual treatment is a major factor in the shift of power from the private sphere to undemocratic public institutions. Individual treatment in any strong sense is impossible in the areas of activity typically covered by anti-discrimination law and is best approximated by turning prospective decisions into retrospective ones. In practice this means subjecting primary decision-makers in the private sphere to the second guessing of quasi-judicial public guardians. In doing so, the ideology of individual treatment substitutes an abstract and rationalistic mode of decision making for the natural empiricism of the private sector. Ironically, as chapter four will show, this leads to less rather than more individual treatment. Institutional and societal transformation, rather than individual treatment, is the true effect of the contemporary emphasis on individual treatment.

Equal Results and the Decline of Action

A major question in virtually all discussions of equality is whether public policy should merely protect members of a target group against direct discrimination as individuals or whether it should also undertake to promote equality of results for the group as a whole. One of the distinguishing characteristics of the division between contemporary liberals and conservatives is their disagreement on this question, liberals tending to favour equal results and conservatives equal opportunity.[21] Neither side in this debate sees it as an either/or proposition, however. In pursuing equal results today's liberals do not usually reject the idea of equal opportunity; to the contrary, they tend to argue that true equality of opportunity leads inevitably to equal results and that existing inequalities testify to the presence of discriminatory barriers. Similarly, modern conservatives who oppose policies oriented directly to the achievement of equal results will often agree that dramatic group inequalities are regrettable and to be reduced if possible. Gone are the days when politically relevant conservative opinion asserted the inevitable and ineradicable superiority of some groups. The disagreement is not so much about whether greater equality of result would be desirable in principle as about how it should be promoted, and about whether it can be perfectly achieved without undermining other important principles, such as excellence and freedom.

One aspect of this disagreement is raised by the fact that group inequalities are caused not only by direct discrimination but also by the disproportionate inability of group members to meet generally accepted standards of excellence or qualification. These standards constitute what are often called "systemic barriers" against groups that are burdened by them. For example, an employment test on which a racial or ethnic group performs poorly relative to other groups may be seen as a "systemic barrier" for that group. Similarly, a minimum height and weight requirement for police work that is too high for the average woman to meet may be considered systemic discrimination against women although it is sexually neutral on its face. The concern with systemic barriers flows from a dissatisfaction with the formally equal opportunity to compete when the standards of competition themselves contribute to inequality of result. As chapter five shows, group variation from these standards can be overcome in two ways. Either the group must be brought "up to standard" or the standard must be changed to accommodate the group. The new war on discrimination uses both strategies.

There is a substantial overlap between the systemic and individual-treatment approaches to discrimination. The prohibition of systemic discrimination can be seen as an indirect way of adding new prohibited grounds and thus of achieving the finer sorting demanded by the individual-treatment model. Thus the repeal of minimum height and weight requirements because of their systemic effect on women can also be understood as an indirect way of challenging unreasonable discrimination against small people, regardless of their sex. Similarly, the direct challenge of a classification based on one group trait because it violates individual treatment can result in the dismantling of a systemic barrier against a group defined by another trait, as when a small man successfully challenges a height and weight requirement because in his case size is not an adequate proxy for strength. Individual treatment, in other words, can achieve not only its own proclaimed ends but also the accommodation of group differences.

Alongside this overlap there is an important difference between the two approaches. Despite its similar practical effect, the systemic approach logically subordinates some groups to others; for example, it subordinates the fate of small people to that of women, thereby establishing a hierarchy of protected groups. By contrast, the individual-treatment model challenges classifications simply because they are *classifications*; it is an approach that does not admit of preferred groups.

A hierarchy of protected groups is inherent in the equality-of-result approach because, as a practical matter, equal results can be pursued only for a limited number of groups. The number of classifications that can be challenged from the point of view of individual treatment is virtually infinite. Not all of these groups can reasonably expect to benefit from an equality-of-result campaign, at least not all at the same time. In fact, the pursuit of equal results is limited to vocal and politically influential "minorities" and does not extend to mere groups or statistical aggregations. The minorities currently benefiting from the equality-of-result orientation include women, racial and ethnic groups, and the handicapped. From the point of view of these preferred groups, categorizations based on other traits are important not in their own right, as violations of individual treatment, but only to the extent that they constitute systemic barriers against a primary group. Furthermore, although the ideology of individual treatment militates against the use of categorizations, achieving equality of result for the preferred groups requires using their defining traits as the basis for distributing benefits. This may be "affirmative" rather than negative discrimination, but it still means that members of these groups are being treated in terms of their group traits rather than as individuals. More importantly, it means that members of other groups may be denied benefits because they lack a group trait that everyone agrees is objectively irrelevant. Discrimination "for" one group is always discrimination "against" others.

The concept of systemic discrimination is the first step in the shift of anti-discrimination policy away from a concern with an undesirable human action towards an exclusive focus on undesirable consequences. A human act is characterized not only by its outward manifestation or consequence but also by its internal quality or intention; this is what enables us to distinguish qualitatively different acts that exhibit similar or even identical external characteristics. An act of courage, for example, is not defined simply by the deed itself. If it were, we would be unable to distinguish between a courageous and a foolhardy act, which may be externally identical. Yet we intuitively know there is a difference. The foolhardy version of the act is characterized by an absence of fear in the face of something inherently fearful; its courageous version is characterized by the overcoming of a sensible fear. The difference lies in the inner qualities that generate the outward behaviour. A human act certainly requires concrete manifestation (it cannot exist as pure potentiality in the form of intention) but it is not defined simply by this outward manifestation; an act is what it is by virtue of both its outer and inner qualities. Thus, to focus on consequence alone is to define discrimination not as a specific kind of act but as any cause, often unintentional, of the targeted consequence—in this case the statistical imbalance of groups.

This result-oriented logic implies a further expansion of the definition of discrimination. Neither direct discrimination nor systemic barriers in the form of employment policies, nor the two combined, can explain all existing statistical imbalance. If statistical imbalance is the true mischief at which anti-discrimination policy is aimed, there is no reason to address only causes of imbalance that take the form of specific employer policy, systemic or otherwise. There are other, societal causes of imbalance that should also be overcome. Among these is the self-segregation of groups. For example, once one has done away with direct employer discrimination and with systemic barriers such as height and weight requirements, one may still find that women do not rush to apply for police work. Perhaps this is due in part to the continuing effect of discriminatory employer policies, direct or systemic, which, by depriving women of role models among police officers, strengthen patterns of socialization that turn them away from this kind of work. However, self-segregation is also due to wider "societal" factors, such as the traditional family structure, which have an influence independent of employer policy. Ultimately, expanding the definition of discrimination to include systemic barriers sets in motion a logic that ends in an even wider, "societal" understanding of discrimination. The latter definition of discrimination is implicit in the more radical formulations of affirmative action. In order to describe the proportional representation of groups as a remedy for discrimination, these formulations imply that discrimination includes not only direct or systemic discrimination but also the wider societal causes of the imbalance to be overcome.

The idea of "societal discrimination" sees society as an all-embracing power that, like God, creates people (its component units) in its own image. This suggests that piecemeal reform is impossible. Any substantial change in human behaviour requires the restructuring of society as a whole. When it confronts the enemy of "societal discrimination," the new war on discrimination is a total war, not a limited-theatre engagement of forces. The affirmative overcoming of societal discrimination represents the ultimate in egalitarian social technology.

Conclusion

To summarize, the traditional liberal concern with discrimination was limited to a small number of similar group traits and was aimed only at direct discrimination on the basis of these traits. Such discrimination could be conveniently described as an infringement of the ideal of individual treatment, but this was not understood to require a comprehensive attack on categorization as such. Discrimination was seen to be a matter for statesmanship, not for permanent technical solution; and even if it was ever completely overcome, equality of result for the specified groups would not necessarily occur because inequality was caused by factors other than discrimination.

Today discrimination is viewed as a problem to be solved and is variously understood as any infringement of the strict logic of individual treatment or as whatever causes the inferior status of certain politically influential minorities. Overcoming discrimination understood in either sense requires social engineering and a consequent transfer of power from private decision-makers to a public domain increasingly dominated by undemocratic institutions. All of this occurs in the name of the liberal notion of rights, which originally implied a free private sphere of social inequality protected by a public domain responsive to consent. Today the idea of rights is the rhetorical vehicle for the sacrifice of political to social equality and private freedom to public administration—in short, of liberal to guardian democracy.

Notes

[1] Hobbes, *Leviathan*, ch. 13; Locke, *The Second Treatise of Government*, section 4. Cf. Harry V. Jaffa, "Equality as a Conservative Principle," in his *How to Think About the American Revolution* (Durham: Carolina Press), 40. Commenting on Locke's emphasis on natural freedom, Jaffa observes that "the proposition that all men are born free is itself an inference from the proposition that all men are born equal. The equality of all men by nature and the freedom of all men by nature differ as the concavity of a curved line differs from its convexity. The two are distinguishable, but inseparable."

[2] Hobbes, *Leviathan*, chs. 13 & 19; Locke, *The Second Treatise of Government*, ch. 9.

[3] *Ibid.*

[4] See Harvey C. Mansfield Jr., "Liberal Democracy as a Mixed Regime," in his *The Spirit of Liberalism* (Cambridge Mass.: Harvard University Press, 1978), esp. 9-10.

[5] Alexander Hamilton, James Madison, John Jay, *The Federalist Papers*, Clinton Rossiter, ed. (New York: Mentor, 1961), 78. Locke, *The Second Treatise of Government*, sections 4, 34, 54. See Leo Strauss, *Natural Right and History* (Chicago: University of Chicago Press, 1953), 234. Cf. Jaffa, "Equality as a Conservative Principle," 43-45.

[6] See Richard E. Morgan, *Disabling America: The "Rights Industry" in Our Time* (New York: Basic Books, 1984), 139.

[7] *Republic*, 415(b).

[8] *Ibid.*, 460(c) & (d).

[9] Cf. Yves Simon, *The Philosophy of Democratic Society* (Chicago: University of Chicago Press, 1951), 222-230.

[10] Cf. *Federalist Papers*, no. 10.

[11] See, generally, Harry V. Jaffa, *Crisis of the House Divided* (Seattle: University of Washington Press, 1973).

[12] I borrow the term from Ward E.Y. Elliot, *The Rise of Guardian Democracy* (Cambridge, Mass.: Harvard University Press, 1974). See also Raoul Berger, *Government By Judiciary: The Transformation of the Fourteenth Amendment* (Cambridge, Mass.: Harvard University Press, 1977), 313-314.

[13] Joseph Cropsey, "Conservatism and Liberalism," in his *Political Philosophy and the Issues of Politics* (Chicago: University of Chicago Press, 1977), 124-125.

[14] *Ibid.*, 122.

[15] Friedrich A. Hayek, *Law, Legislation and Liberty: Volume I, Rules and Order* (Chicago: University of Chicago Press, 1973), ch. 1. Cf. Thomas E. Flanagan, "Hayek's Concept of Constructivism," in J.M. Porter (ed.), *Sophia and Praxis: The Boundaries of Politics* (Chatham, N.J.: Chatham House, 1984).

[16] My understanding of technology owes much to the writings of George Grant. See especially, *Technology and Empire: Perspectives on North America* (Toronto: Anansi, 1969); *English-Speaking Justice* (Toronto: Anansi, 1985); and *Technology and Justice* (Toronto: Anansi, 1986).

[17] Grant, *English-Speaking Justice*, 3.

[18] See Leo Strauss, "The Three Waves of Modernity," in Hilail Gildin, ed., *Political Philosophy: Six Essays by Leo Strauss* (New York: Pegasus, 1975).

[19] See Grant, *English-Speaking Justice*, 86: "In so far as the contemporary systems of liberal practice hold onto the content of free and equal justice, it is because they still rely on older sources which are more and more made unthinkable in the very realisation of technology." See generally Part III of this book. See also George Grant, "Abortion and Rights," in E. Fairweather and I. Gentles, eds., *The Right to Birth: Some Christian Views on Abortion* (Toronto: Anglican Book Centre, 1976), 2.

[20] Robert Fulford points to the examples of Northrop Frye, Robertson Davies, and George Woodcock, "[n]one of [whom] had a Ph.D. or ever tried to get one." He adds that "it would be a brave and foolhardy young scholar who set out to follow their example today." See "Varsity Blues," *Saturday Night* (Sept. 1987), 8. It has apparently been suggested in Australia that possession of a Ph.D. is not a genuine job-related qualification and that advertisements for academic jobs should no longer require it. See L.J.M. Cooray, ed., *Human Rights in Australia* (Epping NSW: ACFR, 1985), 114.

[21] It should be obvious from the context that "contemporary liberals" are not the "classical liberals" discussed above. Indeed, classical liberals are today's conservatives. See my comments on the evolution of political language in the preface. It would be clearer, but more awkward, to find new terms for the modern political partisans. I have chosen to avoid awkward neologisms and to let the context convey my meaning.

II

POLICY DEVELOPMENT

In 1982 Canada entrenched the *Charter of Rights and Freedoms* in its formal constitution. Not all of the *Charter* was immediately applicable however; section 15—the "equality rights" section—did not come into effect until April 17, 1985, three years after the main body of the *Charter*. This was a dramatic episode in a forty-year development of the legal control of discrimination. Other milestones in this history were the adoption of comprehensive human rights codes in all thirteen Canadian jurisdictions, the establishment of human rights commissions to administer them, and the enactment of quasi-constitutional bills of rights at the federal level and in three of the provinces. The story is far from over. The horizons of existing anti-discrimination law are continually being expanded through both interpretation and formal amendment. Thus human rights statutes now prohibit not only intentional discrimination against an expanding list of protected groups but also neutral rules that have a "disparate impact" on these groups, such as height and weight requirements that few women can meet; some commentators are urging a similar interpretation of section 15(1) of the *Charter*. Section 15(2) of the Charter permits, though it does not require, "affirmative action" programs designed to provide special benefit to disadvantaged groups, and such programs are increasingly being established. This chapter describes the historical development and current status of this complex of equality policies.

Human Rights Legislation

Canadian concern with the legal protection of "human rights" has its roots in the Second World War and the years immediately following it. There were scattered attempts to control discrimination before this time, but the war was a watershed, marking the beginning of a steady growth and consolidation of anti-discrimination policies. The horrors of racial, ethnic and religious discrimination were made graphically evident by the Nazi atrocities in Europe. Nor could discrimination be considered a foreign virus against which Canadians were immune. Canada had a long history of discrimination against Orientals, for example, in which the massive internment and relocation of Japanese Canadians during the war was only the most recent and dramatic example. Coming close on the heels of this wartime experience, the oppression of Jehovah's Witnesses in Quebec during the 1950s confirmed liberal sensitivity to the problem of discrimination.[1]

Discrimination may be practiced by both the state and such private actors as employers, landlords and shopkeepers. The enactment of human rights legislation was the common response to the phenomenon of "private discrimination." This legislation developed in three stages, roughly corresponding to the three decades after 1940. The 1940s saw the enactment of "quasi-criminal" prohibitions of discrimination, such as Ontario's *Racial Discrimination Act*, enacted in 1944, and the anti-discrimination provisions in Saskatchewan's 1947 *Bill of Rights*. The Ontario legislation applied only to the public display of discriminatory signs or symbols. The Saskatchewan *Bill of Rights* was much broader in scope; in addition to guaranteeing rights against state infringement, it prohibited private discrimination in several areas of activity, including employment and accommodation. Both statutes incorporated the criminal-law model of regulation: discrimination was made an offence subject to penalties such as fines or imprisonment, and enforcement was left to the traditional machinery of the police and the courts.[2]

In the 1950s the volume of anti-discrimination legislation increased steadily, with most of the provinces entering the field. More importantly, an administrative model of enforcement came to replace the "criminal-law" approach. The perceived weaknesses of the latter model have been summarized by Walter Tarnopolsky:

> There is reluctance on the part of the victim of discrimination to ini-
> tiate the criminal action. There are all the difficulties of proving the
> offence beyond a reasonable doubt, and it is extremely difficult to
> prove that a person has not been denied access for some reason other
> than a discriminatory one. There is reluctance on the part of the
> judiciary to convict, probably based upon a feeling that a discrimi-
> natory act is not really in the nature of a criminal act. Without exten-
> sive publicity and promotion, many people are unaware of the fact
> that human rights legislation exists. Members of minority groups
> who have known discrimination in the past tend to be somewhat
> skeptical as to whether the legislation is anything more than a sop
> to the conscience of the majority. Finally, the sanction, in the form of
> a fine, does not really help the person discriminated against in
> obtaining a job or home or service in a restaurant.[3]

Under the new administrative system, traditional prosecution
and the application of penal sanctions were not abandoned but
were to be used only as a last resort. The investigation and conciliation of complaints was the preferred course of action. Only if
this failed would more obviously legal proceedings begin, and
even then the first step was often not a court but an *ad-hoc*, quasi-
judicial tribunal, which had the advantage of more flexible procedures. Typically this process of administrative enforcement was
directed by officials in a governmental ministry. Fair employment
and fair accommodation statutes based on this model were
enacted by most of the provinces in the 1950s. This era also saw
the widespread enactment of "equal pay" legislation, which prohibited discrimination in remuneration on the basis of sex.[4]

The development of anti-discrimination legislation up to this
point was characterized by special purpose statutes, which either
applied to particular areas of activity (housing, employment,
etc.), or prohibited discrimination only on the basis of a single
ground of discrimination (equal pay for the sexes). Enactment of
such special purpose legislation continued sporadically into the
1960s. For example, Quebec did not enact fair employment legislation until 1964.[5] Similarly, British Columbia and Ontario introduced a new kind of "single ground" statute in the mid-1960s,
enacting age discrimination acts in 1964 and 1966 respectively.[6]
By this time, however, the trend in anti-discrimination legislation
had shifted to comprehensive "human rights codes" that prohibited discrimination based on several specified grounds and in a
number of areas of activity.

The first such statute was Ontario's *Human Rights Code*,
enacted in 1962, which consolidated all of that province's anti-

discrimination legislation.[7] By the end of the 1960s all but two jurisdictions had followed suit. Saskatchewan did not consolidate its human rights legislation until 1979. The federal government had enacted the *Canadian Human Rights Act* two years earlier, in 1977.

Ontario pioneered a second important development in human rights legislation. In 1961, a year before it consolidated its legislation, the province established a human rights commission to administer its anti-discrimination statutes. A year later this commission was given the power to administer the comprehensive Code. Although the earlier fair employment and fair accommodation statutes had provided for education, investigation and conciliation, the actual implementation of these functions was considered by many to be perfunctory and inefficient, in part because no full-time body existed with special responsibility for them. Human rights commissions became the common response to this problem. In many instances the establishment of commissions went hand in hand with the enactment of comprehensive human rights codes. This was not always the case, however. Ontario established its commission before it enacted the *Human Rights Code*. Similarly, Saskatchewan's commission pre-dates its code by seven years. By contrast, Prince Edward Island and Newfoundland enacted comprehensive codes several years before they established commissions to administer them. In any case, by the late 1970s all thirteen Canadian jurisdictions had both comprehensive human rights legislation and human rights commissions.

Human rights commissions enjoy significant powers not available to their departmental predecessors. The most important of these is the power of initiating discrimination proceedings rather than just responding to individual complaints. Under fair employment and accommodation legislation the process of investigation and conciliation could be initiated only by the alleged victim of discrimination. As Walter Tarnopolsky points out, this legislation "placed the administrative machinery of the state at the disposal of the victim of discrimination, but it approached the whole problem as if it were solely his problem and his responsibility. The result," Tarnopolsky continues, "was that very few complaints were made, and very little enforcement was achieved."[8] A full-time human rights body is also more likely to publicize the availability and effectiveness of redress for discrimination, and thus to generate more complainant-initiated cases. As might be expected, the establishment of such commissions has led to a steady increase in the number of discrimination cases.[9]

Much discrimination is not touched by the legislation. Although human rights legislation is concerned with private discrimination, it does not reach such purely private matters as choosing one's friends or one's mate. The legislation prohibits discrimination in areas concerning the gaining of a livelihood (employment, contracts), the spending of the proceeds of employment on shelter (housing, rental accommodation), and the consumption of publicly available goods, services and accommodation.

In these areas all of the human rights acts outlaw discrimination based on a list of prohibited grounds. Race, colour, ethnicity[10] and religion[11] were among the first grounds to be specified and are included in the legislation of every jurisdiction. Sex, age and physical handicap were gradually added and are also included everywhere. A host of other grounds has received more scattered protection. Examples include mental handicap, political belief, family status, pregnancy, place of residence, and sexual orientation. Altogether, thirty prohibited grounds of discrimination may be found in Canadian human rights legislation.[12]

In addition to growing lists of explicitly prohibited grounds of discrimination, two Canadian jurisdictions have experimented with open-ended anti-discrimination provisions. In 1973 British Columbia amended its Code to prohibit discrimination in employment or provision of access to public facilities "unless reasonable cause exists." By 1982 thirty-seven percent of complaints laid under the Code were attributable to this provision. In 1984, however, the Social Credit government of Bill Bennett abolished the reasonable cause provision as part of a general overhaul of the legislation. Manitoba has similar reasonable cause provisions regarding tenancy and public facilities.[13] Until 1987 Manitoba also had a similar but somewhat weaker formulation for employment, by which stipulated forms of discrimination were prohibited "without limiting the generality of the foregoing."[14] This has been replaced by a prohibition of employment discrimination "unless the discrimination is based upon bona fide and reasonable requirements or qualifications."[15] The Manitoba Human Rights Commission took assorted complaints to the stage of conciliation under the earlier residual clause but pushed only one employment case, involving sexual preference, to a board of adjudication.[16] Having lost the adjudication, the Commission decided against an appeal to the courts for fear of receiving a ruling that would weaken the residual clause even further.[17] In the area of publicly available rights and privileges, by contrast, the Manitoba Court of Queen's Bench upheld, in 1987, a claim of discrimination without "reasonable cause."[18]

Human rights legislation contains several kinds of exemptions to its general prohibition of discrimination. Non-profit religious, philanthropic, educational, fraternal or social organizations have always been permitted to discriminate.[19] Thus the Catholic Church is permitted to discriminate on the basis of both religion and sex when it hires priests. The employment of domestic labour and the rental of accommodation in situations involving close personal contact between the landlord and tenant have also been exempt.[20] The insurance industry has been the subject of another traditional exemption,[21] although this has come under increasing criticism. Also subject to recent challenge is the tradition of limiting the prohibition of age discrimination to a specified period in the human life cycle (e.g., between eighteen and sixty-five).[22]

Over time all Canadian jurisdictions have replaced or supplemented particularized exemptions in the employment area with a general provision that immunizes discrimination on one of the prohibited grounds if it can be shown to be a *bona fide* (or reasonable)[23] occupational qualification (or requirement).[24] The Supreme Court has determined that to qualify as a BFOQ a requirement must pass both a subjective and an objective test. Subjectively, it must be imposed "honestly, in good faith, and in the sincerely held belief that such limitation is imposed in the interests of the adequate performance of the work involved with all reasonable dispatch, safety and economy, and not for ulterior or extraneous reasons aimed at objectives which could defeat the purposes" of human rights legislation. Subjective good faith is not enough, however; the requirement must also be "related in an objective sense to the performance of the employment concerned, in that it is reasonably necessary to assure the efficient and economical performance of the job without endangering the employee, his fellow employees and the general public."[25]

Section 15 of the Charter

As well as prohibiting "private discrimination," human rights legislation binds the Crown in its capacity as employer, provider of publicly available goods and services, etc.[26] Whether and to what extent "human rights" acts can prevail against clearly conflicting legislation is more controversial.[27] In any case, the common route to protecting rights against infringement by legislation is the enactment of a judicially enforceable "bill of rights." The *Charter* is such a document, and since 1985 section 15 has been available to control discrimination by all levels of government. Prior to the *Charter*, the federal government and three of the provinces had enacted statutory bills of rights applying within their own jurisdictions.[28] Civil libertarians considered them inadequate because of their scattered jurisdictional application and because, lacking entrenched constitutional status, they were not aggressively applied by a judiciary steeped in the tradition of legislative supremacy. The history of jurisprudence under the *Canadian Bill of Rights*, especially as regards its equality provision, was particularly galling to human rights activists.

Enacted in 1960, the *Canadian Bill of Rights* "recognized and declared that in Canada there have existed and shall continue to exist without discrimination by reason of race, national origin, colour, religion or sex," a number of "human rights and fundamental freedoms," including the "right of the individual to equality before the law and the protection of the law." Section 2 of the Bill stated that "Every law of Canada shall, unless it is expressly declared by an Act of the Parliament of Canada that it shall operate notwithstanding the Canadian Bill of Rights, be so construed and applied as not to abrogate, abridge or infringe...any of the rights or freedoms herein recognized and declared...."[29]

Only once during the Bill's first twenty-two years, in the case of *The Queen* v. *Drybones*, did the Supreme Court strike down a law because it conflicted with the Bill.[30] Moreover, to avoid invalidating other laws the Court abandoned the relatively liberal interpretation it established in *Drybones* of the Bill's "equality before the law" guarantee. Writing for the majority in *Drybones*, Justice Ritchie vigorously rejected an interpretation that would guarantee only the equal administration of the law within the categories it established, regardless of the nature of those categories. Under this interpretation, he declared, "the most glaring discriminatory

41

legislation against a racial group would have to be construed as recognizing the right of each of its individual members to 'equality before the law', so long as all the other members are being discriminated against in the same way."[31]

Four years later, in *The Queen* v. *Lavell and Bedard*, the same Justice Ritchie insisted that "'equality before the law' is to be treated as meaning equality in the administration or application of the law by the law enforcement authorities and the ordinary courts of the land."[32] This case arose out of a challenge to section 12(1)(b) of the *Indian Act*, under which Indian women, but not Indian men, lost their status if they married non-Indians. The Court's ruling meant that "equality before the law" was not violated as long as all Indian women who married outside the status community were "discriminated against in the same way." *Lavell* became a *cause célèbre* for Canadian feminists, who played a major role in the drafting of section 15 of the *Charter*.

Feminists were similarly outraged by the Court's decision in *Bliss* v. *Attorney-General of Canada*.[33] This case upheld more stringent qualifications for unemployment insurance benefits for women who were unemployed because of pregnancy; it also sustained the denial of all benefits to women who did not meet these qualifications, even if they would have been eligible for regular benefits had they become unemployed for other reasons. Once again it was Justice Ritchie who wrote the opinion. Among other things, he did not see the issue as one of sex discrimination, but as a distinction between pregnant persons and all other persons, including non-pregnant women, adding that "Any inequality between the sexes in this area is not created by legislation but by nature."[34]

In the fall of 1980 the Trudeau government introduced its proposal to "patriate" the Constitution with the addition of a formal amending procedure and a charter of rights. In its original version section 15 of the *Charter* read:

> (1) Everyone has the right to equality before the law and to the equal protection of the law without discrimination because of race, national or ethnic origin, colour, religion, age or sex.
>
> (2) This section does not preclude any law, program or activity that has as its object the amelioration of conditions of disadvantaged persons or groups.[35]

Except for the addition of age as a prohibited ground of discrimination, the first part of this section essentially replicated the equality guarantees of the *Canadian Bill of Rights*. Fearing that this would simply entrench the jurisprudence of *Lavell*, feminist groups, led by the National Advisory Council on the Status of Women, mounted a concerted and successful campaign to add phrases that would clearly indicate to the courts that the old jurisprudence was no longer acceptable.[36] To override *Lavell*, equality "under the law" was added to the traditional "before the law" phrasing, thereby suggesting that something more than the equal administration of unequal laws was required. Similarly, the guarantee of "equal benefit" was designed to overrule *Bliss*.[37]

Women's groups were also concerned about the inclusion of age in the list of prohibited grounds. Legal distinctions overtly based on race, religion or ethnicity, they thought, would almost always violate section 15, whereas many distinctions based on age would not because they are generally accepted as reasonable. This meant that there would be two tiers or classes of prohibited grounds: those entitled to "strict scrutiny" and those that would be assessed according to more lenient criteria. Feminists worried that sex might be associated with the latter. To address this problem, the Advisory Council suggested an open-ended, general protection against discrimination along with a number of specifically listed grounds. The latter would include sex, but not age, and would receive strict scrutiny; all other classifications, including those based on age, could be challenged under the open-ended wording and would be subject to more relaxed assessment. Once age had been included in the explicit listing of prohibited grounds, however, its deletion proved to be politically impossible; and, indeed, another ground that was likely to attract more lenient scrutiny, "mental or physical disability," was added as the result of vigorous lobbying.[38] At the same time, the Advisory Council's proposal for an open-ended formulation was accepted.[39] Thus section 15 now reads:

> (1) Every individual is equal before and under the law and has the right to the equal protection and equal benefit of the law without discrimination and, in particular, without discrimination based on race, national or ethnic origin, colour, religion, sex, age or mental or physical disability.

> (2) Subsection (1) does not preclude any law, program or activity that has as its object the amelioration of conditions of disadvantaged individuals or groups including those that are disadvantaged be-

cause of race, national or ethnic origin, colour, religion, sex, age or
mental or physical disability.

As in the case of human rights legislation, the constitutional
prohibition of discrimination in section 15 is subject to limits or
exceptions. Section 1 of the Charter permits such "reasonable
limits" as are "demonstrably justified in a free and democratic society." This section does for constitutional equality rights what
BFOQ provisions do for human rights legislation. It should also
be noted that section 15 of the *Charter* is subject to section 33, the
so-called *non-obstante* provision, which allows governments to im-
munize policy from *Charter* review for renewable five-year periods
by explicitly enacting that the legislation shall operate "notwithstanding" the *Charter*.[40]

Most commentators agree that section 15 is the *Charter* section
most likely to pose controversial policy issues, that it "has the potential to be the most intrusive provision."[41] This will be especially true if section 15 is given a systemic interpretation. The three-
year delay in the implementation of section 15 reflects the legislature's awareness of the particularly controversial nature of this
section. These expectations seem to be borne out by the early jurisprudence under section 15. In the first three years after the
Charter's entrenchment, the legal rights sections generated the
bulk of the cases, as everyone had predicted.[42] Since April, 1985,
section 15 cases threaten to outstrip legal rights cases.
Furthermore, "equality rights" cases have been more likely to involve challenges to legislation than have other *Charter* cases,
which often challenged the conduct of public officials.[43]
Interestingly, over forty percent of these cases have been generated by the open-ended, residual aspect of section 15 instead of
the explicitly listed prohibited grounds.[44] This stands in marked
contrast to the recent fate of open-ended formulations in
Canadian human rights legislation. However, the ultimate effect
of section 15's residual wording, and indeed of the section as a
whole, remains unclear; at the time of writing only one case
based explicitly on the section has reached the Supreme Court.

Systemic Discrimination and Human Rights Legislation

The prohibition of intentional discrimination against individuals on the basis of their membership in certain listed groups may be understood as reflecting primarily a concern with formal equality of opportunity. However, with respect to any particular protected group the prohibition of such discrimination cannot achieve equality of result. For example, an employer who ceases to discriminate against members of a racial or ethnic minority but requires qualifications disproportionately lacked by that minority will continue to hire few of its members. The increasing interest in equality of results for the protected groups is demonstrated by the inclusion of "systemic barriers" in the category of prohibited discrimination.

From its inception to the early 1970s, Canadian human rights legislation was consistently interpreted as prohibiting only direct, intentional discrimination against protected groups.[45] In 1972, in *Griggs* v. *Duke Power Co.*, the United States Supreme Court ruled that the *Civil Rights Act* also prohibited the "adverse impact" of actions not intended to discriminate against a protected group. Duke Power Co. would hire only those who had a high school education and could pass a standardized intelligence test. Neither requirement could be met by blacks at the same rate as whites. Chief Justice Burger concluded that these requirements constituted *prima facie* discrimination despite their surface neutrality. "Good intent," he said, "or absence of discriminatory intent does not redeem employment procedures or mechanisms that operate as 'built-in headwinds' for minority groups."[46]

In the last half of the 1970s Canadian commissions and tribunals began to follow the American Court's lead and adopted a similar interpretation of their own legislation. The most significant breakthrough was *Singh* v. *Security and Investigation Services Ltd.*, a 1977 case arising under the *Ontario Human Rights Code*.[47] The company required its employees to be clean-shaven with "hair properly cut," and to wear a hat as part of a uniform. Singh, a Sikh, could not comply with these requirements without violating the tenets of his religion. The board of inquiry concluded that "even though Security bears no ill will towards the Sikh religion, its refusal to offer employment to Mr. Singh because of Sikh dress and grooming practices has the effect of denying Mr. Singh his right to practice the religion of his choice. Discrimination in fact exists even though Security did not intend to discriminate."[48] A series of similar decisions quickly followed.[49]

Prohibitions of systemic discrimination emphasize the unintentional effect of a requirement on a target group. Traditionally, proof of intent was required under anti-discrimination legislation because in its early form legal regulation was aimed as much at the "evil motive" underlying discrimination as at the discriminatory result.[50] The approach was analogous to the criminal law approach to such crimes as murder or fraud, which is concerned not only with the prevention or deterrence of undesirable acts, or with the rehabilitation of the criminal, but also with the "enforcement of morality."[51] For many criminal law offences, in other words, one is punished not simply for having caused harm, but for having engaged in morally reprehensible behaviour. But behaviour is considered morally reprehensible only if one can sensibly be held responsible for it, which is to say only if one did it voluntarily. Someone who causes harm during an epileptic fit is not morally culpable and therefore not guilty of a crime. In brief, the harm-causing behaviour is not sufficient to constitute the offence; *mens rea*, or intention, must be present as well.

Many discussions of "discriminatory intent" equate the term with "evil" or "malicious" motive. It is possible to distinguish intent from motive, however, in the sense that intent designates the conscious desire or will to do something whereas motive refers to the reason underlying that desire or will.[52] Thus the same intention may be formed on the basis of different motives.[53] One may, for example, impose a low fixed retirement age because one dislikes old people and wishes to employ only the young, or because one believes that the nature of the job is such that safety may be jeopardized by older workers. In either case the retirement policy remains one of intentional discrimination on the ground of age, and thus a form of direct discrimination, although the motive is "malicious" in one case and not in the other.

The distinction between motive and intent makes possible a morally neutral definition of the term "discriminatory intent." Such a definition brings more discrimination within the scope of an anti-discrimination law that requires a showing of intent. This transformation was required as anti-discrimination legislation added new and different traits to the list of prohibited grounds.

Direct discrimination against the groups originally protected by the legislation—racial, ethnic and religious groups—is almost always associated with dislike or bigotry. This may also be true of such new grounds as "sexual preference." However, discrimination based on such grounds as age or sex is rarely motivated by dislike or malice. The previously mentioned fixed-age retirement issue is a good example. Similarly, the paternalistic assumptions lying behind much of the differential treatment to which women were subject in the past are difficult to equate with malice.

Some confusion has been generated by cases involving intentional but non-malicious differential treatment. In the early cases of this kind, tribunals and courts often emphasized the fact that evil motive need not be proved as a constituent element of the offence. Sometimes such cases are cited in support of a systemic interpretation of the legislation. However, these cases really represent the adoption of the morally neutral definition of intent, rather than the abandonment of intent as such; they remain examples of intentional differential treatment of specified groups and cannot easily be stretched to cover the disparate impact upon these groups of otherwise neutral rules.

The 1976 case of *Human Rights Commission* v. *College of Physicians and Surgeons of British Columbia* provides an example of this confusion. In this case the board of inquiry had to decide whether a requirement imposed by the College on newly licensed, non-Canadian doctors to practice for a time in medically underserved areas of the province was discriminatory. The board held that, although "the principal motivation of the College in adopting the policy under review was a wholly laudable one,"

> ...[T]he result...is to discriminate against non-Canadian doctors on grounds quite unrelated to their qualifications for the practice of medicine, and in our view this, quite apart from any question of motive, constitutes a form of discrimination without reasonable cause that is prohibited by the Code.[54]

This case has been cited in support of a "consequences or effects definition" of discrimination that includes systemic discrimination,[55] but the factual context does not support this conclusion. One must remember that the "adverse effect" in question is the effect of direct discrimination, which was clearly intentional, although it was not *motivated* by malice.

In order to bring systemic discrimination within the reach of ambiguously worded human rights provisions, something more

than the adoption of a morally neutral definition of intent is required. As Chief Justice Dickson has said, "the imputation of a
requirement of 'intent,' even if unrelated to moral fault, [fails] to
respond adequately to the many instances where the effect of policies and practices is discriminatory even if that effect is unintended and unforeseen."[56] One possibility is further to transform
the definition of intent in terms of one of its lesser-known dictionary meanings. The Oxford English Dictionary provides both an
active and a passive definition of "intent." In its active sense intent is characterized by will or desire; in its passive sense it is syn-
onymous with "attention" or "heed," as in "paying attention" to
something. The latter meaning conveys a sense of observation
rather than will. Using the active meaning of the term, intentional
discrimination would occur only when the unequal treatment was
willed or desired. Under the passive meaning of intent it would
also include unequal treatment that, if not actively willed, was anticipated or foreseeable.[57]

In criminal law, definitions of *mens rea* have been proposed in
which both the active and passive definitions of intent are applicable to a finding of the required mental element. Under such definitions someone who foresees and genuinely deplores the prob-
able consequences of an action, and who nevertheless engages in
that action for other reasons, manifests the degree of *mens rea* necessary to a finding of guilt.[58] The situation of such a person is
precisely analogous to that of the perpetrator of systemic discrimination who is aware of the unequal effects of a policy adopted for
non-discriminatory reasons. A passive definition of intent would
bring such "discrimination" within the scope of a prohibition of
"intentional" discrimination.[59]

But what of the person who actually did not foresee the unequal effects of his action? As an Ontario board of inquiry put it,
a "discriminatory result may exist without any ill-will *or even
knowledge* on the part of the employer."[60] In many cases one may
conclude that such a person *should* have foreseen the result. One
way of solving this problem would be to substitute the hypothet-
ical "reasonable man" for the actual man. However, this is probably unnecessary, for as the same board notes, "the scheme of
[human rights] legislation...provides for a conciliation stage
whereby the discriminatory result is brought to the attention of
the employer."[61]

Although a definition of "intent" that includes its passive meaning would solve many of the problems of those who desire a legal prohibition of systemic discrimination, the preferred course has been to abandon the requirement of intent altogether in favour of a concentration on disparate results or effects. To pursue the criminal-law analogy once more, this involves the application of "absolute liability" to the realm of discrimination. From this point of view, the offence of discrimination is no longer defined, even in part, by the psycho-moral condition of its perpetrator, but solely by its "adverse effect" or result. This approach is implicit in the use of the term "systemic" to describe the opposite of direct discrimination, it being the "system" (of employment criteria, for example) that is at fault. As a corollary of this "absolute liability" approach, the notion that anti-discrimination legislation seeks to punish a moral wrong is abandoned.[62]

It is frequently suggested that the absolute liability approach to the legislation is logically implied by the change from an enforcement mechanism that was quasi-criminal in nature to one that is largely administrative. For example, the Canadian Jewish Congress has argued that

> The approach taken by the Legislature to human rights problems in the [Canadian Human Rights] Act is not criminal or penal in nature but is an administrative, remedial, settlement-oriented, re-education approach. It is submitted that it is inconsistent with such an approach to import into the legislation a notion of mens rea and to confine discrimination only to cases involving intentional acts of employers.[63]

This inconsistency is not obvious, however. It is true that the administrative model was chosen because discriminatory intent is difficult to prove "beyond a reasonable doubt," as the criminal model requires. But it was chosen in part to make proof easier, not to abandon it. Writing in 1968, for example, Tarnopolsky praised the administrative model because it required only a "preponderance of evidence" to prove discriminatory intent. "Since proof of discrimination involves proving a motive which is rather easy to disprove," he said, "it is difficult to prove the act of discrimination beyond a reasonable doubt. It is not so difficult to prove it by a preponderance of evidence."[64] There was no assumption in this that rejection of the criminal-law enforcement model required a transformation of the definition of discrimination. Indeed, Tarnopolsky was quite clear that proof of intent was still required. This was further emphasized by his brief discussion of systemic barriers at the end of the essay. He mentioned them not to show how they are covered as a logical implication of the shift from criminal to administrative enforcement mechanisms, but precisely to lament the fact that they were not yet covered.

> Two assumptions underlie the present philosophy of human rights legislation: 1. Employment qualifications are based upon bona fide criteria; 2. Members of minority groups who suffer discrimination are prepared to meet such qualifications. Both assumptions are often not true. Many employers use sets of standards and other employment criteria which have no valid relation to job requirements. Often these innocently or deliberately serve to disqualify members of minority groups. Moreover, many members of minority groups lack the training necessary to compete on equal terms for jobs or promotional opportunities.[65]

He therefore recommended that "Employers who contract with public agencies should be required to co-operate with the Human Rights Commission to review job requirements and even to provide on-the-job training." Clearly, there was no necessary connection between the move to an administrative enforcement structure and a transformation of the legal definition of discrimination. The latter cannot easily be piggybacked on the former; it requires separate justification. The most common justifications are canvassed in chapter six.

By 1982 the absolute liability reading of human rights legislation had come to prevail among commissions and quasi-judicial tribunals. In that year, however, the Ontario Divisional Court struck a blow at this interpretation in the case of *O'Malley* v. *Simpsons-Sears*.[66] Theresa O'Malley had become a Seventh Day Adventist in October, 1978. As a full-time sales clerk for Simpsons-Sears Ltd., she was required to work a rotation that included two successive Saturdays followed by one Saturday off. She had done so without complaint for several years, but upon her religious conversion she informed Simpsons-Sears that she would no longer be available for work on Friday evenings and Saturdays. Simpsons-Sears responded by offering her a part-time position, with consequent loss in pay and benefits. Full-time clerks, the company argued, had to be prepared to work at the store's busiest times. Mrs. O'Malley accepted the part-time offer but lodged a complaint with the Ontario Human Rights

Commission, alleging that her employer had discriminated on the ground of religion in contravention of the *Ontario Human Rights Code*. There was no question of intentional discrimination against Seventh Day Adventists, and the charge was therefore that an employment policy enacted for neutral reasons constituted a systemic barrier against Saturday sabbatarians. The Divisional Court, however, concluded that the legislation prohibited only direct, intentional discrimination "because of" membership in a protected category. This decision was subsequently upheld by the Ontario Court of Appeal.[67]

During the same period of time Canadian National Railways was having similar difficulties with one of its employees. K.S. Bhinder, a Sikh, was employed as an electrician by the company. In 1978 CNR required everyone who worked in its coachyards to wear a hard hat, but Bhinder refused because his religion required the wearing of a turban and forbade any other headgear. As a result he was fired. He too complained of systemic discrimination, only to discover in 1983 that in the opinion of the Federal Court of Appeal the *Canadian Human Rights Act*, like the Ontario Code interpreted in *O'Malley*, did not cover such discrimination.[68] Both cases were appealed to the Supreme Court of Canada.

The restrained interpretation of the legislation manifested by the Ontario and Federal courts was not limited to the judicial sphere. The Special House of Commons Committee on Visible Minorities thought in 1984 that systemic discrimination was not prohibited outside Ontario. Perhaps not surprisingly for a legislative body, the Committee considered the latitudinarian interpretations of the commissions and tribunals an incursion into the legislative realm, even though the Committee itself supported the legislative prohibition of systemic discrimination. "This is an instance," it noted, "where Human Rights Commission practice and Tribunal decisions have bypassed an inadequate legislative framework—they have dealt with systemic or constructive discrimination although not mandated to do so."[69]

The events that gave rise to *O'Malley* occurred in 1978-79. In 1981, four years before the case reached its conclusion in the Supreme Court of Canada, Ontario amended its Code to include an explicit prohibition of systemic discrimination. Section 10 of the 1981 Code reads:

> A right of a person under Part I is infringed where a requirement, qualification or consideration is imposed that is not discrimination

on a prohibited ground but that would result in the exclusion, qualification or preference of a group of persons who are identified by a
prohibited ground of discrimination and of whom the person is a
member, except where,

(a) the requirement, qualification or consideration is a reasonable
and bona fide one in the circumstances; or

(b) it is declared in this Act that to discriminate because of such
ground is not an infringement of a right.

Until recently section 10 of the Ontario Code was the only explicit prohibition of systemic discrimination in Canadian human
rights legislation.[70] Most jurisdictions are in the position of
Ontario prior to the enactment of the new section 10. As board of
inquiry chairman Edward Ratushny put it in *O'Malley*, the difficulty in determining whether systemic discrimination was covered by the old Ontario Code lay in "the absence of specific legislative guidance. The relevant provisions of the Code [went] no
further than section 4(1)(g), which merely provide[d] that no person shall 'discriminate against any employee with regard to any
term or condition of employment' because of" certain prohibited
grounds of discrimination.[71] This section is similar in wording to
subsection 703(a)(1) of the U.S. *Civil Rights Act*, which makes it
unlawful for an employer

to fail or to refuse to hire or to discharge any individual, or otherwise to discriminate against any individual, with respect to his
compensation, terms, conditions or privileges of employment, because of such individual's race, color, religion, sex or national
origin.[72]

One Ontario board of inquiry argued that the similar wording
justifies a similar interpretation, and that since section 703 has
been interpreted by the American Supreme Court as prohibiting
systemic discrimination, the same interpretation should apply in
the case of section 4(1)(g) of the old Ontario Code.[73] But *Griggs*
was based not on subsection 703(a)(1) but on subsection
703(a)(2), which makes it illegal "for an employer to limit, segre-
gate, or classify his employees in a way which would deprive *or
tend to deprive* any individual of employment opportunities or otherwise *adversely affect* his status as an employee, because of such
individual's race, color, religion, sex or national origin...."[74] It is
the italicized language that most clearly supports the *Griggs* interpretation, and both subsection 703(a)(1) of the *Civil Rights Act* and
section 4(1)(g) of the old Ontario Code lack this phrasing. In such

cases human rights commissions have often resorted to the assumption that if systemic discrimination is not explicitly excluded from the scope of their legislation it must be included.[75] Buttressing this assumption is the argument that remedial legislation ought to receive a large and liberal construction, and, indeed, that interpretation statutes require such a reading.[76]

The federal Human Rights Commission relies on sections 7 and 10 of the *Canadian Human Rights Act* as the source of its mandate to attack systemic discrimination. Section 7 states that "It is a discriminatory practice, directly or *indirectly,* (a) to refuse to employ or continue to employ any individual, or (b) in the course of employment, to differentiate adversely in relation to an employee, on a prohibited ground of discrimination."[77] The Commission argues that the clause applies to systemic discrimination because of the word "indirectly." But this word is open to more than one interpretation. According to the Federal Court of Canada, "...it refers to the manner in which the conduct described [in section 7] is carried out rather than the manner in which it produces its discriminatory effect." The Court thus found that the section applied only to direct discrimination.[78]

Section 10 of the *Canadian Human Rights Act* makes it a "discriminatory practice for an employer...to establish or pursue a policy or practice...that deprives or tends to deprive an individual or class of individuals of any employment opportunities on a prohibited ground of discrimination." The language of this section is similar to subsection 703(a)(2) of the U.S. *Civil Rights Act*, on which the *Griggs* decision was based. The two clauses differ in one significant respect, however: although both use the words "deprive or tend to deprive," the American version adds the phrase "or otherwise adversely affect." The Federal Court of Canada concluded that the latter phrase is the necessary "anchor" of an interpretation that would bring systemic discrimination within the scope of the prohibition of section 10.[79] Whether or not one agrees with this, one must concede that even with the requisite anchor, subsection 703(a)(2) of the *Civil Rights Act* is not nearly as explicit on the matter of systemic discrimination as is section 10 of the new Ontario Code or section 1 of the English *Sex Discrimination Act*.[80] Indeed, there is evidence to suggest that American legislators did not intend or expect subsection 703(a)(2) to extend to systemic discrimination.[81]

In the event, the Supreme Court of Canada upheld the appeals of both O'Malley and Bhinder on the issue of whether intent was a required component of prohibited discrimination. In a twin set of judgments that rank as the Canadian *Griggs* v. *Duke Power*, the Court declared that both the federal *Human Rights Act* and the old Ontario Code—and thus, effectively, the similarly worded legislation of other Canadian jurisdictions—covers systemic discrimination.[82] Writing for the Court, Justice McIntyre asserted that human rights legislation "is of a special nature, not quite constitutional but certainly more than ordinary," and that as such it is entitled to a broad and purposive interpretation.[83] Its fundamental purpose, moreover, "is not to punish the discriminator, but rather to provide relief for the victims of discrimination. It is the result or the effect of the action complained of which is significant."[84] Justice McIntyre concluded: "An employment rule honestly made for sound economic or business reasons, equally applicable to all to whom it is intended to apply, may yet be discriminatory if it affects a person or group of persons differently from others to whom it may apply."[85]

The legal remedy to systemic barriers takes two different forms. In some cases the barrier is subject to wholesale challenge because it is seen to reflect the bias of a dominant group rather than a truly neutral standard of excellence; in other cases the neutrality and legitimacy of the standard is accepted but special exemptions are made for members of certain target groups. The latter has come to be known as "reasonable accommodation."

The "reasonable accommodation" remedy to systemic discrimination is illustrated in Justice McIntyre's *O'Malley* opinion. He pointed out that where, in the case of direct discrimination, "a working rule or condition of employment is found to be discriminatory on a prohibited ground and fails to meet any statutory justification test, it is simply struck down." However,

> In the case of discrimination on the basis of creed resulting from the effect of a condition or rule rationally related to the performance of the job and not on its face discriminatory a different result follows. The working rule or condition is not struck down, but its effect on the complainant must be considered, and if the purpose of [the legislation] is to be given effect some accommodation must be required from the employer for the benefit of the complainant.[86]

This requires a flexible balancing of the right of the employee and the "right of the employer to proceed with the lawful conduct of his business." Thus the employer has a "duty to accommodate" but not to the point where it causes "undue hardship" to the business.

The extent to which reasonable accommodation is required by human rights legislation that does not explicitly cover it has been a matter of considerable controversy.[87] The question turns on the proper interpretation of the BFOQ exemption. According to one interpretation, a BFOQ is a requirement of the occupational category as such and may legitimately be required of all who wish to enter or remain in it. Thus a successful BFOQ defence immunizes the employer not only from the charge of discrimination but also from any duty of reasonable accommodation. Others argue that the principles of reasonable accommodation should be built into the definition of BFOQ. In this view, while a requirement may be sensible as a general rule applicable to most employees, it can be a BFOQ for certain individuals only if the employer can show that making an exception would cause undue hardship. This interpretation orients the BFOQ defence to the particular circumstances of individual employees rather than to the general requirements of an occupational category; it holds that where reasonable accommodation is possible, it is required by the BFOQ standard itself.

The incorporation of reasonable accommodation into the definition of BFOQ was accepted by the dissenting opinion of justices Dickson and Lamer in Bhinder's Supreme Court appeal. It was rejected, however, by the two opinions representing the rest of the seven-judge panel in that case. Justice McIntyre insisted that the words "occupational requirement...refer to a requirement of the occupation, not a requirement limited to the individual," and that a BFOQ is, "by its nature, not susceptible to individual application."[88] Justice Wilson agreed. The purpose of the BFOQ provision, she wrote, is to "make the requirement of the job prevail over the requirement of the employee. It negates any duty to accommodate by stating that it is not discrimination."[89]

The Supreme Court did not completely reject the principle of reasonable accommodation, however. We have seen that in *O'Malley* Justice McIntyre, writing for a unanimous court, found a duty to accommodate up to the point of undue hardship in the Ontario legislation. More exactly, he found that the duty of reasonable accommodation was implicit in anti-discrimination provisions that were not explicitly subject to a BFOQ exemption. Although the Ontario legislation contained a BFOQ provision, it did not apply to "creed," which was of course the ground of discrimination at issue in *O'Malley.* Justice McIntyre saddled the employer with the onus of proving that O'Malley could not have been better accommodated without undue hardship and found that this onus had not been met. Thus, while Bhinder lost his case, O'Malley won hers.

Systemic Discrimination and the Charter

At the constitutional level the question of systemic discrimination is far from settled. Section 15 did not come into effect until April, 1985, and at the time of writing the Supreme Court has yet to decide a case based primarily on this section. The question has been a matter of much scholarly speculation, however, and it has arisen indirectly in cases under section 2 of the *Charter.*

In *The Queen* v. *Big M Drug Mart*, the Supreme Court found that the *Lord's Day Act* violated the *Charter* and was thus "of no force or effect."[90] Although the participating judges were unanimous in supporting this conclusion, there was some disagreement about the proper reasons for reaching it. Chief Justice Dickson, writing for all but Madame Justice Wilson, stressed the fact that the *Lord's Day Act* gave effect to an unconstitutional purpose, namely, the official promotion of one religion to the detriment of all others. Justice Wilson, on the other hand, did not think that the purpose of the legislation was a relevant consideration. If the *Lord's Day Act* infringed on the freedom of conscience and religion protected by section 2(a) of the *Charter,* it did so not "because the statute was enacted for this *purpose* but because it has this *effect.*" The *Charter,* she insisted, "asks not whether the legislature has acted for a purpose that is within the scope of the authority of...government, but rather whether in so acting it has had the effect of violating an entrenched individual right. It is, in other words, first and foremost an effects-oriented document."[91] Although Justice Dickson refused to discard purpose as a test of unconstitutionality, he did not deny the relevance of effect. If legislation embodies a constitutionally permitted purpose, he said, it may nevertheless be challenged because it has an unconstitutional effect. On this basis he subsequently ruled that Ontario's *Retail Holidays Act*, which had a purely secular purpose, had the effect of infringing the religious liberty of non-Sunday sabbatarians, though he found the infringement to be a "reasonable limit" under section 1.[92] Thus, although Justice Wilson was unsuccessful in making effects the sole touchstone of constitutionality under the *Charter*, it has become an important interpretive principle in section 2 cases.

The Supreme Court has also emphasized "effects" in jurisprudence under section 7 of the *Charter*, which guarantees "the right to life, liberty and security of the person and the right not to be deprived thereof except in accordance with the principles of fundamental justice." In its 1988 landmark decision *R* v. *Morgentaler*, the Court struck down the existing Criminal Code restrictions on abortion. The law permitted abortions in an accredited hospital if a therapeutic abortion committee determined that the life or health of the woman was at risk. The committee had to include at least three physicians on the hospital's staff, none of whom could perform the abortion. This meant that many small hospitals would be ineligible. "In other words," wrote Justice Dickson, "the seemingly neutral requirement of section 251(4) that at least four physicians be available to authorize and perform an abortion meant in practice that abortions would be absolutely unavailable in almost one quarter of all hospitals in Canada." The "disparate impact" of this neutral requirement was held to violate the "principles of fundamental justice."[93]

In *Big M Drug Mart*, Justice Wilson's effects-oriented interpretation was not limited to the guarantee of religious freedom in section 2 of the *Charter* but was phrased in general terms. It was the entire *Charter* that was said to be effects-oriented. In fact, however, to the extent that Justice Wilson was thinking beyond section 2, she was probably mainly concerned with section 15, the "equality rights" section. Section 15 is inevitably implicated in freedom of religion cases because religion is included among the prohibited grounds of discrimination, and a violation of religious freedom under section 2 can usually also be described as discrimination on the basis of religion.[94] The opinions in the Sunday closing cases were limited to section 2 because section 15 had not yet come into effect.

That Justice Wilson was thinking of the discrimination issue in her *Big M Drug Mart* opinion is also indicated by the fact that the major precedent she cited in support of the effects-oriented interpretation was *Griggs* v. *Duke Power Co.*, which was a racial employment discrimination case.

The effects-oriented interpretation of section 15 has found considerable favour in both the scholarly and political communities. In October of 1985 the Parliamentary Committee on Equality Rights reported its belief that Section 15 covered systemic discrimination.[95] Similarly, the contributors to a major book on section 15 are unanimous in their view that it applies to systemic barriers.[96] This argument flows from the conviction that the purpose of the section is not just to protect formal equality of opportunity but to achieve equality of results. As the Parliamentary Committee on Equality Rights put it: "Equality is an elusive concept. It is much easier to narrow it down by stating what it does not mean than by trying, initially, to articulate what it does mean. We can safely say that, in our view, it doesn't necessarily mean either sameness of treatment or patent equality." The Committee considered equality of results "to be the proper emphasis in any consideration of equality under section 15"[97] and immediately added that this goal requires the overcoming of unintentional, systemic barriers:

> Consistent with this results-oriented approach, we also believe that the kinds of discriminatory laws to which section 15 relates are those that have the effect, in practice, of discriminating. Therefore, a law that does not single out for adverse treatment members of a group protected by section 15 will nonetheless be discriminatory if that is the inherent result.[98]

In short, systemic barriers must be included in section 15 because the equality of results aimed at by the section could not otherwise be achieved.

In considering the question whether section 15 should be given a systemic interpretation, it should be noted that the Supreme Court of the United States has declined to bring systemic discrimination within the scope of the equal protection clause of the Fourteenth Amendment to the Constitution. In *Big M Drug Mart* Justice Wilson neglected to mention that *Griggs* was not a constitutional equality rights case but a private employment case arising under the *Civil Rights Act*. The United States Supreme Court has drawn a clear line between the two kinds of cases: the *Civil Rights Act* covers systemic barriers, but the Fourteenth Amendment does not. To make out a case of unconstitutional "state action," it is not sufficient, or even necessary, to prove a discriminatory effect; one must above all demonstrate a discriminatory purpose. Whether the Canadian Supreme Court will make a similar distinction or adopt a systemic reading of section 15 remains to be seen. In chapter six I shall argue that there are good reasons for rejecting the latter course and following the American lead instead.

Affirmative Action

The equality-of-result orientation evident in the systemic approach to anti-discrimination provisions is even more dramatically represented by affirmative action, which adds positive measures to the negative prohibition of discrimination in order to achieve a more proportional representation of groups than currently exists. According to one formulation,

> Affirmative Action is a comprehensive planning process designed to ensure not only an equality of opportunity but also an equality of results. Its primary objective is to ensure the Canadian workforce is an accurate reflection of the composition of the Canadian population given the availability of required skills.[99]

Affirmative action is constitutionally protected from the charge of "reverse discrimination" by section 15(2) of the *Charter* and is fast becoming one of the leading policy responses to the political claims of Canadian women and minorities. In June of 1983 Treasury Board president Herb Gray "announced that an affirmative action program, under the direction of the Treasury Board, is being implemented across the Public Service of Canada."[100] Many provincial governments have similar programs, as do a number of municipalities. While these public sector programs are mandatory, affirmative action in the private sector remained voluntary until 1986.[101] Governments were actively promoting private sector affirmative action, however. In 1979 the Affirmative Action Directorate of the Canada Employment and Immigration Commission (CEIC) was established to act as a consultant to private industry in the creation and implementation of affirmative action programs; it did this for businesses under both federal and provincial jurisdiction. Some of the provincial human rights commissions have done the same thing. The response to these initiatives was not overwhelming: from 1979 to 1983 only 49 of the 1130 firms approached by CEIC entered into agreements to establish affirmative action programs, a fact that led the Special House of Commons Committee on Visible Minorities to recommend the imposition of mandatory affirmative action in five years "if insufficient progress is detected under voluntary programs."[102]

In 1983 the federal government appointed Judge Rosalie Abella to sit as a "Royal Commission On Equality In Employment" and directed her to inquire into the feasibility and desirability of mandatory affirmative action programs in federal Crown corporations. Abella's report strongly supported the notion of compulsory affirmative action (she renamed it "employment equity") in both the public and the private spheres.[103]

Depending on how one defines discrimination, affirmative action can be understood either as a remedial response to discrimination or as something separate from and additional to an anti-discrimination policy. In the early days of anti-discrimination legislation, when it was generally thought that the legal prohibition extended only to intentional discrimination "because of" an individual's group affiliation, affirmative action was understood in the latter sense. Since not all group underrepresentation could be attributed to direct discrimination, the prohibition of such discrimination could be expected to have a less-than-adequate impact on the problem of disproportionality. A policy designed to bring about proportional representation had therefore to be understood as overcoming factors other than legally prohibited discrimination, not as a remedy to such discrimination. It followed that the enforcers of anti-discrimination legislation had no authority to compel affirmative action; at best they could recommend voluntary implementation. Peter Robertson, a consultant to CEIC, recalls that this was the understanding with which he began his career in the enforcement of anti-discrimination legislation. Upon his appointment as Executive Director of the Missouri Human Rights Commission, he was briefed by a group of experts, one of whom told him, "If all you do is remedy discrimination, you will fail. The wave of the future is affirmative action." Says Robertson,

> Thus, I started out in this field with the idea that affirmative action was entirely different from remedying discrimination and that it was really a sort of quasi-charitable activity which I would ask employers to engage in—out of the kindness of their hearts; but which I could not insist that they implement to comply with the law.[104]

The second way of understanding affirmative action—as a remedy for discrimination[105]—requires an expanded definition of discrimination.[106] One must include in the concept those factors other than direct intentional discrimination that contribute to the underrepresentation affirmative action is designed to overcome. Proponents of affirmative action argue that such a transformation of the definition is logically required by the purpose to which anti-discrimination policy is directed. In this view the legislation was enacted precisely to bring about greater proportionality, and the discrimination it prohibits must therefore be defined in a manner adequate to this end. Again Peter Robertson summarizes this thinking:

> ...when we in the U.S. initially confronted the different unemployment rates, occupational distribution, and disparate income levels of minorities and women we attempted to change the situation by making it illegal to discriminate. When we discovered that eliminating discrimination (as it was then defined) was having no impact on the problem we began to talk about affirmative action and to perceive that action as something above and beyond eliminating discrimination. [However] that failure to change the underlying facts which had confronted Congress was not a failure of the anti-discrimination legislation but was, instead, a failure to understand the real nature of discrimination. It was only when we began to perceive discrimination in a totally different fashion that we began to have a real impact on the problem...on the facts.[107]

The concept of discrimination was expanded mainly by extending it to include systemic barriers. Affirmative action, understood as a policy of increasing the proportional representation of groups, is generally described as a response to this kind of discrimination. One CEIC report, for example, defines affirmative action as "a comprehensive result-oriented plan adopted by an employer as a remedy for employment discrimination with special emphasis on systemic discrimination."[108] Another states that

> The affirmative action approach to the problem of inequity and inefficient utilization of target group workers is based on the concept of systemic discrimination. That is, this approach identifies discrimination in the workplace in terms of the impact of employment practices on the employment of target group members.[109]

According to CEIC an affirmative action program cannot achieve its goal of proportionality unless it is composed of both an "equal opportunity response" and "special measures." By an "equal opportunity response" CEIC means the cessation of direct discrimination and the dismantling of systemic barriers in favour of practices that do not have a disparate impact on target groups.

Special measures are of two types: remedial and support. "A remedial measure is any action designed to redress past discrimination by providing a preferential benefit to a designated group." Examples of such measures include the preferential hiring of women from a pool of otherwise equally qualified applicants, and special training programs for natives to help them qualify for certain jobs. A support measure is designed to alleviate "an employment problem specifically affecting a particular group" but is not preferential because members of non-target groups can avail themselves of the benefit. An alcoholic counselling program, for example, may have been designed with the problem of a particular minority in mind, but would be available to any alcoholic, whatever his group affiliation.[110] Whereas equal opportunity responses, and some support measures, constitute permanent changes in employment practices, remedial measures are usually conceived of as being temporary.

The reason affirmative action must include both "equal opportunity" and "remedial" measures is that it "has as its primary objective a change in the existing employment distribution. Equality of results is of paramount concern,"[111] and such "results" cannot be achieved by an equal opportunity response alone. Equality of opportunity gives free rein to actual inequalities and leads inevitably to inequality of result. To the extent that actual inequalities are not natural but the consequence of past discrimination, equality of opportunity perpetuates the effects of past injustice. The mere cessation of discrimination is therefore not enough. As one commentator observed in 1983, "The federal Public Service Commission, after four years of implementing an equal opportunity program, reported little improvement in women's status, and an actual decrease in some occupational areas."[112]

If an equal opportunity response is not sufficient for the achievement of affirmative action's goals, it is nevertheless necessary. A remedial program designed to upgrade the qualifications of a particular group will not achieve the desired result if the employer continues to base hiring decisions on prejudiced stereotypes, or if systemic barriers, such as seniority systems, prevent the promotion of the program's beneficiaries.

In addition to an equal opportunity response and special measures, most of the literature stresses that a properly constructed affirmative action program must set numerical goals or targets and establish timetables for achieving them. The Commons Committee on Visible Minorities distinguished between voluntary and mandatory affirmative programs partly in terms of the emphasis placed on achieving these goals. "While it is not obligatory [in a voluntary program] to meet the goals, good faith efforts to hire minorities must be demonstrated." In a mandatory program, on the other hand, "An employer is obligated to employ a fixed number or percentage of visible minority workers."[113] Although such goals are to be flexible even in mandatory programs, the success of a program is measured in terms of achieving them, and program managers are evaluated in terms of this measure of success—if they don't get results, they must expect to be penalized. Thus one of the criteria for evaluating Treasury Board's affirmative action programs is "the level of attainment of the quantitative goals set by departments and agencies..."; success "will be considered a priority item in evaluating the performance of deputy heads."[114] For CEIC such "accountability" is important even in voluntary private sector programs.[115]

In March of 1985, in response to the Abella Commission's recommendations, the federal government announced a significant expansion of affirmative action policy.[116] Designating women, aboriginal peoples, persons with disabilities, and visible minorities as the target groups for affirmative action, the new policy had three main components. First, it would strengthen the existing Treasury Board program in the federal civil service. Second, an *Employment Equity Act* would be introduced to extend affirmative action to federal Crown corporations and federally regulated businesses with more than 100 employees. (This legislation was enacted in 1986.)[117] Third, a "Federal Contractors Program" would require businesses and institutions with more than 100 employees to commit themselves to implementing affirmative action as a condition of bidding for federal contracts over $200,000. These policies make affirmative action mandatory outside the civil service for the first time.[118] Through the "contract compliance" program, moreover, they reach contractors outside the ambit of federal regulatory power.[119]

All of the central elements of affirmative action as described in the literature are embodied in these policies. Employers have a duty to identify and eliminate "employment barriers against persons in designated groups" (an equal opportunity response).[120] They must institute "such positive policies and practices and

[make] such reasonable accommodation as will ensure that persons is designated groups achieve" a more proportional representation in the workforce (remedial measures).[121] And, finally, employers are required to prepare annual plans setting out numerical goals and timetables for the achievement of increased target-group representation.[122]

Conclusion

The history of human rights legislation in Canada has been one of expansion and consolidation. Scattered "fair employment" and "fair housing" statutes, which did not even use the rhetoric of "rights," have been replaced by comprehensive human rights codes that cover these and many other areas of activity. In its early form the legislation prohibited discrimination only on the basis of race, ethnicity and religion; taken together Canadian human rights codes now specify thirty prohibited grounds, including occasionally an open-ended list. Section 15 of the *Charter* provides a similar far-reaching prohibition of public discrimination. Chapter three suggests a way of classifying this lengthy list of prohibited grounds.

In addition to protecting a growing list of groups against direct discrimination, human rights legislation also prohibits systemic discrimination against the specified groups. Whether section 15 of the *Charter* will also receive a systemic interpretation remains an open question.

Whereas the steady expansion of the list of explicitly prohibited grounds of discrimination reflects the influence of the rhetoric of individual treatment, the prohibition of systemic discrimination tries to achieve equality of result. The latter end is also served by affirmative action programs, which use remedial measures and ameliorative preferences to achieve pre-determined numerical goals. Chapters four through seven examine these two orientations and their policy manifestations in detail, arguing that both are imbued with the assumptions of constructivist rationalism and that they provide the guardian elite with substantial projects in social technology.

Notes

[1] See Walter Surma Tarnopolsky, *The Canadian Bill of Rights,* second revised ed., (Toronto: McClelland and Stewart, 1975), 3-7; Peter H. Russell, "The Political Purposes of the Canadian Charter of Rights and Freedoms," *The Canadian Bar Review* 61 (1983), 33; Roy Romanow, John Whyte and Howard Leeson, *Canada Notwithstanding: The Making of the Constitution 1976-1982* (Toronto: Carswell/ Methuen, 1984), 220-221.

[2] Walter Surma Tarnopolsky, *Discrimination and The Law in Canada* (Toronto: Richard De Boo, 1982), 26-27; Ian A. Hunter, "The Origin, Development and Interpretation of Human Rights Legislation," in R. St. J. Macdonald and John P. Humphrey, eds., *The Practice of Freedom: Canadian Essays on Human Rights and Fundamental Freedoms* (Toronto: Butterworths, 1979), 80.

[3] Walter S. Tarnopolsky, "The Iron Hand in the Velvet Glove: Administration and Enforcement of Human Rights Legislation in Canada," *Canadian Bar Review,* XLVI (1968), 568-69.

[4] Tarnopolsky, *Discrimination and the Law,* 27-29.

[5] *Ibid.,* 28.

[6] *Ibid.,* 29.

[7] *Ibid.,* 30; Hunter, "Origin and Development," 81.

[8] Tarnopolsky, *Discrimination and the Law,* 29-30.

[9] Ontario Human Rights Commission, *A Life Together: A Report on Human Rights in Ontario* (Toronto: Queen's Printer, 1977), 10.

[10] What I here call "ethnicity" encompasses such grounds as national and ethnic origin, ancestry, place of origin, nationality, and perhaps citizenship. One or more of these is found in every Canadian human rights act.

[11] This ground is variously forumulated as religion, religious belief, and creed.

[12] The full list, in approximate order of their frequency of appearance in the various acts, is as follows: race, colour, sex, marital status, age, physical handicap, religion, national and ethnic origin, mental handicap, creed, ancestry, place of origin, political belief, family status, nationality, pregnancy, pardoned offence, criminal record, source of income, citizenship, language, état civil, sexual orientation, drug and alcohol dependency, public assistance, religious belief, attachment of pay, social origin, social condition, place of residence, without reasonable cause.

[13] S.M. 1987, c.45, s.13(1) and s.16(1).

[14] S.M 1976, c.48, s.6; 1977, c.46, ss. 2 & 3; 1982, c.23, s.9.

[15] S.M. 1987, c.45, s.14(1).

[16] *Chris Vogel* v. *Government of Manitoba* (1983), 4 C.H.R.R. D/1654.

[17] Interview by Thomas Flanagan with Darlene Germscheid, then Executive Director of the Manitoba Human Rights Commission, December 13, 1983.

[18] *Gryba* v. *Scott* (1987), 8 C.H.R.R. D/3674.

[19] See, for example, s.19(1) of the British Columbia Human Rights Act, S.B.C. 1984, c.22; and s.23(1)(a) of the Ontario Human Rights Code, S.O. 1981 c.53.

[20] See, for example, sections 20(1) and 23(1)(c) of the Ontario Code.

[21] See s.21 of the Ontario Code.

[22] Such a limit is imposed by s.9(1)(a) of the Ontario Code. In *McKinney* v. *University of Guelph* (1988), 9 C.H.R.R. D/4573, the Ontario Court of Appeal found that this limit violated section 15 of the *Charter* but that it was saved, in the case

of a university mandatory retirement policy, as a "reasonable limit" under section 1. In British Columbia, by contrast, the Court of Appeal, again in the context of a university retirement requirement, found that the age limit in the B.C. act (between 45 and 65) could not pass the section 1 test. See *Connell* v. *University of British Columbia* (1988), 9 C.H.R.R. D/4557.

[23] The term *"bona fide"* is used in most legislation; some jurisdictions, however, such as Saskatchewan, substitute the term "reasonable."

[24] The federal Act uses the term "requirement" rather than "qualification."

[25] *Ontario Human Rights Commission et. al.* v. *The Borough of Etobicoke* (1982), 3 C.H.R.R. D/781 at D/783.

[26] Tarnopolsky, *Discrimination and the Law,* 380.

[27] *Ibid.,* 476-482.

[28] These were Saskatchewan, Alberta and Quebec.

[29] 8-9 Elizabeth II, c.44.

[30] [1970] S.C.R. 282.

[31] *Ibid.,* at 297.

[32] [1974] S.C.R. 1349 at 1366.

[33] (1979), 92 D.L.R. (3d) 417.

[34] *Ibid.,* at 422.

[35] Peter W. Hogg, *Canada Act Annotated* (Toronto: Carswell, 1982), 52.

[36] Romanow, Whyte and Leeson, *Canada Notwithstanding*, 253-255.

[37] See Leslie A. Pal and F.L. Morton, "Bliss v. Attorney General of Canada: From Legal Defeat to Political Victory," *Osgoode Hall Law Journal* 24:1 (1986).

[38] Romanow, Whyte and Leeson, *Canada Notwithstanding*, 253-255.

[39] Another victory for the feminist movement was the insertion of s.28 into the Charter. This section, which guarantees Charter rights "equally to male and female persons," "notwithstanding anything in this Charter," was intended to prevent the application of the s.33 legislative override to the s.15 guarantee of sexual equality.

[40] Section 33 applies to sections 2 and 7 to 15 of the Charter. But see the previous note on the application of section 33 to the section 15 prohibition of sex discrimination.

[41] Peter Hogg, *Constitutional Law of Canada*, 2nd. ed., (Toronto: Carswell, 1985), 797.

[42] F.L. Morton and M.J. Withey, "Charting the Charter, 1982-1985: A Statistical Analysis," *Canadian Human Rights Yearbook 1987,* 72-74.

[43] *Ibid.,* 75.

[44] *Ibid.,* 76.

[45] William Black, *Employment Equality: A Systemic Approach* (Ottawa: Human Rights Research and Education Centre, 1985), 25-26.

[46] 401 U.S. 424, (1971), 432.

[47] A year earlier, in a famous equal pay case—*Re Attorney General for Alberta and Gares* (1976), 67 D.L.R. (3d) 635— Justice McDonald of the Alberta Supreme Court wrote (at 695) that "it is the discriminatory result which is prohibited [by Alberta's equal pay provisions] and not a discriminatory intent." But as William Black points out "Statutory provisions concerning equal pay are worded differently from other anti-discrimination provisions…and the new approach might have been confined to this area." Black, *Employment Equality,* 26.

[48] Unreported at 19.

[49] Black, *Employment Equality,* 27.

[50] Walter Surma Tarnopolsky, *Discrimination and the Law,* ch. 4.

[51] Patrick Devlin, *The Enforcement of Morals* (London: Oxford University Press, 1965).

[52] As Chief Justice Dickson has said, in the early forms of anti-discrimination statutes "The word 'intent' was deprived of its meaning in common parlance and was used as a surrogate for 'malice.' 'Intent' was not the simple willing of a consequence, but rather the desiring of harm." See *Action Travail des Femmes* v. *Canadian National Railway Co.* (1987), 8 C.H.R.R. D/4210 at D/4224. (S.C.C.)

[53] For a slightly different discussion of this distinction see William Black, "From Intent to Effect: New Standards in Human Rights" (1980), 1 C.H.R.R. C/1, at C/2-C/3.

[54] Tarnopolsky, *Discrimination and the Law,* 115.

[55] *Ibid.,* 113-122.

[56] *Action Travail des Femmes,* D/4225.

[57] The passive definition of intent was used as a fallback position, pending the Supreme Court's decision in the *Bhinder* appeal, by the tribunal in *Action Travail des Femmes* v. *Canadian National* (1984), 5 C.H.R.R. D/2327 at D/2373. See also Black, "From Intent to Effect," C/2-C/3.

[58] Graham Parker, *An Introduction to Criminal Law,* 2nd ed. (Toronto: Methuen, 1983), 155-158.

[59] The United States Supreme Court rejected the passive definition of intent in *Personnel Administrator of Mass.* v. *Feeney,* 442 U.S. 256 (1979). This case concerned a "veteran's preference" that benefited mainly men. The court conceded that the legislature was aware of the disparate impact on women, but insisted that only an active intent to discriminate against women could invalidate the law. See William Black, "Intent or Effects: Section 15 of the Charter of Rights and Freedoms," in Joseph M. Weiler and Robin M. Elliot, eds., *Litigating the Values of a Nation: The Canadian Charter of Rights and Freedoms* (Toronto: Carswell, 1986), 128.

[60] *O'Malley* v. *Simpsons-Sears Ltd.* (1981), 2 C.H.R.R (Bd. of Inquiry) D267 at D267. Emphasis added.

[61] *Ibid.*

[62] Saskatchewan Human Rights Commission, *Affirmative Action News* (January 1981): The systemic approach "removes guilt and blame from the social arena ."

[63] Factum of the Canadian Jewish Congress in the case of *Bhinder* v. *Canadian National Railway,* (Case file, S.C.C.) 4.

[64] Tarnopolsky, "The Iron Hand in the Velvet Glove," 585.

[65] *Ibid.,* 589-90.

[66] (1982), 3 C.H.R.R. D/796; reversing (1981), 2 C.H.R.R (Bd. of Inquiry).

[67] (1982), 3 C.H.R.R. D/1071.

[68] *Canadian National Railway* v. *Bhinder* (1983), 4 C.H.R.R. D/1404; reversing (1981), 2. C.H.R.R. D/546 (Tribunal).

[69] Bob Daudlin, Chairman, Special Committee on Visible Minorities in Canadian Society, *Equality Now* (Ottawa: Queen's Printer, 1984), 77.

[70] Manitoba added a provision explicitly addressing systemic discrimination in 1987, S.M. 1987 c.45, s.9(3).

[71] *O'Malley* v. *Simpsons-Sears* (1981), 2 C.H.R.R. D/267 at D/268.

[72] 42 U.S.C. 2000e-2(a)(1).

[73] *Bone* v. *Hamilton Tiger Cats Football Club* (unreported), quoted in *Mears* v. *Ontario Hydro* (1984), 5 C.H.R.R. D/1927 at D/1937-D/1938.

[74] 42 U.S.C. 20003-2(a)(2). See Griggs v. Duke Power Co. 401 U.S. 424 at 426 (1971). Emphasis added.

[75] Confidential interview with a senior human rights commission staff person.

[76] See e.g., *O'Malley* v. *Simpsons-Sears* (1981), 2 C.H.R.R. D/267 at D/268.

[77] S.C. 1976-77, C.33 amended by 1977-78, C.22, 1980-81-82-83, C.111, 143. Emphasis added.

[78] *C.N.R.* v. *Bhinder* (1983), 4 C.H.R.R. D/1404 at 1413.

[79] *Ibid.*, D/1405.

[80] 1975 (Eng.), c. 65. Section 1 reads as follows:

1(1) A person discriminates against a woman in any circumstance relevant for the purposes of the Act if;

(b) he applies to her a requirement or condition which he applies or would apply equally to a man; but

(i) which is such that the proportion of women who can comply with it is considerably smaller than the proportion of men who can comply with it; and

(ii) which he cannot show to be justifiable irrespective of the sex of the person to whom it is applied; and

(iii) which is to her detriment because she cannot comply with it.

[81] Hugh Steven Wilson, "A Second Look at Griggs v. Duke Power Company: Ruminations on Job Testing, Discrimination, and the Role of the Federal Courts," *Virginia Law Review* 58(1972) 852-858.

[82] *O'Malley* v. *Simpsons-Sears Ltd.* (1986), 7 C.H.R.R. D/3102 at D/3106; *Bhinder* v. *Canadian National Railway Co.* (1986), 7 C.H.R.R. D/3093 at D/3095 and D/3096.

[83] *O'Malley* (1986), D/3105.

[84] *Ibid.*

[85] *Ibid.*, D/3106.

[86] *Ibid.*, D/3106-D/3107.

[87] Some jurisdictions have recently enacted explicit reasonable accommodation requirements. See section 9(1)(d) of the Manitoba Code and s.16(1a) of the Ontario Code, enacted in 1987 and 1986 respectively.

[88] *Bhinder* (1986), 7 C.H.R.R. D/3093 at 3096.

[89] *Ibid.*, 3097. This approach was followed by the Alberta Court of Queen's Bench in *Central Alberta Dairy Pool* v. *Alberta Human Rights Commission* (1987), 8 C.H.R.R. D/3639, and by the Supreme Court of British Columbia in *Central Okanagan School District No. 23* v. *Renaud* (1988), 9 C.H.R.R. D/4609. But see *Saskatchewan Human Rights Commission* v. *City of Moose Jaw* (1987), 8 C.H.R.R. D/4201, in which the Saskatchewan Court of Appeal finds that the "reasonable occupational qualification" defence in the Saskatchewan Act, as legislatively elaborated in regulations, differs significantly from an undefined "bona fide occupational qualification" defence and requires the individualized assessment of reasonable accommodation.

[90] *The Queen* v. *Big M. Drug Mart Ltd.*, [1985] 18 D.L.R. (4th) 321.

[91] *Ibid.*, 372.

[92] *Edwards Books* v. *The Queen*, [1986] 2 S.C.R. 713 at 766 and 783. The same approach was used by the majority of the Court in *R.* v. *Jones*, [1986] 2 S.C.R. 284.

[93] *Morgentaler* v. *The Queen* (1988), 44 D.L.R. (4th) 385 at 409.

[94] William Black, "Religion and the Right of Equality," in Bayefsky and Eberts, eds., *Equality Rights*, 132-133.

[95] In its response to this report, the government is not clear as to whether it considers the overcoming of systemic discrimination to be required by section 15, or whether it is one of the things that governments should do to promote equality and social justice over and above what is constitutionally required of them. In any case, it is clear that the government thinks systemic discrimination ought to be overcome. See, *Toward Equality: The Response to the Report of the Parliamentary Committee on Equality Rights* (Ottawa: Department of Justice, 1986), 3-4.

[96] Bayefsky and Eberts, eds., *Equality Rights*.

[97] *Equality For All: Report of the Parliamentary Committee on Equality Rights* (Ottawa: Supply and Services Canada, 1985).

[98] *Ibid*.

[99] Rhys D. Phillips, "Affirmative Action As An Effective Labour Market Planning Tool of the 1980s." (Labour Market Development Task Force Technical Studies Series, No. 29, 1981).

[100] Treasury Board of Canada, News Release, June 27, 1983, 1.

[101] Human rights commissions generally have the power only to approve affirmative action programs, not to impose them. In some cases, however, boards of inquiry or tribunals engaged in the quasi-judicial resolution of cases that cannot be settled by the commission may have the power to order an affirmative action remedy. Judge Rosalie Abella, Commissioner, *Report on the Commission on Equality in Employment* (Ottawa: Supply and Services, 1984), 197-198. See also *Action Travail des Femmes* v. *Canadian National Railway Co.* (1987), 8 C.H.R.R. D/4210 (S.C.C.).

[102] Daudlin, *Equality Now*, 33.

[103] Abella, *Equality in Employment*, ch. 6.

[104] Peter C. Robertson, "Some Thoughts About Affirmative Action in Canada in the 1980s" (CEIC, 1980), 4.

[105] The following is a typical statement: "Affirmative action has no meaning outside the context of discrimination, the problem it was created to remedy." *Affirmative Action in the 1980s: Dismantling the Process of Discrimination* (A Statement of the United States Commission on Civil Rights, Clearinghouse Publication 70, 1981), 1. See also Saskatchewan Human Rights Commission, *Newsletter* (Oct.-Nov. 1984), 2: "An affirmative action program is a comprehensive strategy developed to counteract and eliminate discrimination and to remedy the effects of past discrimination."

[106] See Saskatchewan Human Rights Commission, *Affirmative Action News* (January, 1981).

[107] Robertson, "Some Thoughts About Affirmative Action," 4-5.

[108] CEIC, *Affirmative Action: Definitions and Terms* (1979), 1.

[109] CEIC, *Affirmative Action Technical Training Manual* (1982), 41.

[110] CEIC, *Affirmative Action: Definitions and Terms*, 3.

[111] *Ibid.*, 1.

[112] Mary Bruce, "Equal Opportunity, Affirmative Action—The Toronto Experience," *Affirmation*, 4:3 (1983), 2.

[113] Daudlin, *Equality Now*, 33.

[114] Treasury Board of Canada, "Affirmative Action in the Federal Public Service," News Release, June 27, 1983, 3.

[115] CEIC, *Affirmative Action: Technical Training Manual*, 54.

[116] A series of news releases and "notes for statements" of various ministers was issued on March 8, 1985. These are summed up in "Employment Equity: A response to the Abella Commission of Inquiry on Equality in Employment—General summary."

[117] S.C. 1984-85-86, c.31.

[118] It was estimated that about one million employees outside the public service would be affected. See the news releases mentioned in note 116.

[119] For example, universities.

[120] S.C 1984-85-86, c.31, s.4(a).

[121] *Ibid.*, s.4(b).

[122] *Ibid.*, s.5. For similar requirements in the contract compliance program see Employment and Immigration Canada, *Employment Equity Federal Contractors Program: Information for Suppliers*, 1986.

III

THE PROTECTED GROUPS

Contemporary human rights policy protects a growing and bewildering variety of groups from discrimination. Many, though not all, of these groups demand and receive protection because they see themselves, and are seen by others, as oppressed minorities. This involves accepting a special understanding of the term "minority," because women, a numerical majority, are now included.[1] The newly protected groups and "minorities" differ in important respects from those of concern to earlier anti-discrimination policy. Their addition to the protected list is a prominent feature of the new war on discrimination.

What is a Minority?

The word "minority" is derived from the Latin *minor*, meaning "smaller" or "fewer." It can refer to a purely quantitative or statistical relationship, as in the sentence "Only a minority of votes was cast for the proposal." It can also refer to a condition of inferior status or power, as in the expression "age of minority." The dimensions of quantity and status are often so intertwined that meaning can be unraveled only through a specific analysis of usage in social context.

When John Stuart Mill borrowed the phrase "tyranny of the majority" from Alexis de Tocqueville, he had in mind the danger to the "instructed minority."[2] Mill believed that under contemporary conditions people of critical intelligence and cultivated sensibility would be few in number and thus exposed to danger in a democratic age where numbers amounted to power.

Certain aspects of Mill's view were reversed, while others were retained, when "minority" became a common term of political discourse in twentieth-century North America. The social context was the massive immigration around the turn of the century, which brought so many Eastern and Southern Europeans to both the United States and Canada, accompanied by the debate over nature and nurture that took place in the first two decades of this century.[3] The hereditarians, reading Darwin and Mendel in a certain way, saw the newcomers as inferior races who threatened the genetic purity of the dominant "great race" in North America. Advocates of cultural determinism, on the other hand, saw the immigrants as culturally distinct groups that could readily be assimilated if society was tolerant enough to accept them.

The term "minority" was proposed in 1932 by Donald Young as a way of transcending the hereditarian implications of the word "race," which at that time was in popular as well as scientific use to refer to what today would be called ethnic groups:

> There is, unfortunately, no word in the English language which can with philological propriety be applied to all...groups which are distinguished by biological features, alien national cultures, or a combination of both. For this reason, the phrases, "minorities of racial or national origin," "American minorities," or "minority peoples" are here used as synonyms for the popular usage of the word race.[4]

This was a brilliant innovation for the cultural determinists. "Minority" purported to be a neutral, scientific term without the obnoxious connotations of race, but it had its own connotations derived from the liberalism of thinkers such as Mill. A minority was a group that through no fault of its own was put in jeopardy by the politics of democracy. Mill's paradigm of a minority jeopardized by an intolerant majority survived, but now the minority was not a cultivated elite but a congeries of low-status immigrant groups of different cultures.

Once these fundamentals were established, studies proliferated under the rubric of minority relations in conjunction with ethnicity, prejudice, and discrimination. Definitions of "minority" multiplied within this framework. Louis Wirth wrote:

> We may define a minority as a group of people who, because of their physical or cultural characteristics, are singled out from others in the society in which they live for differential and unequal treatment and who therefore regard themselves as objects of collective discrimination.[5]

(Note that this definition does not even raise the question of numbers). In 1958 Charles Wagley and Marvin Harris constructed a more elaborate ideal type of minorities:

> 1. Minorities are subordinate segments of complex state societies;
>
> 2. minorities have special physical or cultural traits which are held in low esteem by the dominant segments of the society;
>
> 3. minorities are self-conscious units bound together by the special traits which their members share and by the special disabilities which these bring;
>
> 4. membership in a minority is transmitted by a rule of descent which is capable of affiliating succeeding generations even in the absence of readily apparent special cultural or physical traits;
>
> 5. minority peoples, by choice or necessity, tend to marry within the group.[6]

Wagley and Harris went further than Wirth in including in their definition what was tacitly assumed by all writers on the subject: that minorities were ethnic groups. This linkage still survives in the literature of sociology; introductory textbooks routinely treat minorities in a larger chapter on ethnicity, employing some version of the definitions of Wirth or of Wagley and Harris.

The intellectual ascendancy of this perspective helped to justify the American civil rights movement of the 1950s and 1960s. However, the very success of this movement in removing the legal disabilities of racial and ethnic groups has undermined the consensus about what a minority is. Inspired by the dramatic gains of blacks in the United States and Francophones in Canada, nonethnic groups also have begun to portray themselves as victimized minorities, the targets of stereotyping, prejudice, and discrimination.

The decisive breakthrough was made by the women's movement, as illustrated by the publication in 1976 of *The Minority Report: An Introduction to Racial, Ethnic, and Gender Relations*, by A.G. and R.J. Dworkin. Treating women alongside traditional ethnic minorities, the authors deliberately constructed a more comprehensive definition of a minority as a "group characterized by four qualities: identifiability, differential power, differential and pejorative treatment, and group awareness."[7] Mere statistical categories, such as left-handed people, can become genuine minority groups if they become aware of their powerlessness and mistreatment at the hands of the statistical majority, and if they can gain a degree of public recognition of their group trait. The

Dworkins explicitly raised the possibility of an infinity of other minority groups, such as homosexuals, communists, or prison inmates. Their approach accurately reflects the politics of the 1970s and 1980s, which have seen the multiplication of *soi-disant* minorities claiming redress for discrimination. Women and the aged have had particular success, as witnessed by the entry of the terms "sexism" and "ageism" into the English language. Homosexuals, welfare recipients, the handicapped, and many others are not far behind in travelling the same path.

Minorities, Groups and Aggregations

In the realm of "human rights" the term minority is a political one, referring not primarily to the numerical size of a group but to the supposed oppression of the group by others. The group consciousness that many authors discuss is not sufficient; a group is a "minority" only if its self-awareness includes consciousness of oppression. In an important sense a "minority" is constituted by those outside the group; without its perception of oppression by others, a group would be just a group, not a minority.

It is important to note that not all groups of concern to the human rights movement are minorities in this sense. Some groups are mere statistical aggregations, which are objectively identifiable but whose members do not share a significant group consciousness. Other groups are characterized by a self-conscious group identity but may not see themselves as oppressed. While the addition of new prohibited grounds to anti-discrimination provisions often reflects the emergence of new minorities, protection is also extended to less political groups and aggregations. For example, people who are married (or unmarried) do not appear to constitute a minority in the political sense described above, yet all Canadian jurisdictions prohibit discrimination on the basis of marital status. The same may be said of small people, parents, children (legitimate or otherwise), and pregnant women—all of which receive human rights protection in some jurisdictions. To the extent that discrimination on the latter grounds disproportionately affects political minorities, its prohibition is often tied to a more fundamental concern with the fate of these minorities. Prohibiting discrimination based on physical size or pregnancy, for example, is often justified in terms of the beneficial effect it will have for women. However, the protection of groups and aggregations may also reflect the logic of individual treatment, which, as I have suggested, is hostile to categorization as such, regardless of the political status and consciousness of the groups involved.

Three Kinds of Protected Groups

Although the subjective sense of oppression is essential to the current political meaning of the term minority, there must be one or more shared objective traits that identify members of the minority both to each other and to their alleged oppressors. Blacks need not be a political "minority" in white society; if they are, it is as much because of their common "blackness" as because of their common sense of oppression—indeed the latter could not exist without the former. In the case of less political groups or aggregations the identifying trait is the only consideration. The objective traits that have become prohibited grounds of discrimination in human rights provisions may be roughly grouped into three categories: "stigmatic," "life-cycle," and "life-style" traits. Table one categorizes the thirty existing criteria under these headings.

In simplest terms, stigmata are group characteristics that are regularly passed from one generation to another through genetic or social inheritance. They relate to the "origin" of group members rather than to their behaviour. Race, colour, and ethnic origin are common examples of stigmatic traits. These persistent traits mark off or "stigmatize" the group. Under normal conditions it is not within the power of the group members to divest themselves of their stigmata. These traits are furthermore disadvantageous because they identify unfavorable stereotypes in the minds of outsiders and will often lead to harmful discrimination. Discrimination against stigmatic groups is almost always associated with dislike or malice.

Life-cycle traits are biologically based but are not transmitted or distributed in the same way as stigmata. Sex, age and handicap are examples. Women do not give birth solely to women, whereas Indians give birth to Indians. Age denotes a series of conditions through which we all pass at different times if we continue to survive. Physical and mental handicaps are conditions

TABLE ONE

A Classification of Prohibited Grounds of Discrimination

Stigmata	Life Cycle	Life Style
Race	Sex	Pardoned offence
Colour	Marital status	Criminal record
Nationality	Family status	Sexual orientation
National/ethnic origin	État civil	Drug/alcohol dependence
Ancestry	Pregnancy	Political belief
Place of origin	Age	Source of income
Religion	Physical handicap	Public assistance
Creed	Mental handicap	Attachment of pay
Citizenship		Social origin
Language		Social condition
		Place of residence

"Without reasonable cause"

produced by a number of biological causes, including genetic inheritance, disease, accident, or aging. They are not transmitted in a direct way like race or national origin. Most deaf children are born to hearing adults, and most deaf adults have hearing children. Nevertheless, life-cycle traits resemble stigmata to the extent that they are rarely within the power of the individual to alter. Although discrimination against life-cycle groups may be based on malice, it is more likely to flow from less blameworthy motives. Discrimination against women, for example, has historically been based more on paternalistic protectiveness than on misogyny. Similarly, discrimination against the old or the young cannot adequately be explained by a dislike on the part of the middle-aged "majority" for either of these "minorities."

Life-style traits are acquired through social learning, both conscious and unconscious, or through deliberate choice. They include beliefs, attitudes, and opinions as well as overt behaviour. Life-style traits differ from stigmatic and life-cycle traits in being less determined by the uncontrollable events of birth, accident, and physical development, though they may be strongly influenced by or correlated with these events. For example, it is difficult to divest oneself of the beliefs and practices and habits inculcated during early childhood in the family. Similarly, there may be genetic dispositions to such life-style phenomena as alcoholism. Unlike the stigmatic facts of one's origin, however, childhood habits can be overcome, beliefs can be rejected, and genetic dispositions can be successfully resisted. An incipient alcoholic need not become one in fact, nor need an actual alcoholic continue to be a heavy drinker. The same might be said of criminals, whether their "criminal tendencies" are socially or genetically induced. Membership in life-style groups, then, especially as they involve overt behaviour, is not always permanent.

Although this threefold classification is useful, some of the prohibited grounds do not fit comfortably under just one of the headings. This is either because they are general formulations that embody different kinds of traits, or because the traits themselves are ambiguous and seem to straddle categories. Analysis requires classification, but reality is always too messy to fit perfectly. A more detailed discussion is necessary to refine and clarify the differences between group traits.

Stigmata. Common examples of stigmatic traits are race, colour, ancestry, and religious, ethnic or national origin. One is born into groups identified by such traits and one's membership in these groups is usually permanent. Colour provides the clearest example. Race is more problematic. Although one is born into a particular race, the definition of the boundaries of a racial category is as much social as biological. For example, what proportion of one's "blood" must be traceable to a particular racial group to qualify one for membership in that group? Such social definitions of race vary from one society to another and may change from time to time in a single society. Under any given set of definitions, however, birth is the most common route to membership in a racial group, and since one cannot choose the conditions of one's birth, membership is permanent and involuntary.

The involuntary character of membership in racial groups seems to be contradicted by people who, according to the prevailing social definitions of race, objectively belong to one race but may easily "pass" as belonging to another. Such people can apparently choose their racial affiliation. This choice is only apparent, however. A person who can "pass" as a member of a race other than the one to which he is consigned by prevailing social definitions and norms may escape the consequences of his membership in the "official" category, but cannot escape the reality of that membership. For example, if a minority is subject to discrimination, a person with the ability to "pass" escapes discrimination not by becoming a member of another group but by successfully hiding his very real membership in the oppressed group.

Membership in groups defined by religious, ethnic and national *origin* is similarly defined by birth and is thus also involuntary and permanent. The emphasis here is on the word "origin" rather than on later voluntary adherence to religious, ethnic, or national communities. On one level, religion, ethnicity and nationality are social phenomena in which voluntary adherence plays a significant role. One can choose to renounce one's religion and adopt another one, just as one can choose to assimilate to another ethnic or national community. In this respect religion, ethnicity, and nationality are life-style traits. On another level people are born into specific religious, ethnic, and national communities, and this fact of birth cannot be chosen or changed, though it may be disguised or denied. From the point of view of the oppression of minorities, stigmatic origin can often be more important than life-style choice. Thus Jews who assimilated to Christianity in Germany in the early part of this century could not change the fact that they had been born Jews, and this was enough to mark them as objects of persecution for the Nazis.

The *Charter* and all thirteen Canadian human rights statutes forbid discrimination based on race or colour. Beyond that, all add some combination of the terms ancestry, national or ethnic origin, or place of origin. Religious *origin* is nowhere specified as such but is clearly included in the more general prohibitions of discrimination on the basis of "religion" or "creed."

Table one also lists the term "nationality" under the stigmata. Like religion it is ambiguous, meaning either "national origin" or "citizenship." It is stigmatic only in the former sense. Citizenship, like religious belief or practice, does not fit well into the stigmata. It is natally acquired, either through inheritance from parents or location at birth, but it can be voluntarily renounced or taken away by an act of state authority. An individual can also acquire a new citizenship through legal procedures. Citizenship, therefore, can be as much a matter of personal choice as of inheritance. The term "nationality" appeared in the original

Ontario Human Rights Code and was later adopted in three other jurisdictions. It was clearly intended to embrace the stigmatic concept of "national or ethnic origin," but three Ontario boards of inquiry interpreted it as also encompassing citizenship.[8] Eventually the Ontario Legislature dropped "nationality" from the Code and replaced it with both "ethnic origin" and "citizenship."

There is less difficulty in seeing language, if that means mother tongue, as one of the group stigmata. One's mother tongue is acquired unconsciously in early childhood; it cannot be deliberately forgotten, and one hardly ever acquires another language with equal facility. However, language in this sense is so intimately tied to ancestry or ethnic origin that a complaint could usually be made under those grounds. Only Quebec has seen fit to incorporate language into its human rights legislation. In spite of the many language conflicts in that province, no grievances based on language have yet come to adjudication, perhaps because the *B.N.A. Act* and the *Charter of Rights* provide more powerful means of redress.

Life Cycle. The life-cycle category includes a number of biological criteria related to the maturation of individuals and the reproduction of the species. As with stigmata, there are some borderline cases that need careful consideration.

Sex, understood as biological gender rather than sexual preference, has been incorporated into all Canadian human rights legislation. Although occasionally invoked by male complainants, it generally has worked to the advantage of females. It has also spawned a series of related criteria because experience has shown that simply prohibiting discrimination based on sex leaves women still exposed to certain disadvantages. For example, a financial institution may refuse credit to a married woman without her husband's cosignature. To deal with such situations all jurisdictions have now outlawed discrimination based on marital status. Three have explicitly brought pregnancy into the definition of sexual discrimination, and four have resorted to the concept of "family status" (*situation de famille*), which includes a variety of relationships such as marriage, divorce, pregnancy, parenthood, consanguinity, cohabitation, and perhaps others. Finally, Quebec uses the technical civil law term *état civil*, which is of somewhat uncertain reach but certainly includes elements of marital and family status as well as aspects of age.[9]

The escalation of the campaign against sexual discrimination borders on invoking life-style criteria. Under contemporary conditions, getting married and having children are more akin to voluntary decisions than to natural inevitabilities. Putting marital or family status into legislation may be defended in terms of protecting the family, but in fact it works just as much in the other direction by hindering employers, landlords, and merchants from showing preference to conventional families. Pushed to the limit, such legislation tends to promote individualism rather than family cohesiveness. Cohabitation becomes as respectable as legal marriage, childlessness as important as parenthood. All become matters of personal choice or life style.

Age is the criterion that best fits the concept of life cycle. Its introduction into human rights legislation initially reflected concern for the employment opportunities of older persons, those in the range of forty or forty-five to sixty-five. Some jurisdictions still define age in this way. Others have lowered the minimum threshhold of concern to eighteen or nineteen, thereby opening up new questions such as the leasing of apartments to young tenants. The absence of boundaries of any sort on age in the *Manitoba Human Rights Act* has led to successful challenges to mandatory retirement. The future tendency may be to "uncap" age as a human rights variable because the *Canadian Charter of Rights and Freedoms,* which will override all other legislation, mentions age in an unlimited way.[10]

Physical and mental handicaps are also related to the individual life cycle. They can be thought of as the failure to attain, or the premature loss of, certain capacities characterizing the normal adult. They are organically caused and not generally the result of personal choice, except by reckless exposure to risk. One cannot ordinarily divest oneself of them, though a person may be able to mitigate their effects through medication, rehabilitation, or use of mechanical aids. All jurisdictions except the Yukon now have accepted physical handicaps into their legislation. Mental disability is also covered in most jurisdictions, although this has been a slower and more recent development.

A look at the definitions of mental disability in the *Ontario Human Rights Code* helps explain the hesitation:

> (ii) a condition of mental retardation or impairment,
>
> (iii) a learning disability, or a dysfunction in one or more of the

> processes involved in understanding or using symbols of spoken language, or
>
> (iv) a mental disorder.[11]

Learning dysfunctions are poorly understood conditions that are not always easy to distinguish from low general intelligence, personality disorder, lack of application, or bad teaching. Mental disorder is an equally imprecise term. It surely must include major psychosis but may also comprehend neurotic character traits and sociopathic belligerence.

Life Style. The life-style category is much more heterogeneous. Without too much distortion, however, it can be subdivided into two classes: moral and economic. Moral criteria are those in which a person's choices involve serious conflict with commonly held views of right and wrong. Canadian human rights legislation includes political opinion, criminal record and/or pardoned offence, alcohol and drug dependency, and sexual orientation. Some aspects of marital or family status are also moral criteria. Economic criteria may also have some moral overtones, but they generally apply to situations in which an employer, landlord, or merchant sees a threat more to his own pocketbook than to the moral fabric of society.

Political belief is the most commonly adopted moral criterion. It generates some old-fashioned, patronage-style complaints where moral issues are not of primary concern. It also leads to contentious cases involving radical or revolutionary ideologies and alleged risks to national security. The most interesting cases come from the highly politicized environment of Quebec.[12]

The many traditional forms of discrimination in favour of conventional marriages and against common-law relationships are also based on moral disapprobation. The traditional family is often described as the moral foundation of society and any departure from its norms is viewed with intense suspicion. Common-law relationships are covered under the marital and family status provisions found in several Canadian jurisdictions.

The dimension of moral conflict is obvious in the case of criminal record and sexual orientation. In each instance, inclusion in human rights legislation is an attempt to shield individuals from the social disapprobation attached to violations of law or of deeply ingrained rules of conduct.

Alcohol and drug dependency is a more complicated case. The federal government has introduced this criterion into its act under the heading of disability:

> "disability" means any previous or existing mental or physical disability and includes disfigurement and previous or existing dependence on alcohol or a drug.[13]

However, it strains credibility to lump alcoholism and drug dependency in with mental and physical handicaps. Abuse of alcohol and drugs is a behaviour pattern. As Alcoholics Anonymous long ago discovered, these are "diseases" whose remedy is spiritual rather than physical.

The economic criteria are quite varied. In contemporary society religious practices cause problems for the faithful not because they attract direct discrimination based on moral dislike but because they conflict with rules and procedures adopted to further economic gain or such societal goals as safety. Gone are the days of signs reading "No Jews need apply." The typical complaint today involves a Sikh who will not wear a hard hat at a construction site, a Seventh Day Adventist who will not work on Saturday, or a member of the Worldwide Church of God who wants time off to attend his annual convention.

Similarly, pregnant women are not discriminated against because they are disliked but because pregnancy and childbearing are perceived to create additional costs for employers or to pose health risks to the pregnant employee. The same is true of the discrimination practiced by some employers in favour of older, married women whose childbearing years are over and whose child-rearing responsibilities are diminished or perhaps non-existent. This is rarely based on moral disapproval of younger women but on the assumption that women whose family status has not yet stabilized, and whose childbearing or childrearing years still lie ahead, are less likely to provide stable, long-term, continuous service.

The tendency towards transforming religion into a life-style criterion will be accelerated if the word "creed" ever comes into its own. Ontario and the Northwest Territories specify creed rather than religion in their human rights statutes, while several provinces mention "creed" or "religious creed" in addition to religion. Until now, creed has been interpreted as meaning "religious creed" only, as is spelled out in the Saskatchewan statute. But one authority predicts that under the heading of creed in the 1981 *Ontario Human Rights Code* "protection will almost certainly extend to deistic religions and, probably, to atheistic or agnostic beliefs."[14] Thus movements such as Scientology or Ethical Humanism may be able to claim protection under legislation which mentions "creed" as a prohibited ground of discrimination. Personal convictions unconnected to organized groups may also claim protection some day.

Place of residence is a prohibited ground of discrimination only in the Northwest Territories and there only with respect to employment. It has not been interpreted in reported decisions. Attachment of pay and social origin are unique to the Newfoundland Human Rights Act. Neither has led to reported cases. The words "social origin," appearing in the phrase "ethnic, national or social origin of such person or class of person,"[15] may have been intended merely as a fulsome statement of group stigmata, but they clearly have the potential for economic interpretation. Better understood are the concepts of source of income, found in Manitoba and Nova Scotia, and receipt of public assistance, found in the *Ontario Human Rights Code* in respect of tenancy only. Both criteria function chiefly to prevent landlords from refusing to rent to welfare recipients as a category. Finally there is the omnibus term "social condition" (*condition sociale*) in the Quebec legislation. Without much success, complainants have raised under it issues such as pregnancy, single parenthood, receipt of public assistance, and criminal record (e.g., a man with a conviction for car theft who wanted to work as a parking lot attendant).[16]

Overlapping Groups

The groups defined by the expanding list of prohibited grounds are not mutually exclusive. For example, an old, parapalegic, native woman is a member of several protected groups. Furthermore, some groups overlap with others to a significant degree. Thus the group of pregnant "persons" is a subset of the group of women—all pregnant persons are women, though not all women are pregnant. A more common overlap occurs when it is possible to be a member of either group without being a member of the other, but when in fact a substantial proportion of each group is found in the ranks of the other. Not all small people are women, for example, nor are all women small, but women are disproportionately small just as small people are disproportionately female. Similarly, some ethnic groups are disporportionately young or old, well or poorly educated, or more or less predisposed to certain diseases.

When discussing the inequality of any particular minority it is important to distinguish between the trait used to define the group and secondary, overlapping traits, which may be possessed by many but not all of its members. These two kinds of traits define what may be called "primary" or "target" groups and "secondary" or "overlapping" groups. Actual or perceived overlaps between primary and secondary groups pose two of the central issues in human rights policy, issues that form the central themes of this book.

First, direct discrimination against the target group may serve as a convenient proxy for discrimination against undesirable overlapping groups. This is often the case when discrimination is based on stigmatic traits. Thus the refusal to hire members of a racial minority may be based on the perception that most members of that group are shiftless, lazy, and unreliable. In this case it is disproportionate membership in the group of the unreliable—which contains members of other races—that triggers or justifies the discrimination. Likewise, discrimination against women may be a proxy for discrimination against short and light people or against actual and potential childbearers. Most commonly, membership in a stigmatic group is used as a proxy for membership in a life-style group, whereas sex is used as a proxy for other life-cycle traits. Sex may also serve as a proxy for life-style traits, however, as when young men have to pay higher automobile insurance rates than young women. Similarly, discrimination on the basis of age may be a proxy for both physical and mental decline or for certain life-style traits (e.g., lack of responsibility among the young). Such "proxy" discrimination raises the issue of individual treatment. Whenever someone falls into the primary group but not the overlapping group, he is not being "treated as an individual."

Second, discrimination against secondary groups may contribute to inequality of results for specified target groups. An employment policy that discriminates directly against the "undereducated," rather than against an ethnic or racial minority whose members tend to be poorly educated, may not exclude all members of that minority but will still exclude many and perhaps most of them. The prohibition of direct, intentional discrimination against members of a target group will not further the substantive equality of the group as a whole as long as its members remain disproportionately represented in significantly overlapping groups that are subject to discrimination.

The inequality of minorities protected by human rights law is affected by many overlapping group traits that are not yet explicitly included in the list of prohibited grounds. Discrimination on the basis of physical size or strength, for example, is nowhere explicitly covered but has obvious implications for the equality of women. Similarly, the effects of discrimination based on level and kind of education are disproportionately distributed among racial and ethnic groups, but such discrimination is not directly prohibited.

Such unlisted overlapping traits are indirectly covered by human rights legislation to the extent that it prohibits systemic discrimination. A prohibition of direct discrimination on certain specified grounds leaves intact the right to discriminate on the basis of non-specified grounds. It allows discrimination on the grounds of height, weight, literacy, grooming, the days on which one is available for work, etc. In other words, it permits direct discrimination on the basis of membership in unspecified groups: e.g., the groups of the short, the illiterate, etc. A prohibition of systemic discrimination, on the other hand, calls into question direct discrimination on the basis of any characteristic that is unevenly distributed among the specified groups. In effect, it indirectly extends the prohibition of direct discrimination to groups identified by legislatively unspecified characteristics.

Unlisted grounds of discrimination may be included not just indirectly, through a prohibition of systemic discrimination, but also directly, through an open-ended formulation of anti-discrimination provisions, such as British Columbia's "reasonable cause" wording and the residual part of section 15 of the Charter. Such provisions can be used both to challenge discrimination against groups that overlap explicitly protected minorities and to protect new *sui generis* minorities. In British Columbia, for example, such new minorities as the physically handicapped and homosexuals gained protection under the reasonable cause provisions. Pregnancy, physical size, family status, and linguistic competence—all traits that define groups overlapping political minorities, not new minorities—were also brought in through the door of reasonable cause.

Political Dynamics

Why has the purview of anti-discrimination provisions expanded so rapidly, even at the risk of changing its character? Some new grounds reflect the emergence of new, self-conscious, political minorities. This was true of the addition of such traits as sex, age, handicap and sexual preference to the original list of grounds in human rights legislation. In other cases, however, an added trait merely defines an aggregation or group and is included to promote the equality of a primary "minority" defined by a different but substantially overlapping trait. Pregnancy and certain aspects of marital and family status are examples. In the next chapter I shall argue that a major cause of expansion is the unfolding logic of individual treatment. The rest of this chapter explores some political and institutional causes that also deserve consideration.

First, the creation of human rights commissions with permanent staff members establishes regulatory agencies with a vested interest in expansion. In the absence of a criterion of profitability, success in the bureaucratic world means to deliver bigger programs, provide more services, spend larger budgets, and supervise more employees. There is no reason to think that human rights professionals are less motivated by self-interest or ambition than the rest of us, and their self-interest is served by amplifying their mandate.[17] Commissions pursue their bureaucratic ambitions by suggesting expansionary amendments to the responsible cabinet minister. They may also take steps to promote such amendments in their annual reports or other public statements. This is not to suggest that such amendments are not also motivated by high-minded idealism, only that idealism and bureaucratic self-interest are as likely to fuel each other in human rights commissions as in other organizations.[18]

In short, the commissions are not neutral agencies of enforcement. They are active centres for promoting human rights, which has meant adding criteria of discrimination to the legislation. They continue to lobby in this direction even though, probably without exception, they feel themselves to be without adequate resources to enforce anti-discrimination law in its present "restricted" form.

Second, the existence of many jurisdictions in a federal system is an important factor contributing to this additive model of legislative change. The commissions keep in touch with what the others are doing, a task made much easier by the establishment of the *Human Rights Reporter* in 1980. They meet regularly in the Canadian Association of Statutory Human Rights Agencies (CASHRA). An amendment in one jurisdiction is soon likely to be imitated elsewhere—a process that Jack Walker, commenting on the policy process in American states, has termed "diffusion."[19] Apparently, to professionals in other jurisdictions each addition to a human rights code is an advance to be incorporated as soon as possible into their own code. It may not be accomplished immediately because of political resistance in the cabinet or among the politically appointed commissioners. Sooner or later, however, the opportunity is likely to come for legislative amendment.

Third, the existence of commissions provides a target for lobbying by organized pressure groups who feel they can advance their cause if they can get it accepted as a human rights issue. For example, incorporation of physical characteristics into the *Alberta Individual's Rights Protection Act* was preceded by long consultation with organizations representing the handicapped. Similarly, when the Manitoba Human Rights Commission held public hearings on a new code in 1983, the gay community applied pressure through public statements and an organized letter-writing campaign.

However, the importance of such pressure-group activity should not be overstated. It is by no means always successful. Further, the majority of amendments to legislation are generated through spontaneous recommendations of the commission to cabinet, and pressure politics may well only reinforce what would have happened anyway.[20]

Fourth, politicians themselves sometimes inject human rights issues into campaigns. Thus the Alberta Conservatives promised the *Individual's Rights Protection Act* as part of their 1971 campaign against the governing Social Credit party. In 1979 Joe Clark promised to amend the *Canadian Human Rights Act* so as to prohibit mandatory retirement, although his government was not in power long enough to accomplish this objective. Again, the importance of this factor should not be overestimated since discrimination does not have the electoral weight of such economic issues as inflation, unemployment, and interest rates.

Only in the four Western provinces, where politics is competitive and ideologically polarized between the NDP on the left and the Conservatives or Social Credit on the right, does human rights legislation have an identifiable relationship to party politics. The NDP has almost always been the party which expands the mandate of human rights commissions.[21]

This pattern does not exist in the absence of competitive, ideologically polarized provincial politics. In the Maritimes both Conservative and Liberal governments have created commissions and expanded their purview. The Quebec Commission was created by the Liberals in 1975 and its powers were enlarged several times by the government of René Lévesque. And in Ontario, which has one of the most comprehensive acts of all, almost the entire history of the Human Rights Commission has occurred under Conservative governments.

Human rights is, after all, an adaptable issue. It can be couched in the socialist rhetoric of equality, the liberal rhetoric of freedom, or the conservative rhetoric of paternalism (looking after the less fortunate). Thus it is not surprising that human rights commissions have been created and have seen their purview enlarged in all sorts of party systems: in two-party competitive and ideologically polarized systems (British Columbia, Saskatchewan, Manitoba, Quebec); in a two-party competitive but not polarized system (Maritimes); and in one-party dominant systems (Alberta, Ontario). This suggests that party competition may foster the proliferation of minorities in some circumstances but is neither a necessary nor sufficient condition for this purpose. Rather, the expansionist tendencies of bureaucratic agencies, once established, seem able to work in almost any political environment and appear to be a more important explanatory factor.

However, the self-interest of public servants cannot be invoked as a fully satisfying cause. Sustained enlargement of the regulatory mandate can be sold to the cabinet and the legislature only if it is broadly acceptable to the current state of articulate public opinion. The political acceptability of human rights expansion is related to what Yair Aharoni has termed the "no-risk society." In his words:

> The state has become a huge insurance agency seemingly trying to guarantee a no-risk society. Government insurance covers not only natural disasters but risks stemming from political or technological changes, lack of information, and even individual folly.[22]

Anti-discrimination policy approaches this description as it progressively embraces life-cycle and life-style criteria. It seeks to protect individuals from some of the risks of getting married, having children, growing old, embracing unconventional moral, religious or political ideas, or relying on public assistance.

More precisely, it seeks to control the reactions of employers, landlords, and businessmen towards those whose life-cycle or life-style traits connote risk. However, the risk itself continues to exist. Pregnant women do require time off, the handicapped may be less efficient at their work, single mothers on welfare may have difficulty in controlling their children in rented housing. What happens, then, is the socialization or dispersal of risk. The costs of "reasonable accommodation" by employers show up in final prices. Rents or insurance rates will ultimately be higher, *ceteris paribus*, to the extent that landlords are impeded in protecting themselves against the riskiest tenants and insurance companies are forced to accept dangerous drivers on equal terms with others.

It is useful to think of "equality of opportunity" not as manna from heaven but as a way of collectivizing risk, which involves the redistribution of costs and benefits. This redistribution is more obviously justifiable in the case of ethnic group stigmata than in the case of the life-cycle and life-style criteria now in vogue. Because their bureaucratic self-interest coincides with fulfillment of their moral goals, and because they find it easy to ignore the costs they create for others, it is not surprising that the professionals consistently favour expansion of their own powers.

Notes

[1] According to one author, the use of the term "minority" to refer to women is "prompted primarily by the desire to avoid unduly burdensome language," but also because it is "consistent with the fact that despite their numerical advantage, women share many of the political and economic disadvantages experienced by cultural and other minorities." See Béatrice Vizkelety, *Proving Discrimination in Canada* (Toronto: Carswell, 1987), 2, fn. 8.

[2] John Stuart Mill, *Considerations on Representative Government* (Chicago: Henry Regnery, 1962), 161.

[3] Derek Freeman, *Margaret Mead and Samoa* (Cambridge: Harvard University Press, 1983), 3-61.

[4] Anthony Gary Dworkin and Rosalind J. Dworkin, *The Minority Report* (New York: Praeger, 1976), 14.

[5] Ralph Linton, *The Science of Man in the World Crisis* (New York: Columbia University Press, 1945), 347.

[6] Charles Wagley and Marvin Harris, *Minorities in the New World* (New York: Columbia University Press, 1958), 10.

[7] Dworkin and Dworkin, *The Minority Report*, 17.

[8] Walter Tarnopolsky, *Discrimination and the Law* (Toronto: Richard De Boo, 1982), 175-176.

[9] *Ibid.*, 301-304.

[10] See, for example, the successful challenge to the age limit (45-65) in the British Columbia Act in *Connel* v. *University of British Columbia* (1988), 9 C.H.R.R. D/4557.

[11] *The Human Rights Code*, 1981, S.O. 1981, c.53, s.9(b)(ii-iv).

[12] Tarnopolsky, *Discrimination and the Law*, 320-322.

[13] *Canadian Human Rights Act*, s.20; S.C., 1980-81-82-83, c.143, s.12.

[14] Judith Keene, *Human Rights in Ontario* (Toronto: Carswell, 1983), 63.

[15] Newfoundland Human Rights Code, R.S.N. 1970, C. 262, s. 7(1).

[16] *La Commission des Droits de la Personne du Québec agissant en faveur de Michel Wilkinson* v. *La Ville de Montréal*, 4 C.H.R.R. D/1444 (1983).

[17] William A. Niskanen, Jr., *Bureaucracy and Representative Government* (Chicago: Aldine-Atherton, 1971), 36-42.

[18] This notion raises few eyebrows when it is applied to other public and private bureaucracies (including, for example, the police); indeed, bureaucratic self-interest is often understood to be one of the chief dangers to rights and freedoms. As Ian Hunter has pointed out, however, human rights agencies and activists are often seen as "on the side of the angels" and thus as exempt from the kinds of criticisms that apply to ordinary mortals. James Madison has aptly argued that "if men were angels, no government [including, presumably, human rights commissions] would be necessary." But Madison understood that the government that was required to control our non-angelic natures would itself be composed of non-angelic beings. Thus "the great difficulty" in "framing a government which is to be administered by men over men" lay not just in enabling "the government to control the governed" but in obliging "it to control itself." However this latter objective is to be achieved, it is certainly not by treating our governing agencies (again including human rights agencies) as if they were above and beyond the nor-

mal human influences and temptations. See Alexander Hamilton, James Madison, and John Jay, *The Federalist Papers*, Clinton Rossiter, ed., (New York: Mentor, 1961), 322.

[19] Jack Walker, "The Diffusion of Innovations Among the American States," *American Political Science Review* 63 (1969).

[20] Interview by Thomas Flanagan with Dale Gibson, then Chairperson of Manitoba Human Rights Commission, December 14, 1983. Many of the changes sought by the Manitoba Commission since 1983, including the addition of sexual orientation as a prohibited ground, were incorporated in a new Human Rights Code in 1987 (S.M. 1987, c.45).

[21] A few examples: NDP governments introduced "reasonable cause" into the British Columbia legislation in 1973 along with other new proscribed grounds of discrimination; created the Human Rights Commission in Saskatchewan in 1971 and expanded its powers in 1978; created the Human Rights Commission in Manitoba in 1969 and repeatedly increased its powers. In contrast, Conservative or Social Credit governments in the West have often held commissions in check by tactics such as appointment of less activist commissioners or even leaving appointments vacant; refusing to appoint tribunals to hear complaints; and rejecting proposed amendments. Premier Bennett's attack in 1983 on the British Columbia commission and enforcement apparatus was the strongest measure so far. In Alberta, a Conservative government created a commission but its powers remain the most restricted.

[22] Yair Aharoni, *The No Risk Society* (Chatham, N.J.: Chatham House Publishers, 1981), 4.

IV

INDIVIDUAL TREATMENT

Anti-discrimination policy was originally directed against actions stemming from the irrational dislike of stigmatic groups. We have seen that discrimination on stigmatic grounds is often a proxy for discrimination against secondary, overlapping groups, and that the attack on this kind of discrimination is justified in part by an appeal to the principle of individual treatment. This way of formulating the attack on discrimination pervades the human rights literature. To give just a single example, a textbook issued by the Alberta Human Rights Commission declares:

> When prejudice is directed against people of a certain race, ethnic-cultural group, colour or religion, there is a tendency to lump together all members of the group and to think of them as types (stereotypes) rather than as individuals.[1]

This appeal to individual treatment is an attractive way to formulate the opposition to stigmatic discrimination, but it portends much more. The inherent logic of individual treatment is hostile not just to the use of stigmatic categories as a way of predicting future performance or behaviour but to the use of predictive categorization as such. Except in close personal relationships prediction is always statistical in nature and is based on projections from group characteristics. The categorizations used for prediction will be more or less relevant or refined and thus more or less reliable as forecasting devices; but no matter how refined they are, there will always be individual exceptions who will thus not be treated as individuals. As Dale Gibson points out, even statistically valid generalizations violate individual treatment precisely because they are *generalizations*. Indeed, valid generalizations often pose the most dangerous threats to the ideal of individual treatment:

> But even stereotypes based on statistically valid generalizations (e.g. that there is a higher incidence of alcoholism among Canadian Indians than among the general Canadian population; that women are, on average, physically weaker than men; that older people tend to be less agile than younger people) may be fallacious when applied to any individual member of the groups identified. The particular job applicant might well be a teetotalling native, a female weight lifter, or an elderly mountain climber; and to assume otherwise without further personal information about the individual would be unfair. Statistically sound stereotypes are the more dangerous ones, in fact, because they are more likely to be given wide credence, and to be acted upon when decisions are being made.[2]

Gibson's examples show that individual treatment is violated not just by inaccurate generalizations that are associated with malice but by generalization as such. Predictive generalizations based on age or sex are not usually rooted in malice and may have greater statistical validity than many stigmatic generalizations, but they nevertheless infringe the ideal of individual treatment. Thus, although the rhetoric of individual treatment was originally used to challenge stigmatic discrimination, its logic extends to discrimination on non-stigmatic grounds as well. The addition of life-cycle and life-style traits to the list of prohibited grounds in anti-discrimination law may be explained in part as an attempt more fully to implement the logic of individual treatment.

In the areas of decision making governed by human rights law, individual treatment can be most closely approximated when decisions about individuals are retrospective rather than prospective in character, when they reward or punish for directly relevant past performance rather than predict future performance in one area on the basis of past or present performance in another. Such decisions involve less predictive generalization and thus more individual treatment. However, statistical prediction based on group characteristics is an inescapable fact of life in such areas as employment, and individual treatment in the literal sense is thus not an achievable goal. In practice, the goal of treating people as individuals is really a rhetorical way of demanding the finer sorting of groups. Stated differently, it is a demand to judge people as members of groups defined by characteristics that are truly relevant to the decision being made rather than by irrelevant group traits. Clothing this demand in the rhetoric of individual treatment, however, turns this finer sorting into an endless process. There will be individual exceptions even to more refined and hence relevant categorizations, and viewed from the vantage point of these exceptions, the categorizations will be open to renewed challenge in the name of individual treatment. The logic of individual treatment thus points beyond the explicit addition of new traits to the list of prohibited grounds; it ultimately implies open-ended anti-discrimination provisions that are retrospectively applied by secondary decision-makers who substitute rationalist for empiricist decision making.

The Paradox of Individualism

The word "individual" is derived from the Latin *dividere*, "to divide," combined with the negative prefix *in*. Its sense, like the Greek *atomos*, is "that which cannot be cut." The individual, therefore, is conceived to be a sort of social atom, a fundamental unit of the species humanity. Note that the use of the term individual implies some common identity in the units inasmuch as they belong to the same general category or group. We would not usually think of a man and a dog as individuals in relation to each other since they do not belong to the same species.

On what grounds do we differentiate individuals from one another? The first and indispensable criterion is physical separateness. Two individuals cannot occupy the same space at the same time. This condition is necessary but not sufficient for speaking of "individuals." When referring to inanimate objects, we might use "individual" as an adjective, as in the sentence "He picked up individual grains of rice with his chopsticks," but we would never call a grain of rice "an individual." We use the word as a noun only in referring to human beings.

These linguistic facts suggest two further criteria for being "an individual." First is the capacity for freedom or self-determination. A grain of rice or a pebble makes no choices about its future, whereas humans do. Some determinists think the choices are themselves caused in such a way as to undercut any claim to freedom, but that is beside the point in this context. Even if we are deceived, we experience our lives as a series of choices and act as if our choosing had important consequences.

The second criterion for being "an individual" is our perception of differences. Most grains of rice strike us as very much the same, whereas members of our own species strike us as infinitely varied, both in physical appearance and in behaviour. Since we perceive the differences as great, we emphasize the significance of individual identity, most obviously by giving a unique name to each human being.

Self-determination and variability come together in our concept of "individualism." The term was introduced into English by the first translator of Alexis de Tocqueville's *Democracy in America.* Tocqueville defined individualism as

> A mature and calm feeling, which disposes each member of the community to sever himself from the mass of his fellows, and to draw apart with his family and friends; so that, after he has thus formed a little circle of his own, he willingly leaves society at large to itself.[3]

The phenomenon to which Tocqueville pointed would now probably be called alienation resulting from mass society, or something similar. In contemporary usage individualism is usually considered praiseworthy. Although John Stuart Mill thought he was challenging public opinion, he would today find wide agreement that "in proportion to the development of his individuality, each person becomes more valuable to himself and is, therefore, capable of being more valuable to others."[4] Individualism today is both a fact (diversity of persons) and a moral imperative (self-determination).

The wide acceptance of Mill's doctrine has not, however, settled all problems. Granting that each individual is unique, in what does this uniqueness consist? One answer is biological. We now know that the makeup of all human beings is governed by the genetic code. That one has blue eyes and another brown eyes is due to the particular assortment of DNA inherited from one's parents. The same is true for a vast number of other physical and probably mental characteristics.[5] The DNA structures are chemically the same in all human beings; each person is an individual because he is composed of a unique combination of universal building blocks.

Even if we had not partially unveiled the mysteries of the genetic code, there is a common-sense view that yields similar results. We clearly perceive other persons as unique; we have an extraordinary ability to distinguish one person from another by recognition of face, voice, and mannerisms. Yet we can only talk about unique individuals in terms of general concepts. If I am asked to describe person A, I may say that he is six feet tall, balding, blue-eyed, deep-voiced, slightly paunchy, and a fisherman. All of these traits are shared with other persons. It would be impossible to describe a characteristic that was *sui generis*, because others, having no experience of it, could not recognize it. Part of what makes someone an individual is a unique combination of a myriad of general characteristics.

This does not mean that there is no residuum of individuality that somehow infuses the shared universals possessed by an individual. As Brian Martine observes,

> After we have said as much of Hamlet as can possibly be said, there remains a stubborn and palpable residue which is Hamlet…All of the universals by which he can be characterized are shot through and through with his individuality, an individuality which remains perfectly irreducible to a series of generals, no matter how complete…There is a quality that might be called "Hamletness" which lingers about each of the general features ascribable to Hamlet. He is indecisive in a way that only Hamlet could be, though indecision itself is certainly a common enough feature of human character.[6]

This core of individuality is difficult to convey to strangers in articulated terms and can be "known" only through close personal acquaintanceship. For precisely this reason, however, knowledge of the individual in any deep sense cannot govern impersonal relations and decisions, such as those that typify most modern hiring processes.

We may call this the paradox of individuality. While each person is unique and can enter into face-to-face relationships with others based on his uniqueness, he can only be known impersonally to others as an assembly of shared group characteristics. Individuals and groups are dialectically and indissolubly connected.

We often lose sight of the paradox through loose modes of speaking. It would not surprise us, for example, if a woman said, "I'm not a weak woman, I can lift 200 pounds. Treat me as an individual." But she shares her ability to lift 200 pounds with an indefinite number of other persons, both male and female. Under the guise of demanding individual treatment, she is really pleading for finer sorting of categories and for use of categories more directly relevant to the problem at hand, say being hired as a shipping clerk. She wants to abandon crude categories such as (strong) men and (weak) women in favour of more differentiated categories such as persons who can lift x, y or z pounds. She is proposing a new and, she believes, a superior categorical standard against which to be measured. She is actually not demanding treatment as an individual; she is demanding a different set of groups in which to be placed. Her claim is that all persons capable of lifting x, y or z pounds should be eligible for the job.

Knowledge and Decisions[7]

The paradox of individualism may be further clarified on the basis of distinctions relating to a) the type of decision made and b) the kind of knowledge employed. First is the distinction between retrospective and prospective decisions.[8] A retrospective decision is one in which person A rewards or punishes person B in proportion to a series of actions that B has performed. Examples might be a teacher assigning a mark to a student at the end of a course, a judge sentencing a convicted criminal, or a parent deciding how to discipline a misbehaving child. A's problem in each case is to confer a benefit or cost upon B that is justified by the course of B's conduct. When B is a single individual, this is an exercise in retributive justice. Where there are many B's, the exercise becomes distributive justice: to share out something in proportion to the relative merit of the actions of B(1), B(2),...B(n).

By contrast, a prospective decision is one in which A does something to B in the hope of reaping future benefits for himself and/or the other. Examples would be employing a worker, renting an apartment to a tenant, selling insurance to a customer, or deciding to send a child to a private school. A's problem in each case is to choose the right person B or the right treatment for a given B so as to maximize future benefits. The past is only prologue. It provides background information for the decision but does not determine it. A parent, for instance, might send to private school a child who had done very well or very poorly in public school. The reasoning would be different in each case, but the determining factor would be an estimation of expected future benefits to the child.

Retrospective and prospective decisions overlap to some extent. A prospective decision is always based on information gathered from previous experience (e.g. reports from other parents about advantages of private schools). Retrospective decisions, while emphasizing the past, are often made for at least an implicit future purpose. Criminals are said to be punished to deter them and others from committing similar crimes in the future. Schools and universities employ marking systems as an aid to learning as well as to label people for the convenience of future educators or employers. In a universe where the past cannot be repeated and the future is always upon us, no decision can be purely retrospective.

But even if prospective and retrospective decisions overlap, the distinction between them emphasizes the different importance given to past and future considerations. They also are based on correspondingly different constellations of knowledge. A retrospective decision is based on a closed universe of facts, which in principle can be exhaustively known by the decision-maker. The teacher should have read all the students' assignments before awarding the final mark, and the judge should have read the criminal's file before passing sentence. One could always do a better job of reading and reflecting, but the possible improvement is in the nature of an asymptotic approach to an objectively given result. There is a "right answer" to be reached in retrospective decisions as long as the decision rules are consistently followed. In comparison, prospective decisions are made on an information base that is never even remotely adequate because one can never know the future until it happens. Even the best-informed prospective decision is a guess about the unknowable, a projection of probabilities.

The second distinction that must be drawn is between personal knowledge of intimate family and friends and impersonal knowledge of strangers or casual acquaintances.[9] When we live in close proximity to someone for a length of time, we build up, through observation and shared experience, a fund of knowledge about that person's behaviour. Based on a longitudinal sample of the individual's life, the knowledge is rarely articulated in abstract propositions. It exists as a "feel" for the other person, a tacit ability to predict his reactions in various circumstances, based on having seen him behave in analogous circumstances in the past.

We must also make assessments of people about whom we know little or nothing. When we walk a dark street at night, we can't help making guesses about who is a likely mugger. When we enter a store, we have to decide who is a clerk and who is another customer. These problems are solved by reference to images of group characteristics. We know in advance how clerks should look and act in stores (neatly dressed and alert), and we also have some ideas about muggers (young not old, male not female). These images form the basis for decisions even though we have never seen the particular clerk or mugger in our lives. They are cross-sectional summaries of group experience rather than longitudinal summaries of individual experience.

This distinction is perhaps best understood as one of degree rather than of kind. There is a spectrum of familiarity in personal relations, ranging from family (through friends, work colleagues and casual acquaintances) to strangers. Our knowledge of family is predominantly personal, whereas our knowledge of strangers is by definition impersonal. In the middle of the spectrum we probably employ personal knowledge as far as we have it, supplemented by general images of how groups (men, women; young, old; workers, executives) behave. The two types of knowledge— longitudinal and cross-sectional—are generically separate but often intermixed in particular cases.

Combination of our two distinctions yields a fourfold matrix of logical possibilities shown in Figure one. Each cell of the matrix contains an appropriate example, except the first cell, for which real-world examples are hard to find.

FIGURE ONE: Knowledge and Decisions

KNOWLEDGE

	personal	impersonal
retrospective	1)	2) Judicial Sentencing
prospective	3) Buying Gift For Spouse	4) Hiring Employees

DECISIONS

Let us examine each of the four typical situations more carefully, with a view to establishing what it means in each to "treat the person as an individual."

Type One (Personal/Retrospective). The difficulty in finding an example of a retrospective decision based on personal knowledge is that personal knowledge arises from an intimate, continuing relationship. As long as the decision-maker wishes the relationship to continue, his judgment must be heavily influenced by prospective considerations. A parent disciplining a child is in a position very different from that of a judge passing sentence, for the parent and child will continue to live in the same household. Pure examples of personal, retrospective decisions are rather bizarre, as of the legendary Roman father who put his own son to death for crimes against the republic.

If examples of pure type one situations are rare generally, they seem especially improbable in the areas covered by human rights law. Human rights codes cover such things as employment, tenancy, and access to public services. Decisions in these areas do not fit the type one category because they are generally prospective in nature and tend to be based on impersonal knowledge. This is a matter of degree, however. Some decisions covered by human rights law embody a greater retrospective element than others, and to this extent the knowledge on which they are based may be more personal. For example, the punishment or reward of existing employees differs significantly in these respects from the initial hiring process. Short of outright dismissal, the discipline of an employee is heavily laden with prospective calculations, as are such rewards as promotion. In both cases the employer will continue in an ongoing relationship with the employee and the rewards or punishments are calculated to maximize future benefits to the firm. Punishment is designed to induce better future performance, and promotion embodies the judgment that excellence at one level portends similar excellence at the next. On the other hand, there are also substantial elements of retrospective justice in such decisions. Furthermore, the knowledge on which they are based is often grounded in actual, ongoing experience with the individual employee. The extent to which this knowledge attains to true personal knowledge will vary with the situation, but it will almost always approximate personal knowledge more closely than the knowledge on which initial hiring is typically based.

In sum, type one situations do not exist in their pure form in areas covered by human rights law, and the individual treatment they imply is thus not possible in a strong sense. Nevertheless, some decisions in these areas exhibit more type one elements than others, and to this extent they more closely approximate the ideal of individual treatment.

Type Two (Impersonal/Retrospective). When a judge sentences a person convicted of a crime, he is already constrained within a categorical framework. The offender, having been found guilty, is classified as a criminal, the law provides the upper and lower boundaries of the sentence that may be imposed, and so on. However, there is within this framework room for judicial discretion and thus for a sort of individual treatment. The sentencing decision is retrospective to the extent that the judge considers a unique combination of facts from the offender's history, such as age, family status and employment prospects, prior criminal record, motive for the offence, and evidence of contrition. (The decision may also be partly prospective, as when a judge justifies an especially severe sentence by invoking the need to deter other would-be criminals.)

This approach to individual treatment through compilation of the offender's case history is necessarily limited by circumstances. Judge and offender are usually strangers or at best casual acquaintances; if they were closely acquainted, the judge would have excused himself from the case. The case history gives a concatenation of categories rather than a true "feel" for the person. Never more than a partial selection of facts from the person's past, it is far removed from the personal knowledge that is possible in intimate circumstances. Moreover, the rule of law demands that the judge try to treat like cases alike. Justice means not only proportioning the punishment to the offence (retribution) but passing similar sentences on offenders in terms of group characteristics.

Overall, the sentencing decision is individualized in the limited sense that its retrospective character requires the cumulation of several group characteristics of the offender. The absence of intimate knowledge combined with the prospective requirements of deterrence and the rule of law necessitate even more emphasis on categorical thinking.

Type Three (Personal/Prospective). When a wife buys her husband a present, it is a prospective decision meant to bring pleasure to the recipient, not to reward him for particular actions. In selecting the gift, she can rely on the tacit knowledge built up in years of mutual experience. She will know that he likes, say, neckties, not because men in general are reputed to like them but because she has seen him take pleasure in them. She probably cannot say in advance what kind of tie she will buy, but her tacit knowledge will allow her to recognize a suitable item when she sees it in a store. She can match the store's stock of ties against her knowledge of her husband's wardrobe as well as of his personal taste. A decision of this type seems to be about as close as one can come to the pure conception of treating a person as an individual.

Type Four (Impersonal/Prospective). The above stands in marked contrast to the initial hiring of an employee. Unless the employer is hiring family members or close friends, the job applicant is unknown to him. He must make the best estimation he can of the applicant's future usefulness to the enterprise. Occasionally employers proceed on an almost random basis, as when a contractor drives past an unemployment office and picks up day labourers; but this seemingly random method of recruitment is actually based on knowledge of group characteristics. It is known to both workers and contractors that unemployed men willing and able to do physical labour congregate in certain places. When the employer's work is sporadic and difficult to predict in advance, this may be his most efficient method of hiring.

However, employers in most cases attempt to compile a longitudinal history of the applicant. Being interviewed and filling out a questionnaire provide facts such as sex, age, education, and work history. Further detail can be provided by letters of reference and mental or physical examinations. But all of this information is like the case history used by a judge in sentencing an offender; it is a concatenation of categories providing a skeletal outline of the person, not a flesh and blood portrait. It is a composite "what," not a "who." Even the most complete personnel file is an impoverished account of the individual compared to the richness of personal knowledge derived from intimate acquaintance.

Moreover, an employer is interested not in doing justice retrospectively but in forecasting performance prospectively. Since he inevitably lacks abundant experiential knowledge of individual applicants, he must rely on cross-sectional comparisons for his predictions. He must compare the applicant's group characteristics to those of past employees as well as to any fund of common knowledge bearing on the problem.

Suppose, for example, that a university wishes to hire a junior faculty member to engage in teaching, research, and administration. Information will be accumulated on candidates' degrees, work experience, and previous publications; letters of reference will also be added to the files. From this pool of applicants, who may all be personally unknown to the selection committee, a short list of candidates will be selected through categorical comparison of group traits. Questions will be asked such as: How does a Ph.D. from institution X compare to one from institution Y? What is the professional performance of the students of supervisor Z? What is the significance of having published one or two articles as a graduate student? Those who are placed on the short list will usually be invited to an interview lasting one or two days. This allows the selection committee to develop some tacit "feel" for the individuals, but this interview generally plays a limited part in the entire process. In the end the successful candidate is selected through a complex weighing and adding of predictions based on group characteristics. It must be stressed that group comparison is essential. A candidate who is the only Ph.D. ever produced by the university he attended is at a grave disadvantage because there is no reference group of graduates to provide meaning to the abstract characteristic of being a Ph.D. from that institution.

Other hiring processes are different in detail but similar in principle. They always involve basing predictions on group characteristics, and indeed it is only the existence of group characteristics that makes prediction possible. Knowing that a large percentage of Harvard Ph.D.'s has gone on in the past to become productive scholars is a helpful piece of information. If each young Ph.D. had to be considered as a unique case, comparisons would be impossible and so would prediction. In the absence of tacit knowledge based on long acquaintance, hiring would be reduced to a random process of trial and error, extremely inefficient in comparison to using comparative, categorical data.

What is true of employment decisions applies to other business situations as well. A landlord assessing possible tenants or a contractor considering which of several suppliers to rely on goes through much the same mental process of making prospective decisions without any fund of tacit knowledge to draw on, although a continuing contractual relationship will allow some longitudinal knowledge to develop.

The purest model of prospective decision making is perhaps the underwriting of insurance. No one knows when he will die or next have an automobile accident; if one knew, insurance would not be necessary because one could save against the anticipated event. Insurance is desired as protection against the risks of an unknown future. The seller also has no idea when the customer will die or suffer an accident, but he can collect actuarial data on large numbers of policy holders. Thus he can establish the statistical life expectancy of a man or woman at any age or the probability of insuring a loss through accident in a given period of time. Customers can then be rated according to their group characteristics. Cumulation of categories (age, sex, marital status, previous accidents, prior traffic convictions, driver training, business or pleasure use of car) can lead to a highly sophisticated rating system with thousands of internal possibilities. In Ontario in 1977 there were 5040 rating cells for public liability automobile insurance.[10] This approach, however, is self-limiting. Categories cannot be piled up without end because the population in rating cells would become too small to provide statistical confirmation of the expected claims. At the limit, if each individual occupied a separate cell, insurance rating would become impossible because of the lack of group data. As numerous commentators have pointed out, it is self-contradictory to talk of treating people as individuals for insurance purposes.[11] If there is no grouping, there will be no insurance, except the most primitive sort of coverage based on an undifferentiated pool of unassigned risks.

Insurance has often been considered an exceptional case, and existing human rights statutes exempt the industry in whole or in part.[12] However, if the preceding analysis is correct, insurance is not an exception but an exemplar of prospective decision making.

Before carrying the analysis forward it is worth drawing certain points together:

1) The distinctions between prospective and retrospective decisions and personal and impersonal knowledge are analytical. Most real-life decisions have both retrospective and prospective aspects and use elements of both personal and impersonal knowledge.

2) Decisions based on personal knowledge can be considered individual in the strong sense of relying upon a tacit "feel" for the

unique individual, based upon a long period of observation and shared experience.

3) Decisions based on impersonal knowledge always tend to be categorical in nature. In the absence of extensive longitudinal knowledge of the unique individual, decision-makers must rely on categorical knowledge of characteristics, which are always shared with groups.

4) This categorization is heightened in prospective decision making where the concern is for prediction. Comparison with the known behaviour of groups provides the ability to make predictions of individual behaviour that, even though not perfect, are better than random guesses. The predictions may be improved by cumulating the individual's group traits, which is far from treating him "as an individual."

5) Under conditions of impersonal knowledge, retrospective decisions can be more individualized than prospective ones, but only in the weak sense of being based on a skeletal, longitudinal case history. At least the universe of relevant data is closed because the decision is based on past events. Since prediction of the future is not necessary, the decision-maker can focus more on the unique concatenation of facts in the case history than on cross-sectional comparisons of these facts taken as group traits.

Strategies for Promoting Individual Treatment

Canadian human rights law generally covers decisions that are strongly prospective and based on impersonal knowledge. Situations where personal knowledge is a major factor are often expressly exempted from application of the legislation (e.g., retention of domestic servants, rental of rooms within a home, membership in private clubs and societies). Individual treatment, on the other hand, is associated with retrospective decisions and/or personal knowledge. In practice the rhetoric of individual treatment requires that decisions be based on a closer approximation of personal knowledge, or that decisions become more retrospective in nature, or both. There are three possible strategies for accomplishing this. These involve moving type four decisions in the direction of one of the other alternatives.

Toward Type Three Decisions. One strategy would be to leave the prospective nature of most business decisions untouched but base these decisions on truly personal knowledge—in effect to transform type four into type three decisions. This strategy might be at least partly realizable in a small, face-to-face society where everyone knows everyone else, but it is difficult to institute in a populous, impersonal and mobile society such as our own. Furthermore, the mechanisms for enforcing this ideal are themselves in tension with it. Human rights commissions are regulatory agencies that must proceed on the basis of publicly ascertainable evidence—records, documents, written policies, etc. Personal knowledge, which is a "feel" for a unique individual, loses its tacit character when it is articulated, as in a proposition linking concepts together. Human rights officers would never be content with the statement "I refused to hire George because I was sure he wouldn't do." One would have to give reasons: George was too young, too old, alcoholic, on welfare, etc. Each of these articulated reasons is essentially a prediction of future behaviour based on cross-sectional comparison of group traits. Thus the very process of investigation is bound to turn an exercise of personal knowledge into an arbitrary-appearing act of categorical discrimination.

Additionally, the human rights regulatory process is a highly intellectualized one, which puts a premium on articulated reasons.[13] At the highest level the dominant figures are lawyers who are professionals in making arguments and giving reasons. At lower levels the personnel are usually trained in social work, personnel administration, or one of the social sciences. It is, to say the least, an unpromising environment within which tacit, personal knowledge might be appreciated.

Finally, human rights ideology is hostile to the ways in which personal knowledge actually and most realistically influences employment decisions. Employers are aware of the more comprehensive, and hence individualized, nature of personal knowledge and are quite prepared to make use of it when the costs are not too high. This is what leads to the pervasive influence of "old boys" networks. But this is surely not what human rights advocates of individual treatment have in mind.

Toward Type One Decisions. A more promising strategy for increasing the degree of individual treatment in areas covered by human rights law is to make the decisions more retrospective in nature. Such decisions embody a more detailed and comprehensive knowledge of the individual's relevant past than more purely prospective decisions and thus also come closer to the ideal of personal knowledge. In the employment sphere this might be done by giving initial employment decisions the characteristics of promotion decisions. Instead of hiring employees on the basis of certain pre-employment traits, such as educational level or test scores, one could hire on a first-come, first-served basis and then discharge those who didn't measure up. Such decisions could be relatively personal if an extended probationary period allowed a longitudinal body of knowledge about the employee to develop. This strategy moves type four decisions closer to the type one model.

Even if such randomized selection were feasible, it might not be desirable. As Alan Goldman points out, it "downgrades accomplishments culminating the first twenty-five years or so of a person's life...," thereby removing one of the incentives for the pre-employment pursuit of educational excellence. Could randomly hired employees "be expected to perform well," asks Goldman, "having never found the need to do so earlier and possibly not having the capacity to do so?" Goldman also emphasizes the resentment likely to be caused by the "series of firings and hirings" that would be required to find the truly competent.[14]

Toward Type Two Decisions. It is generally conceded that the use of probationary periods is not always practical. However, this does not mean that the ideal of retrospectivity must be abandoned. It can also be achieved by allowing a secondary, quasi-judicial agency retroactively to reconsider more purely prospective primary decisions. In this case an employer might legitimately use group characteristics to predict future performance, but individual exceptions to his statistical predictions could appeal to a human rights agency, which could force a reconsideration of the decision based on a more comprehensive, retrospective look at the individual situation. This strategy transforms type four situations into the kind of type two situation exemplified by judicial sentencing, which is highly congenial to the lawyers who dominate the regulatory process, for they are professional specialists in type two situations. Legal contests, whether criminal or civil, are premised on documenting a sequence of events and distributing proportional rewards or punishments. In practice human rights proceedings are inevitably pushed in that direction. A complaint will generate a quasi-legal investigation in which the emphasis will be on the question of whether the employer (landlord, etc.) was fair to the complainant. The respondent will have to establish fairness by demonstrating that his conduct conformed to the provisions of the code. Prospective considerations of "business necessity" may be allowed in certain exceptional circumstances, but in general they are subordinated to retrospective considerations of fairness.

This strategy is attractive in the sense that it is congenial to the regulatory personnel. It is also feasible in that there is no *a priori* limit to the number of prospective decisions that can be reconstructed as problems of retrospective justice. The only limit is provided by the availability of resources to devote to the task. However, the enterprise is fundamentally at variance with the necessity of economic calculation. The cost of such large-scale second guessing transcends the direct cost of the regulatory activity. Each time a prospective decision is overturned on the quite different grounds of retrospective fairness, a network of expectations is upset. To minimize the disruption, employers and businesses in general have to devote resources to making themselves "human rights proof."[15] They must hire their own specialists to write appropriate policy documents, keep the required records, and defend them in case of challenge.

The second and third of these strategies—the greater use of retrospective procedures in primary decisions, and the subjecting of primary decisions to second guessing by human rights agencies—are not mutually exclusive alternatives for maximizing individual treatment. Even decision making that involves some degree of retrospectivity is subject to review on the grounds that the retrospective elements did not go far enough and that the knowledge involved in the decision was thus not sufficiently detailed or comprehensive, that it did not approximate personal knowledge closely enough. The crux of the matter is not so much the retrospectivity of the decision as the greater accuracy of knowledge that retrospectivity affords. Retrospectivity promotes accuracy but does not ensure it; by the same token, where probationary assessment is not a practical alternative, accuracy of knowledge can nevertheless be improved, often through secondary review. The two strategies are thus really part of a more general concern with improving the accuracy of knowledge on the basis of which decisions about individuals are made.

The Limits to Individual Treatment

The practical implications of the demand for greater accuracy of knowledge are illustrated by a series of cases arising under the reasonable cause provision of British Columbia's pre-1983 Code. These cases also point to the natural limits of the ideal of individual treatment. [16]

In *Wilson* v. *Vancouver Vocational Institute* [17] the challenged decision was based on a probationary period, but the judgment makes clear that mere probation is not enough; individual treatment requires acknowledgement of the difference between fast and slow starters. The complainant claimed that she was discriminated against because of her sex and age, and without reasonable cause. She was enrolled in a graphic arts program and was subsequently terminated because of poor performance in the practical aspects of the program. The majority of the board of inquiry found that discrimination did occur, in particular on the basis of age and without reasonable cause. The chairman claimed:

> It is my opinion that the Respondent has contravened Section 3(1) of the Human Rights Code. In view of the short time that elapsed from the complainant's enrollment to her termination, I do not feel she was given an adequate opportunity to become proficient in the use of the machinery. Further, no extra time was extended to her to complete assignments or use the machinery and no special effort was made by the instructors to teach her the practical work even though they saw she was having some difficulty with parts of the course.

Here we have a decision based on knowledge of actual individual performance. Still, it did not meet the requirements of individual treatment because the probationary period was not long enough or conducted fairly enough to permit adequate assessment of Wilson's true abilities. Knowing someone well enough to treat him or her as an individual must not only be based on retrospective experience with that person, but that experience must be sufficiently long-term to permit real knowledge. What must be known is a person's ultimate ability to perform a task, and that may not be accurately measured by how quickly one masters its rudiments. As in the old tale of the tortoise and the hare, those who start slowly and plod along may finish more strongly.

The knowledge required for individual treatment must distinguish not only between fast and slow starters but also between those aspects of performance for which the individual is responsible and those that are due to circumstances beyond his or her control. This part of the individual-treatment logic is illustrated in *Lopetrone et. al.* v. *Harrisons and Juan de Fuca Hospital Society,*[18] another reasonable cause case. The complainant was employed at the Juan de Fuca Hospital and was released when the facility was taken over by the provincial government. Employees were told they could re-apply and that their applications would be given "full consideration." The new personnel administrator at the hospital was not pleased with the condition of the facility prior to the takeover, and since it was to be upgraded from a nursing home to an extended care facility, she wished to improve the quality of the staff. The administrator was particularly concerned about the poorly run kitchen and attributed part of the responsibility for its condition to Mrs. Lopetrone, one of the kitchen staff. Accordingly, Lopetrone's application for re-employment was refused.

Mrs. Lopetrone persuaded the board of inquiry that her competence had not been accurately assessed. In particular, the administrator had not considered the poor conditions under which Lopetrone worked. For example, she had insufficient help and poor equipment. Furthermore, the administrator had falsely held Lopetrone responsible for the menus and portions served to patients, over which she in fact had had no control. The board concluded that the administrator "reacted unfairly. She asked for no explanation from Mrs. Lopetrone. Indeed, she made no further enquiries of any kind beyond her inspection of the kitchen." If she had "looked into the matter further," she would have understood that Mrs. Lopetrone "did well under the circumstances." The respondent was held to have discriminated without reasonable cause.

Part of the problem in Lopetrone's case arose from the fact that although the decision was more retrospective than most initial hiring decisions, the decision-maker was new on the scene. She had not been involved in an ongoing employment relationship with Lopetrone and thus did not know her individual situation well enough. In short, although the decision was partly retrospective, the knowledge on which it was based did not sufficiently approximate the ideal of comprehensive personal knowledge. Under the circumstances true personal knowledge was impossible, but the administrator could have made the effort to inform herself more accurately. This failure was remedied by the second and more comprehensive review of Lopetrone's situation by a human rights tribunal.

No doubt the administrator of the Juan de Fuca hospital acted in good faith and in the honest belief that Mrs. Lopetrone was responsible for the poor state of the kitchen. Clearly the fact that her knowledge was objectively deficient was more important than her "honest belief." Individual treatment requires not only that the proper distinctions be made but also that the conclusions reached be based on accurate knowledge rather than honest belief. This dimension of the individual-treatment ideology is clearly displayed in *Jorgenson* v. *B.C. Ice and Cold Storage Ltd.*[19] The complainant, a female employee, was denied a transfer to a more physically demanding class of work because of certain disabilities her employer thought she possessed. She taped her wrists regularly and on a few occasions complained of back pain. The employer attributed her apparent ill-health to the work she was doing and on this basis refused her request for more arduous employment. It was determined at the board hearing that the back pain was due to an implanted intra-uterine device and that wrist taping was commonly done for protection and added strength even by male employees. Whether or not the employer's perception of disability was based on "honest belief" was never determined, but the board asserted that, even if it existed, "honest belief" was no substitute for objective accuracy, and that differential treatment based on objective mistakes would constitute discrimination without reasonable cause:

> ...even if the Employer held an honest belief...such honest belief would not constitute reasonable cause if the alleged facts upon which such honest belief were based did not in fact exist, or were not as the Employer believed.[20]

Wilson, Lopetrone, and *Jorgenson* all underscore the conclusion that individual treatment requires highly accurate knowledge of the individual, based on long experience, attention to all relevant contextual circumstances, and a willingness to probe deeply for the most precise explanations of behaviour rather than jumping to conclusions, even to "good faith" conclusions based on "honest belief." In short, individual treatment requires employers to make the "right" decision—i.e., the decision that would be made if *all* relevant information were available.

The practical limits to the attainment of such knowledge, and thus the limits to the ideal of individual treatment, are demonstrated in *Andruchiw* v. *Corporation of the District of Burnaby.*[21] Like *Jorgenson*, this case concerned the objectively mistaken perception of a job-related physical disability. Andruchiw had applied for a position as a fireman in Burnaby and, having passed the initial screening, was required to undergo a medical examination, including back x-rays. The x-rays revealed an interarticularis defect (separation of vertebrae) on one side of the L-2 vertebra. The effect of this defect on Andruchiw's performance as a fireman was the central issue. The employer's doctor referred to a 1964 medical report on the risks of injury for different types of work and used its evaluation of back defects to recommend that Andruchiw not be hired. As was discovered at the board hearings, however, more recent medical evidence had rendered the 1964 report "outdated and of questionable value." These up-to-date studies suggested that, located where it was in Andruchiw's spine, this back defect would not adversely affect a fireman's ability or jeopardize safety. Andruchiw was subjected to a false standard and was thus treated in terms of his (falsely) presumed characteristics rather than in terms of his actual abilities. The employer had tried to treat him as an individual but had failed because of outdated and inadequate knowledge.[22]

Andruchiw differs from the previous cases inasmuch as the decision involved was more purely prospective. The decisions in *Wilson, Lopetrone,* and *Jorgenson* also involved prospective prediction, but these predictions were based on some degree of experience with or knowledge of the employees' past performance. In *Andruchiw* the employer had no direct knowledge of the applicant's performance in similar or substantially related work.

In other respects *Andruchiw* closely parallels *Jorgenson*, except that recourse was had to medical expertise. In both cases alleged or actual "honest belief" was found to have an inadequate grounding in objective fact, but in *Andruchiw* respectable medical research rather than surmise provided the basis for the honest belief. For the board in Andruchiw this difference was decisive. The 1964 report was obsolete, but the employer "did not have the benefit of that perspective." The employer was "obliged to maintain high selection standards, including high medical standards," but since "the complainant's back was both revealed and determined through medical opinion to be potentially troublesome," reasonable cause existed for the refusal to employ.

The key factors seem to have been the effort made by the employer to seek out objective evidence, and the expert certification of the evidence, rather than its objective accuracy. This is a common-sense view and it represents the victory of practicality over the pure logic of individual treatment. The fact is that the information on the basis of which decisions were made was just as deficient in *Andruchiw* as it was in *Jorgenson*. That it was based on expert testimony in Andruchiw's case does not mean that his rejection violated the ideal of individual treatment any less than Jorgenson's. If there was "reasonable cause" in this case, it flowed not from the accuracy of the knowledge underlying the differential treatment but from the "honest belief" that was rejected as a sufficient ground for "reasonable cause" in *Jorgenson*. The logic of *Jorgenson*—that objective accuracy rather than honest belief is the touchstone of individual treatment— remains unimpeached by the more respectable ground of the honest belief in *Andruchiw*. The greater respectability of medical expertise, as compared to mere hunch, provided more compelling reasons to depart from or place limits on the logic of individual treatment in *Andruchiw*; but the true implications of that logic for such cases, when countervailing considerations of practicality are set aside, were spelled out by a minority opinion in the subsequent case of *Cook v. Noble*:

> Reliance on a medical opinion may or may not provide an employer with reasonable cause, depending on all the circumstances. The question in the end is whether assessment of an applicant was based on his abilities as an individual rather than upon his sharing a particular characteristic with other persons where there are common preconceptions about that characteristic. In my view, such preconceptions may arise in a number of ways (including, possibly, in medical literature) and may operate on the thinking of a professional medical person as much as on anyone else. As may be seen, I do not agree with the Board in the Andruchiw case if what the Board is saying is that reliance on a medical opinion is enough to establish reasonable cause in every case.[23]

The reluctance of tribunals to push the logic of individual treatment as far as the minority report in *Cook* probably flows from a perception of the difficulty of always achieving the degree of knowledge necessary for true individual treatment. Even expert knowledge, such as that possessed by medical doctors, is usually incomplete, and prospective predictions based on such knowledge will thus always remain statistical predictions, to which there will be individual exceptions. To the extent that prospective prediction must be used in employment situations, good faith and honest belief must at some point be permitted to triumph over objective accuracy.

The practical limits to the logic of individual treatment become still more apparent when one realizes that even the more individualized knowledge provided by retrospective experience with the individual, such as performance during a probationary period, is used to make prospective, statistical predictions. The knowledge gained by probationary periods, even when they are much longer than the one in *Wilson*, is statistical knowledge when it is used to predict future performance. Like any other basis of categorization, initial or present performance is an imperfect predictor of future performance for any given individual. Once this is recognized, it becomes apparent that the logic of individual treatment can never be perfectly realized. The longer a probationary period is, the more accurately will past performance predict future performance. Still, one rarely has the perfect knowledge necessary to make this prediction with certainty. Often people of superior natural talent compare poorly with their less gifted colleagues because of character traits such as laziness. As time goes on such character flaws tend to become more entrenched, thus lending credence to the prediction of their future continuation. Yet dramatic personal reform is possible and does occasionally occur. One can never be certain that a talented person who has performed poorly in the past might not become the best performer in the future. The ideology of individual treatment prefers retrospective to prospective knowledge because it is likely to be more accurate knowledge of the particular individual. But inasmuch as retrospective knowledge is used for prospective prediction it remains statistical and thus imperfect with respect to the individual. The only perfect retrospective knowledge comes at the end of a lifetime, at which point it is of use only to God and historians.

Individual Treatment and Secondary Review

Given that true individual treatment is a practical impossibility, the operational effect of the notion is to "individualize" prospective judgments by requiring decision-makers to invoke more numerous and more relevant group characteristics. The shift from pre-employment predictive categories to performance on the job during a probationary period is one such refinement. Those who perform well during the probationary period share a group characteristic that is likely to predict future performance more accurately, but to which there will still be individual exceptions. Where probation is not a practical alternative, the rhetoric of individual treatment requires an assessment of the predictive reliability of pre-performance categorizations and urges the substitution of more finely tuned groupings for grosser and less reliable generalizations.

The finer sorting of groups implied by the logic of individual treatment is reflected in the gradual addition of new prohibited grounds to anti-discrimination legislation. Each new ground represents a new kind of generalization that is deemed presumptively illegitimate. In the final analysis, however, the logic of individual treatment points not to the addition of new grounds to an explicitly enumerated list but to open-ended anti-discrimination provisions, such as the "reasonable cause" formulation used in British Columbia until 1983. The kinds of generalizations that can be used in decisions covered by human rights legislation are virtually endless, and any generalization is open to challenge from the point of view of individual treatment. Generalizations that "unreasonably" infringe the ideal of individual treatment cannot be exhaustively known and listed in advance. The logical solution is to use open-ended language that may be applied to any generalization.

Although the logic of individual treatment is hostile to predictive generalization as such, generalization is inevitable in the primary decisions covered by the law. An open-ended anti-discrimination law would make it possible to challenge any generalization, but it could not eradicate the phenomenon of generalization. In any particular case the question would be whether the discrimination was "reasonable," as the "reasonable cause" wording implies. Determining whether a generalization is reasonable involves balancing the requirements of individual treatment against the costs of acquiring sufficiently accurate knowledge about particular individuals. Every generalization is "unreasonable" in its application to individual exceptions, but the perspective of the exception cannot be the only consideration. Andruchiw was not treated as an individual, but the discriminatory generalization used by the employer was reasonable. Given the state of knowledge available to the employer, and the care taken to acquire relevant knowledge, the classification represented a predictive sorting of applicants that was precise enough to pass muster.

At least where malicious, stigmatic prejudice is not at work, the economic market tends to an "economically rational" balance between individual treatment and its countervailing costs. Employers have an interest in choosing their employees from the largest possible pool of qualified employees. If they define qualifications too narrowly, they restrict the supply of labour to their own disadvantage. On the other hand, expanding the supply of labour by abandoning restrictive qualifications eventually becomes too costly. First-come, first-served hiring, with ultimate selection based on satisfactory performance during a probationary period, provides the widest possible labour supply and achieves the most accurate selection of the truly qualified, but even the most committed proponents of individual treatment concede that this strategy is often too costly to be reasonable.

Although human rights advocates accept the need to balance individual treatment against the cost of achieving it, they tend to reject the idea that the balance struck by "economic rationality" is "reasonable." In this view the kind of balance achieved by a businessman responding to the market gives too little weight to the individual-treatment side of the ledger. Human rights ideology thus tends to emphasize the review of primary decisions by secondary agencies that are institutionally committed to individual treatment and that do not bear its costs. Open-ended anti-discrimination provisions permit all generalizations to be challenged from the point of view of the individual exception; secondary review ensures that the interest of individual exceptions will be given greater weight in reaching a "reasonable" balance. Secondary review also furthers individual treatment by bringing the perspective of retrospective justice to bear on the case.

Rationalism and Depersonalization

Not all decisions, of course, can reasonably be subject to such retrospective review, and the vast majority of decisions will thus continue to be prospective in nature, making use of probabilistic reasoning based on statistical categories. However, the number and kind of categories that can legitimately be used for prospective decision making are gradually being whittled away. Although this battle against categorization has been waged in the name of individual treatment, its paradoxical result is radically to depersonalize the individual by stripping away all his recognizable characteristics until he becomes, like the hero of Robert Musil's novel, *Der Mann ohne Eigenschaften* (The Man without Qualities). Far from promoting individual treatment, this depersonalization actually undermines it.

Under Canadian legislation and its amplifying regulations and guidelines, it has become unlawful for an employer to request a photograph from an applicant; to inquire into age or sex; to ask if the applicant is married, has children or plans to have children; to require a medical examination; to inquire into any facts that might have a bearing on religion or ethnic origin (place of birth, birth certificate, mother tongue, citizenship, membership in clubs); and much more. Some of this information can be collected after an offer of employment is made (knowledge of sex, age, family status, and perhaps a medical exam will be necessary for fringe benefits), but it is not supposed to influence the hiring decision in any way.

It is hard to see this as a victory for individual treatment. An employer can scarcely visualize as an individual human being a person whose age, sex, family status, ethnic background, height, weight, and health are deliberately concealed or ignored. The protection of human rights has come to mean the deletion of information, reducing applicants to abstract dossiers.

In the extreme this logic would prohibit the practice of face-to-face interviews. For example, employers in Saskatchewan may ask job applicants "whether they have a physical disability which will interfere with their ability to perform the job," and "if the answer is 'yes', [they] may ask what functions cannot be performed and what accommodations could be made which would allow them to do the work adequately." However, "an employer may not ask, at any time during the pre-employment inquiry or on an application form, about the nature or severity of a physical disability, should one exist."[24] The logic of the last requirement suggests that personal interviews should probably be avoided lest "the nature or severity" of a disability be too obvious. Does such depersonalization further individual treatment?

This development, in the name of treating people as individuals, reveals a clash between different conceptions of decision making. The human rights movement espouses a rationalist model of decision making that assumes that precise requirements for a job can be specified beforehand. If we want a policeman, we should be able to say exactly what skills are necessary to the job: ability to read at a tenth grade level, to bench press 150 lbs., etc. In case of dispute we should be able to prove in articulated terms to external reviewers that our requirements are "really" essential. We must not resort to vague reasons such as "experience suggests..." Hiring thus becomes a process of selecting the person who scores highest on some combined total of these specified attributes. In principle the decision could be entirely objective, because if we could specify the criteria so exactly, we could also specify their relative weights as well as methods of measurements. The rationalist assumption that the world can be effectively ordered by articulated rules, and that the information on which to base such rules is readily available, is a central feature of constructivism.

By contrast, empirical methods of decision making assume that it is impossible to spell out all job requirements, let alone to measure and weight them. Employers who bear the risk of the business should be free to use information from all sources, including not only such scraps of personal and longitudinal knowledge as they may glean from interviews or acquaintanceship but also cross-sectional predictions based on their experience of group performance. An employer may not be able to prove in articulated terms that being middle-aged and married are assets to a secretary, but he may know from experience that middle-aged, married women generally have been satisfactory employees in the office pool. A non-rationalist approach to decision making would let him use such information even if its validity cannot be defended in articulated terms to skeptical third parties. It is, after all, his business, not theirs; and if he is wrong, he will confer an advantage upon competitors who are not hindered by his preconceptions.

Neither the rationalist nor the empiricist approach can really claim to provide individual treatment in type four business situations, for the personal knowledge required for individual treatment is largely absent. But the rationalist approach identified with the human rights movement is, if anything, even less individualized than the empiricist. It reduces persons to diagrams containing relatively few points of reference, whereas empiricism allows many more factors to be considered, even if they are categorical in nature and based on personal experience rather than on allegedly scientific evidence.

The demand to treat people as individuals, as formulated by the human rights movement, is animated by an eschatological vision of a world of perfect information, where tasks and assignments can all be specified in articulated terms. It holds that individuals may differ randomly in their characteristics, but that these differences are not importantly related to biological, cultural, or family background. Matching of persons and social roles is seen as a technical process of assessing merit. If the world we live in does not resemble this rationalist utopia, it is said to be because of discrimination. Differential achievement of groups, whether defined by race, religion, sex, age, or anything else, is not thought to show that the group traits are valuable bits of information; it only shows the ubiquitous presence of discrimination. The "solution" to the "problem" is accordingly the reconstruction of society along rationalist lines, using coercive authority delegated by the state to reformist intellectuals. In the new war on discrimination, "individual treatment" is a rhetorical vehicle for constructivist social technology.

Notes

[1] Alberta Human Rights Commission, *Human Rights: Respecting our Differences, Students' Manual* (Edmonton: School Book Branch, 1984), 8.

[2] Dale Gibson, "Stereotypes, Statistics and Slippery Slopes: A Reply to Professors Flanagan and Knopff and Other Critics of Human Rights Legislation," in Neil Nevitte and Allan Kornberg, eds., *Minorities and the Canadian State* (Oakville: Mosaic Press, 1985), 126.

[3] Alexis de Tocqueville, *Democracy in America,* tr. Henry Reeve (London, 1864), Vol. II, Book II, ch.2. See in general Friedrich A. Hayek, "Individualism: True and False," in *Individualism and Economic Order* (Chicago: University of Chicago Press, 1948), 1-32.

[4] John Stuart Mill, *On Liberty* (Indianapolis: Bobbs-Merrill, 1956), 6.

[5] Charles J. Lumsden and Edward O. Wilson, *Promethean Fire: Reflections on the Origin of Mind* (Cambridge, Mass.: Harvard University Press, 1983), 73-74.

[6] Brian John Martine, *Individuals and Individuality* (Albany: State University of New York Press, 1984), 78-79.

[7] The following analysis is inspired by Thomas Sowell, *Knowledge and Decisions* (New York: Basic Books, 1980).

[8] *Ibid.,* 28.

[9] *Ibid.,* 23-30.

[10] Ontario Legislative Assembly, Select Committee on Company Law, *The Insurance Industry: First Report on Automobile Insurance* (1977), 105. I make no comment on the fact that 5040 is also the population of the city described in Plato's *Laws*!

[11] *Ibid.,* 110.

[12] All provincial and federal human rights legislation exempts group benefits provided in connection with employment. In addition, Manitoba, Ontario, and Quebec provide exemptions in varying degree for insurance sold in the private market.

[13] Sowell, *Knowledge and Decisions,* 334-336.

[14] Alan H. Goldman, *Justice and Reverse Discrimination* (Princeton, N.J.: Princeton University Press, 1979), 47.

[15] The management consultants Reed Stenhouse Associates Ltd. offer to perform a "human rights audit" for their clients. *Alberta Report,* August 6, 1984.

[16] This section draws heavily on Thomas Bateman, "The Law and Politics of Human Rights in British Columbia, 1983-84" (M.A. Thesis, Department of Political Science, University of Calgary, 1988) ch.3.

[17] Unreported, June 4, 1976.

[18] Unreported, March 31, 1976.

[19] 2 C.H.R.R. (1981), D/289.

[20] *Ibid.,* at D/293.

[21] 3 C.H.R.R. (1982), D/663.

[22] On the appeal of this case, Justice McKay expressed his opinion that the board's finding that the medical report was out of date was based on "rather skimpy, inconclusive and one-sided evidence." See *Andruchiw v. Corporation of the District of Burnaby* (1983), 4 C.H.R.R. D/1182 at D/1185 (S.C.B.C.). Whether or not this is true is beside the point in the present context.

[23] *Cook* v. *Noble* (1983) 4 C.H.R.R. D/1510.
[24] See Saskatchewan Human Rights Commission, *Newsletter,* 16:2 (Fall, 1987), 1.

V

EQUALITY AND DIFFERENCE

The logic of individual treatment is indifferent to the nature of the generalizations it calls into question. It does not matter whether the trait on which a generalization is based defines a genuine political minority, a social group, or a statistical aggregation: each kind of generalization violates individual treatment in the same way. Discrimination against non-political groups and aggregations can be challenged not only from the point of view of individual treatment, however, but also in terms of its impact on overlapping minorities. The phenomenon of overlapping groups poses not only the problem of discrimination by proxy, which sets in motion the rhetoric of individual treatment, but also the opposite problem: the effect on a target group of direct discrimination against a secondary, overlapping group. Individual treatment is only one prong of the new war on discrimination; the other is achieving equality of result for specified minorities. The pursuit of equal results is the subject of this and the next two chapters.

The inferior status of any particular minority is caused not only by intentional discrimination against its members but also by discrimination against secondary, overlapping groups and aggregations. This problem affects especially women and the stigmatic minorities. There are many secondary life-cycle or life-style traits that are disproportionately possessed by these minorities. Women bear children and tend to play the dominant role in rearing them; they also assume a disproportionate share of other domestic responsibilities. Men are generally more aggressive and competitive than women. Some groups outperform others at school. Often groups "specialize" in certain academic and occupational pursuits. Some ethnic and religious groups cluster geographically and form long-term, tightly knit communities; others disperse and are more likely to assimilate into the wider community. Average family size varies dramatically among ethnic groups, so that some groups are younger than others and possess less education and experience. These and other differentiations contribute to the statistical inequalities among groups.

The prohibition of direct discrimination against a minority assures its individual members of formally equal rights; but given the unequal distribution of secondary characteristics, equal rights for individuals do not lead to equal results for groups as a whole. The fact that more women than men are homemakers may not affect the *right* of women to engage in certain occupations or to hold certain public offices, but it is central if one asks why so few women avail themselves of these rights. The smaller average size of women does not affect the *right* of large women to enter police work, but it surely plays a role in the underrepresentation of women on police forces with height and weight requirements. The *right* of well-educated natives or blacks to pursue high-status occupations is not affected by the poor scholastic performance of these groups as a whole, but the overall representation of natives and blacks in such occupations is.

Not surprisingly, there are two kinds of egalitarian responses to the problem posed for minorities by discrimination against overlapping groups. The first does not challenge the way in which existing standards of excellence or qualification exclude overlapping groups but seeks to reduce the overlap itself. Deploring the secondary difference between the minority and the majority, this approach explores ways of eradicating it; it is "conformist" in orientation. The second approach recommends the reduction of discrimination against the overlapping groups; instead of requiring target groups to measure up to the prevailing standards, it wishes to change the standards. This "accommodationist" approach accepts the reality and persistence of group differences and attempts to promote equality of result by requiring benefit-distribution systems to accommodate to these differences. The new war on discrimination pursues both strategies, especially in the prohibition of systemic discrimination and the numerical goals of affirmative action programs. Before examining these policies in detail, this chapter explores in a more general way the differences between conformist and accommodationist responses to group differences.

Three Kinds of Conformity

Promoting equality of result by reducing or overcoming the differences among groups implies the acceptance of common standards of excellence. Sometimes these standards are understood as those of a superior group, which ought to become the model for other groups. Historically this was often the perspective of politically dominant groups. It has appropriately been called the "dominant-conformity" or "absorption" model of assimilation.[1] A second way of achieving common standards is to "amalgamate" the standards and ways of all existing groups into a common mixture. This is the famous "melting pot" model of ethnic assimilation.[2] The metallurgical image suggests that differences should not be overcome by absorbing "inferior" groups into the "superior" group, but by "melting" down all groups, including the dominant group, into a common culture that incorporates the best elements from all of its contributors. Although this "amalgamation" model seems more egalitarian than the dominant-conformity model, it too ultimately points to a superior culture. Like many metallic alloys, the mixture that emerges from the cultural "melting pot" is alleged to be stronger and better than any of its components.

Both the absorption and amalgamation models imply the eventual establishment of a unified set of standards that ought to pervade both public and private life. This approach has fallen out of favour. Nowadays, when the reduction of differences is recommended as an egalitarian strategy, it is almost always in the name of neutral standards or necessities rather than the superiority of a particular group. These "neutral" standards remain "dominant" and they demand "conformity," but the degree of conformity required is allegedly much more modest than that implied by either of the first two approaches. The very idea of "neutral" standards implies the continued existence of different cultures or religions; presenting common standards as neutral is attractive because it suggests that in adhering to them one does not abandon one's own particularity. This strategy is commonly associated with the conceptual separation of the public and private realms. The public sphere is considered neutral, and it is only here that conformity is required; in the private sphere pluralism is permitted and even encouraged. I call this the "liberal conformist" approach to group differences.

Liberal conformity is based on the separation of a neutral or secular public realm and a private realm of diversity. This separation is the hallmark of classical liberalism, whose early theorists were preoccupied with solving the problem of religious civil war. According to these theorists religious strife would be overcome by establishing separate private and public spheres and banishing religion to the private sphere. The public sphere was to devote itself not to promoting the "good life" but to securing the conditions of life itself so that different versions of the "good" could be privately pursued. Since life itself was the universal condition of all versions of the "good life," public devotion to its requirements was neutral as between competing visions of the good; in accepting public rules oriented to security and liberty, one did not have to abandon the pursuit of one's particular good.

From the liberal conformist perspective it is not just religion that must be banished from the public sphere to ensure civil peace. The idea that the state should serve a particular culture is as productive of strife as the theocratic approach to religion. In both cases the establishment of the standards of a particular group would arouse the intransigent opposition of others. The parallel was well expressed by Pierre Trudeau: "In days gone by religion had to be displaced as the basis of the state before the frightful religious wars came to an end. And there will be no end to wars between nations until in some similar fashion the nation ceases to be the basis of the state."[3] Again this implies the cultural (or national) neutrality of the state and the relegation of culture to the private realm.

Liberal conformity is wedded to the modern technological view of the world. The liberal separation of public from private and the limitation of the public sphere to securing the means to private happiness was undertaken in the name of realism. For the early liberal theorists the ancient emphasis on the "good life" over "mere life" as the goal of the political community was both unrealistic and dangerous: unrealistic because the standards of higher "good" could not be known with any certainty; dangerous because making the best way of life the central public goal produced civil strife. Lowering the goal of public life to means rather than ends, and making ultimate ends a purely private question, solved both problems. Moreover, the public pursuit of the means to life was considered to be an inherently more achievable goal.

This liberal transformation of the goals of political life went hand in hand with, and was supported by, a transformed paradigm of knowledge. The ancients placed the "good life" at the heart of the political agenda because they thought that the standards of good could be known. The modern paradigm of knowledge denies that reason can tell us anything about "good" and "evil." These are transformed into "values," which are the product of our will and are not rooted in nature. The "nature" we can know is "value free." This means that reason becomes the servant of our wills, the way in which we discover how to accomplish ends that are not themselves discovered by reason but are merely willed. Moreover, because nature is "value free" and our values are unconstrained by nature, it becomes possible to conceive of nature as something to be conquered to suit our purposes: knowledge becomes technological. For the ancients, securing the means to life was no more realistic than pursuing the good life, both because the good could be known and because nature could not (or should not) be conquered in the name of mere life. The technological paradigm of knowledge shifted the balance: the good could not be known because it was not natural, but value-free nature *could* be conquered. Securing the means to life became more "realistic" as the public pursuit of higher ends lost its support in reason.

Technology is the way in which modern societies attempt to secure the means to the private pursuit of happiness. As the apparently "value free" servant of human "values" it is the appropriate preoccupation of the "neutral" public sphere. Technology and its social requirements are not conceived as themselves embodying a way of life but as the neutral and universal conditions for many different ways of life. Thus liberal conformity is also technological conformity.

The Accommodationist Reaction

The problem with liberal conformity is that what seems neutral or secular to some will not seem so to others. A flag salute policy for school children, if universally applied, forces Jehovah's Witnesses to engage in a proscribed form of idolatry. To the Amish compulsory public education is heretical. "Public schools" have often looked like "Protestant" schools to Catholics. Hard hat requirements infringe the religious sensibilities of Sikhs. Intelligence tests are often deemed to be culturally biased by groups whose scores are disproportionally low. "Correct" English has been called "white" English by some American blacks. The mandatory use of English in air traffic communications, which appears to many Anglophones to be a requirement of safety, is an expression of invidious ethnic and linguistic prejudice to Canadian Francophones. Such challenges to the neutrality of existing public standards give rise to the accommodationist strategy to group differences. In what follows I will look more closely at the differences between conformism and accommodationism in the areas of religion, culture or ethnicity, and sex.

Religion

The liberal conformist approach to religious differences envisages a pluralism that is virtually unlimited as regards belief but not as regards action. One can believe what one likes, but one can act only on those beliefs that are not proscribed by secular law. This was the position of such classical liberals as Locke and Jefferson.[4] A modern formulation is Justice Frankfurter's dictum that freedom of religion means "freedom from conformity to religious dogma, not freedom from law because of religious dogma."[5] This means that people might have to obey laws that conflict with their religious beliefs, or that impose special burdens on them because of their religious beliefs.

It should be noted that the liberal conformist approach does not deny the legislator the option of granting special *privileges* or exemptions—for example, exemptions from military conscription to conscientious objectors, who would not make good soldiers anyway—but in this view one has no *right* to such an exemption.[6] If the law does not grant an exemption on prudential grounds, one is required to obey.

Liberal conformism subordinates the individual's private judgment of the character of a public rule—whether or not it is truly neutral—to the judgment of the state. Private perceptions of the lack of neutrality in public laws cannot be permitted to override the state's judgment of neutrality and must not undermine generalized enforcement. A *right* to special treatment or exemptions would encourage the theocratic notion that the state should be obeyed only when its laws corresponded to, or at least did not conflict with, God's laws—the very notion early liberalism strove to overcome. For conformist liberalism, secular political truth circumscribes and limits religious truth, not *vice versa*.

The accommodationist approach to religious practices that conflict with public law gives more scope to private judgment. From the perspective of the disadvantaged religious minority, the demand for accommodation is grounded in a denial of the religious neutrality of the relevant law. Accommodationism would have made little headway, however, if it had not found support among members of the majority who are not inclined to question the neutrality of the challenged laws. The latter subscribe to a revised liberalism, which does not deny the existence or desirability of a neutral public sphere, or the secular purpose of the laws to which it wishes to provide exemptions, but which would rigorously apply those laws against private judgment only when the secular end was extremely compelling and when the exemption would substantially undermine it. In this view there is a *right* to an exemption, although that right is not absolute and is subject to reasonable limits.[7]

Determining the "reasonable limits" to the right to an exemption involves balancing the interest in free religious practice against the secular purpose served by the law. If the latter is sufficiently compelling, and if an unlimited exemption would subvert it, the exemption may be appropriately circumscribed. One problem with an unlimited exemption on religious grounds is that people might begin to invent religious justifications for their desire to evade an inconvenient law. If this became widespread, the effectiveness of the law would be undermined. A common solution to this problem is to require those who wish to avail themselves of an exemption to demonstrate that their objection to the law is sincerely religious. Another solution is carefully to investigate the religion in question to determine whether the otherwise illegal practice is doctrinally required or is a matter of mere discretion.

Both the sincerity and the doctrinal necessity tests pose problems for the liberal conscience. There is something distasteful about the state determining either the sincerity or the orthodoxy of religious belief. Both problems are avoided if the exemption can be drafted in religiously neutral terms. Ontario's *Retail Business Holidays Act* provides an example. The Act requires retail businesses to close on specified holidays, including Sundays. However, section 3(4) of the Act allows stores to open on Sunday if they were closed the preceding Saturday. The section is clearly designed to accommodate the religious practices of observers of a Saturday sabbath, but it applies to anyone, of whatever religious persuasion, who chooses to close on Saturday rather than Sunday. Religious practice, sincere or otherwise, and whether or not doctrinally required, is irrelevant. Writing for the majority of the Supreme Court in its review of this legislation, Chief Justice Dickson expressed his preference for such religiously neutral exemptions. He conceded that religiously specific exemptions subject to a sincerity test could not always be avoided, but concluded that neutral drafting was generally preferable.[8]

The neutral drafting of religious exemptions poses problems of its own, however. In particular, it raises the possibility that what is intended to be a narrow exemption, exercised by a small minority, will undermine or transform the rule. If the Ontario Sunday closing exemption is used not only by Saturday sabbatarians but by many others as well, the policy of having a single, common day of rest for the majority will give way to two alternative days. Thus, to save the primary policy, neutral exemptions may themselves have to be subject to further neutral limitations. In the case of Ontario's *Retail Business Holidays Act*, section 3(4) not only granted an exemption to merchants who closed on Saturday but limited that exemption to those whose premises were under a specified size and who operated with no more than seven employees on a Sunday. Anyone who closed on Saturday, and whose business was small enough, could open on Sunday. Of course, the size limitation, being religiously neutral, also excluded large establishments operated by Jews or Seventh Day Adventists. Thus the sincerity and orthodoxy tests were avoided only at the cost of discriminating within the religious groups for whose benefit the exemption was created. Justice Wilson found this more problematic than the sincerity test and preferred a generalized, religiously specific exemption.[9] Finding both alternatives equally problematic and neither more principled than the other, Justice La Forest argued that an exemption was not constitutionally required—that it was a matter of legislative discretion.[10] This points back in the direction of liberal conformity.

Culture

As regards culture, the most obvious challenge to the liberal conformist ideal of a neutral public realm is posed by language. In all political communities a minority of languages—usually just one, occasionally two or three—dominate public life. If language is seen primarily as a vehicle for culture, then this linguistic "establishment" also implies cultural establishment. The Royal Commission on Bilingualism and Biculturalism made this association between language and culture, describing language as a vehicle of culture, and culture as a comprehensive "way of thinking, being and feeling"—in short, as a way of life.[11] In this formulation official bilingualism implies official biculturalism, which in turn means that some ways of life are publicly preferred to others. This combined policy of bilingualism and biculturalism was opposed by non-English and non-French minorities throughout Canada, and by Quebecois nationalists. The former failed to see why their cultures should be symbolically denigrated; the latter did not question the propriety of preferring some cultures to others, but wished to "establish" only French culture (and hence language) in Quebec.

The Trudeau government attempted to blunt such criticisms by denying the connection between "official" bilingualism and biculturalism. In its view language served not only as the vehicle for the transmission of a particular culture but also as a culturally neutral or utilitarian means of communication that allows those of different cultures to participate in the same political community.[12] Because of this dual function, it is possible for governments to treat language and culture separately; indeed, to divorce them for purposes of public policy. By placing the emphasis on the utilitarian aspects of language, government can enact official languages without at the same time legislating official cultures. If this is accepted, the cultural neutrality of the public sphere is maintained. It then becomes possible to have an officially bilingual country that is nevertheless not officially bicultural, but multicultural.[13]

The combination of bilingualism and multiculturalism is rhetorically attractive, but in practice it is difficult to make the cultural neutrality of an "official" languages policy persuasive to linguistically "unofficial" minorities. It is certainly true that language serves culturally neutral purposes of communication, but these are usually performed by the language of the dominant majority in the natural course of things, without any need legally to underline the "official" status of that language. The political emphasis on "official" languages almost always serves the interests of politically powerful linguistic minorities. For these minorities the assimilative force of the majority's language is diminished. Since language is not only a means for utilitarian communication but also a primary vehicle for cultural transmission, as even the Trudeau government was compelled to admit, this means that linguistically "official" minorities are indirectly aided in the process of cultural transmission and maintenance. In Canada Francophone minorities outside Quebec and Anglophones in Quebec enjoy advantages as compared to other language groups. These advantages tend to be justified by reference to the "founding nations" argument, but this argument carries little weight with such groups as the non-English or non-French "founders" of the Canadian West. From the perspective of the latter groups, the official status of French represents not so much the entrenchment of a second vehicle of culturally neutral communication as the accommodation of the cultural transmission needs of one minority among several. This understanding fuels the demand for a more general accommodation of linguistic minorities. The official promotion of multiculturalism, in this view, is impossible without official multilingualism as well.[14]

Ethnic groups differ not only linguistically but in many other ways as well. They often differ in such things as preferred foods, dress, family structures and customs, styles and occasions of celebration, etc. Differences are also apparent in attitudes toward work, education and achievement, and preferred academic and occupational pursuits. Some of these group traits are perfectly compatible with prevailing public standards of excellence and success; others are not. Again, one's approach to conflicting traits will depend on whether the public standards are seen as neutral standards of excellence. If they are, conflicting group traits will be labelled as "backward" or "regressive," as traits to be deplored and to be overcome. This orientation is evident in the writings of John Porter, who saw the forces of "modernization," and the technological "post-industrial" society to which they led, as culturally neutral and, on the whole, as good. He thus opposed multiculturalism to the extent that it strengthened group traits that impeded modernization; certainly he did not think that the standards of modernization should be diluted to accommodate conflicting traits.[15]

The problem with this argument is that the "universal" and "neutral" standards of modernity and post-industrialism that Porter praises are associated with some ethnic groups more than with others. They are the standards of white English-speakers and Northern Europeans. This often impels minorities to ask whether they are indeed being asked to conform to neutral standards or to those of politically dominant groups. As Porter writes, there were fears that what was actually demanded in the North American context was "Anglo-conformity on the part of 'non-Anglo' groups." Porter concedes that such fears were "in a large measure...probably justified" but adds that "it could also be said that what was being advocated was conformity to the values of societies leading in the modernizing process."[16] In other words, what is being demanded is not Anglo-conformity but liberal conformity, which only looks like Anglo-conformity because English-speakers happen to be more liberal.

Again, it is often difficult to persuade minorities that the conformity demanded of them is neutral "liberal conformity" rather than Anglo-conformity. When persuasion fails, existing employment requirements, testing processes, educational standards, and the like come to be seen not as neutral standards of excellence or requirements of technological efficiency but as culturally biased (or racist) rules that require modification to accommodate cultural plurality. This perception sometimes leads to the charge that the use of such standards of judgment is racist. A dramatic example occurred at Cornell University in 1968, when black students held an economics professor hostage because he "was racist in using a Western standard for judgment of the efficiency of African economic performance."[17]

Sex

The most fundamental difference between men and women is biological: women bear children and men do not. It is generally agreed that in the past this division of reproductive labour gave rise to a much broader sexual division of labour, extending beyond biological reproduction to most other productive and social activities. Not only did women bear the children but, in the absence of adequate birth control, they bore them often enough to foreclose serious involvement in non-domestic activities. Women and children were thus dependent on males for protection and the provision of sustenance. Furthermore, in pre-technological societies productive (as opposed to reproductive) labour often required the kind of strength that women lacked. By a kind of natural necessity, women's role of child*bearing* was extended to include the primary role in child*rearing* and in domestic life generally. Similarly, men naturally dominated the public sphere. The division between "public man" and "private woman" was thus rooted in natural necessity.[18]

In older, teleological theories "nature" was associated not only with necessity but also with the "good." Such teleological perspectives have often been used to justify the sexual division of labour. What is generally conceded to have been necessary was also justified as being good. Thus woman's dominant role in the household was not simply a matter of necessity but the foundation of her natural fulfillment. Associated with women's biological monopoly on childbearing were natural psychological dispositions to nurture that made them better childrearers and homemakers than men, and that could not find their proper satisfaction outside the household. By the same token, men (being more abstract, rational, and aggressive) were better suited to the public realm and found their natural fulfillment there.

Modern theories of nature are decidedly non-teleological. As we have seen, the language of "good" has been separated from the language of "nature." Indeed, the language of good has been transformed into the language of "values," which human beings freely "create" for themselves, often against nature. In this view nature is solely the realm of necessity and chance, and the limits it places on human freedom to create and live "values" are to be regretted and, if possible, overcome. The marriage of making and knowing entailed in this technological approach was unknown to the ancients, who never combined *techne* and *logos*. For them the standards of good were natural and thus accessible to human reason, something to be understood and freely embraced, rather than something to be made against nature. For the moderns *logos* is more instrumental, teaching us not what is good by nature but how to actualize our values by conquering nature.

Modern feminism views the sexual division of labour from this technological perspective. Simone de Beauvoir contends that

"Human society is an *antiphysis*—in a sense it is against nature; it does not passively submit to the presence of nature but rather takes over the control of nature on its own behalf."[19] Shulamith Firestone adds that "the 'natural' is not necessarily a 'human' value. Humanity has begun to outgrow nature." Agreeing that the sexual division of labour is rooted in natural necessity, Firestone insists that "we can no longer justify the maintenance of a discriminatory sex class system on grounds of its origins in Nature."[20] Far from being the natural path to fulfillment, the sexual division of labour is stultifying and alienating, and must be destroyed in the name of "human value."

Having separated the natural from the good, feminism emphasizes the technological possibility of liberating women from their undesirable "biological destiny." Indeed, some feminists, such as Firestone, even call pregnancy "barbaric" and look forward to the day when artificial reproduction will replace it, thus truly putting men and women on an equal footing in relation to their children.[21]

Short of artificial reproduction, the physical or biological technology of liberation is largely in place. Effective contraception and techniques for safe, efficient abortion exist and, if readily available, permit women to plan their families or to choose not to have children at all. Women who have children can and do have fewer, and because the average life expectancy is longer today than in the past (another consequence of technology), they are tied to "home and hearth" for much smaller proportions of their lives. Moreover, with appropriate advances in social technology—daycare, reformed job expectations and conditions, sex role reform, etc.—they need not be confined to the domestic sphere even for the childrearing period. In addition, the nature of non-domestic work in modern industrial (and "post-industrial") society is such that the important and desirable positions outside the home do not require "male strength." It is often argued that modern technology has made strength an obsolete requirement even in warfare.

As noted, the sexual division of labour was in the past not only necessary but also socially approved. Women were excluded from the public domain by law and custom as well as by nature. These conventional supports of sex-role differentiation continued, and were sometimes even strengthened,[22] after the supports of necessity had crumbled. The first battle in the feminist war against the sexual division of labour was naturally fought against such direct discrimination against women. Gaining the vote was the first step in this process; beating down the barriers of direct employment discrimination was the second.

Discrimination *against* women was not the only conventional support for the traditional division of labour. Such discrimination perpetuated women's dependence on men and the family unit for economic security. To ensure that these needs for security were met, public policy undertook to support the family and women's position within it in a myriad of ways. The natural concomitant of discrimination against women in the public sphere was to compensate for their resulting weakness and dependence by discriminating *for* them in the family. This discrimination *for* women in the private domain was also challenged by feminists, both out of abstract principle and out of a rejection of the symbolic implications of protective paternalism—namely, that women were by nature weaker and more vulnerable than men. In this view law and policy are symbolic educators, and the symbolism of paternalistic policies reinforces traditional conceptions of women's proper place.[23] This attack attracted the support of men who could see no reason why women should continue to enjoy discrimination in their favour domestically while men lost their public privileges.

The dismantling of negative discrimination in the public sphere and protective paternalism in the private sphere is part of all modern feminist programs. However, the resulting formal equality between the sexes does not lead to equality of result as long as women continue to differ from men in ways that conflict with prevailing requirements and standards of public success. For example, if women generally remain less assertive than men, and if they continue to shy away from academic studies that qualify one for high-status careers, they will not even enter careers that are now formally open to them. Most importantly, if women continue to take the primary responsibility for childcare and housework they will be unable to compete effectively with men who are not similarly "burdened." Indeed, as long as the division of domestic labour persists, formal equality only exacerbates the vulnerability of women. Unable to compete, especially during the childrearing years, women remain dependent on men for their financial security, but law and policy, now officially blind to their relative weakness, no longer compensate for this dependence.

Developments in divorce law illustrate the problem. During the era of protective paternalism the law clearly favoured women. In recognition of the special vulnerability of women the law made it difficult for a man to divorce his wife and guaranteed that if he did he would have to support her until she remarried.[24] This is no longer true. Today the law increasingly assumes that women have no comparative disadvantages and can compete with men on equal terms.[25] However, this assumption does not reflect reality. Married women still sacrifice career to family to a much greater extent than their husbands. This means that upon divorce they are clearly not economically equal to their husbands. Typically their work experience is shorter and less well-paid because they have taken time away from the work force and settled for lower status jobs in order to devote themselves to the family.[26]

As in the case of ethnic inequalities, substantive equality of result for the sexes can be pursued either by overcoming or by accommodating the relevant secondary differences. One way of overcoming them is for women to become more like men. This is analogous to the dominant-conformity approach to the overcoming of ethnic differences, except that women who advocate such conformity do not see the male lives they wish to emulate as representing *male* standards. They are, rather, truly "human" standards, which in the past only men have been able to pursue because they were free from the biological constraints that oppressed women. The better analogy, therefore, is to Porter's contention that the standards embodied by Anglo society are as much the standards of modernity as they are Anglo standards.

This "male conformist" approach to sexual differentiation involves the resocialization of women. If they are less aggressive than men, they must undergo "assertiveness training." Similarly, girls must be taught to take the hard sciences more seriously. Finally, male conformism entails a serious depreciation of motherhood and childcare. This is especially true if women are to accept male standards of success in the elite professions. Getting to the top of these professions requires commitments of time and energy that preclude serious devotion to anything else. Traditionally, married men have been able to make such commitments because their wives raised the children and took care of other domestic responsibilities. Women can succeed in such careers, given their present demands, only if they become like careerist men; that is, only if they delegate childcare and domestic responsibilities elsewhere, or if they choose not to have children at all. Even one or two children can derail a promising career if they distract the mother from full-time absorption in her job.

Male conformism has been criticized by women who question whether the "workaholic" standards of male lives are truly fulfilling, and who point out the elitist and ultimately unrealistic dimensions of the flight from motherhood and the family. Few women can or want to give up these things to the extent that successful men have always given them up.[27] Nor, in this account, should they. Parenting and domesticity have their fulfillments, which women would be foolish to abandon. Furthermore, traditional female traits are not deficiencies to be overcome but virtues to be maintained.[28] This criticism is made both by traditionalists, who support the notion that woman's proper place is in the home, and by feminists. The latter do not wish to keep women at home, but neither do they wish to purchase public equality at the cost of becoming male clones.

The notion that traditional female traits are *virtues* does not necessarily imply that they should continue to be specifically "female." While the "melting pot" has fallen out of favour in the ethnic and cultural realm, its equivalent in the discussion of sexual differentiation is very much alive. Many feminists recommend a sex-role amalgamation, a new androgyny that combines what is good from both of the traditional roles and rejects what is bad. Women must indeed become more like men if equality is to be achieved, but this is only half the story: men must also become more like women. In this view men have a feminine side, which they currently suppress, just as women have masculine inclinations, which they are taught to deny. Both have lived "half lives" of sexual specificity rather than fully human lives of androgyny.[29] As Angela Miles explains,

> To claim women's humanity only insofar as women can show themselves to be like (as good as) men is to challenge men's definition of women but not their definition of humanity. With the insistence that the cares and concerns and values traditionally associated with women, and indeed women themselves, are human, women's demand for access to male areas is transformed. It is no longer merely a claim to be human in limited male terms. It becomes instead part of the wider struggle to transform people as individuals, and the masculine concept of humanity common to the whole spectrum of male politics, society, culture and scholarship.[30]

"In affirming women's specificity," Miles concludes, "feminism articulates new and more universal truths—truths which end narrow, single-sex definitions of the world, and in the process feminize and humanize politics."[31]

Sexual equality of result can be pursued not only by overcoming differences but by accommodating them. Thus an important strand within modern feminism argues that the division of labour as regards childcare will be with us for the foreseeable future and that the prevailing rules should be changed to make the public sphere more hospitable to women as they are. Such accommodations can be either "gender specific" or "gender neutral but sex specific."[32] A gender-specific accommodation is a special exemption or preference granted only to women in recognition of their special needs and vulnerabilities. For example, the fact that women are temporarily incapacitated by childbirth can be offset by "maternity" leave. To accommodate the tendency of women not only to bear the children but also to stay home and nurture them well past the period of actual physical incapacity, such maternity leave might be extended for an appropriate period of time and combined with a guarantee of continued job tenure and no interruption in the accumulation of seniority. The latter accommodation could also be provided in the gender-neutral form of "parental leave" available to either the mother or the father, though it would be sex-specific in the sense that it is designed to accommodate the special needs of women and would be taken advantage of primarily by women. Another gender-neutral-but-sex-specific accommodation would be the expansion of part-time options in jobs where they are currently lacking. Again, such options would be open to both men and women but would serve the needs primarily of women who wish to combine remunerated work with a dominant role in the household.

This accommodationist approach to sexual differences worries some feminists. For one thing, it resembles the old paternalist protectionism in the sense of acknowledging the comparative weakness of women. In the past the special vulnerabilities of women were used to justify their confinement in the private sphere, and today's feminists fear that any public admission of such vulnerability might feed the forces of reaction that would like to return women to their domestic duties.[33] Accommodationist feminists understand and often share these fears but insist upon the different purposes of the two forms of protectionism: paternalistic protectionism was designed to make it possible for women to devote themselves totally to domesticity, whereas the new protectionism seeks precisely to liberate them from total confinement to that sphere. Accommodationist feminists also point out that a reactionary return to the traditional family is highly unlikely. Women today are virtually compelled to work outside the home for financial reasons, and the task is to enable them to do so on more equal terms with men.

A more serious criticism of accommodationism comes from feminists interested in the promotion of androgyny. From this perspective sex-role differentiation should be overcome rather than entrenched through accommodation. For example, the greater availability of part-time work with better benefits and working conditions can be seen as a way of permitting women to continue to play the dominant domestic role while men continue to avoid it.[34] Similarly, permitting homemaking to count as a contribution to "family assets," and thus to influence the division of these assets upon divorce, has been criticized for encouraging women to stay home.[35] Or, again, allowing female naval officers in an "up-or-out" career ladder a "longer period of service before a mandatory discharge for want of promotion" accommodates their ineligibility for combat service, but it may also entrench that ineligibility and the assumptions about sexual difference that underlie it.[36]

This criticism certainly applies to gender-specific accommodations, which imply that the difference being accommodated either cannot or should not be overcome. For example, policies of extended "maternity" leave imply that fathers are not well suited to full-time childrearing during the first months or years of the child's life. The same is true when gender-neutral accommodations "such as part-time work, flextime, and child-care centres are sought as '*women's* benefits'." As Betty Friedan contends, when the sex-specific aspect of these policies is emphasized, "instead of easing the strain between work and family, they actually do the reverse, merely reinforcing the idea that home and family belong to women's sphere rather than being a joint responsibility."[37] On the other hand, gender-neutral accommodations can be understood as a necessary part of sex-role reform. Thus "parental" leave policies entail no formal entrenchment or legitimation of the existing sex-role differentiation, even if, because of that differentiation, it is mainly women who take advantage of the benefit.

Such gender-neutral accommodations may not cause sex-role reform, but they are not symbolically hostile to it. More importantly, they accommodate not only the needs of women as they presently are but also the needs of the anticipated androgynous persons of the future. When as many fathers as mothers wish to play a substantial role in childrearing, or when both partners wish to share the task, they will be able to do so with adequate "parental" leave policies.[38] Similarly, the gender-neutral expansion of part-time work may entrench existing sex roles by making it easier for women to combine work with their traditionally dominant role in the household, but it also meets the needs of men who wish to share the domestic responsibilities more equally. In androgynous families women will be relatively freer to engage in non-domestic work but men will be correspondingly less free. Neither will have the freedom of men in traditional families, and both will have an interest in part-time opportunities.

According to some feminists, gender-neutral accommodations will not only provide a more hospitable environment for androgynous persons but may actually contribute to the process of sex-role reform itself. Accommodations that enable parents to take time out for childrearing without sacrificing career advancement are likely to be invoked primarily by women in the short term. On the other hand, because of career continuity these women will ultimately earn more than they otherwise would, and their incomes will be a more important part of the "family income." Some feminists argue that a man's compulsion to share in housework varies in proportion to his wife's contribution to the family income. On the basis of this assumption Betty Friedan suggests that, simply as a result of more women entering the labour force, men will find themselves doing more of the domestic work.[39] Obviously the more important a woman's income to the family, the greater the psychological pressures on the man to abandon the traditional male role. In any case, to the extent that men assume a greater share of the domestic burden, they will find existing job requirements and demands more onerous. These requirements were established by and for men who had full-time, homemaking wives. Friedan suggests that the increasing number of men who no longer enjoy this luxury will become the natural allies of women in pressing for further accommodations.[40] By further improving the relative economic position of women such accommodations will then generate more sex-role reform in the household, and so forth. Thus it is possible to envision a spiraling transformation as accommodations in the work world begin to change sex roles within the household, which then cause demands for further job-related accommodations.

Conclusion

Constructivist social technology attempts to make society conform to rationally pre-conceived goals. To achieve the goal of equal results, the new war on discrimination makes use of both conformist and accommodationist strategies; it attempts either to change disadvantaged groups to suit society or to change society to suit the groups. The accommodationist approach to target-group differences is most obviously represented by the prohibition of systemic discrimination. Affirmative action, on the other hand, has conformist overtones. Remedial measures, for example, are designed to help target groups "remedy" their "deficiencies." Similarly, numerical targets and ameliorative preferences are often defended as establishing *qualified* role models for currently underrepresented target groups, thereby demonstrating that members of these groups can attain desirable positions and that it is worthwhile pursuing the requisite qualifications. On closer examination, however, both policies turn out to be more complex and ambiguous. The prohibition of systemic discrimination is a protean thing that can be understood to serve many ends other than the accommodation of target-group differences. In some contexts, and given a certain interpretation, it even has conformist implications. Similarly, affirmative action programs often resort quite explicitly to accommodationist devices. What is more, the conformist rhetoric commonly used to justify numerical goals (and especially to distinguish them from "quotas") cannot withstand close scrutiny. The setting of targets inevitably entails an accommodationist challenge to existing standards of excellence. In any case, both affirmative action and the prohibition of systemic discrimination are devices of constructivist social technology and further the interests of "guardian democracy." These matters are the subject of the next two chapters.

Notes

[1] Evelyn Kallen, *Ethnicity and Human Rights in Canada* (Toronto: Gage, 1982), 170.

[2] *Ibid.*, 161.

[3] P.E. Trudeau, *Federalism and the French Canadians* (Toronto: Macmillan, 1968), 157-158.

[4] Walter Berns, *The First Amendment and the Future of American Democracy* (New York: Basic Books, 1976), chs. 1 and 2.

[5] *Board of Education* v. *Barnette*, 319 U.S. 624 at 653 (1943).

[6] Berns, *The First Amendment*; cf. Alexander Bickel, *The Morality of Consent* (New Haven: Yale University Press, 1975), 95.

[7] This approach has been adopted by the Supreme Court of Canada in cases arising under section 2 of the Charter. See *Jack and Charlie* v. *The Queen*, [1985] 2 S.C.R. 332 and *Edwards Books* v. *The Queen*, [1986] 2 S.C.R. 713.

[8] *Edwards Books*, at 780.

[9] *Ibid.*, 808-811.

[10] *Ibid.*, 794-796.

[11] Hugh R. Innis (ed.), *Bilingualism and Biculturalism: An Abridged Version of the Royal Commission Report* (Toronto: McClelland and Stewart, 1973), 4.

[12] *A National Understanding: The Official Languages of Canada* (Hull: Queen's Printer, 1977), 19-20. For an interesting treatment of the dual function of language, see E.D. Hirsch, Jr., *Cultural Literacy: What Every American Needs to Know* (Boston: Houghton Mifflin, 1987), ch. 4.

[13] For further analysis of this position and the opposite position maintained by the Quebec Government, see Rainer Knopff, "Language and Culture in the Canadian Debate: The Battle of the White Papers," *Canadian Review of Studies in Nationalism* 6:1 (1979).

[14] Kallen, *Ethnicity and Human Rights*, 168; John Porter, "Ethnic Pluralism in Canadian Perspective," in his *The Measure of Canadian Society: Education, Equality, and Opportunity* (Toronto: Gage, 1979), 118.

[15] Porter, "Ethnic Pluralism in Canadian Perspective."

[16] *Ibid.*, 125.

[17] Allan Bloom, *The Closing of the American Mind* (New York: Simon and Schuster, 1987), 354.

[18] Shulamith Firestone, *The Dialectic of Sex* (New York: Bantam Books, 1970), 8-9.

[19] Quoted in Firestone, *The Dialectic of Sex*, 10.

[20] *Ibid.*

[21] *Ibid.*, 198-199, 206-209, 221.

[22] Sylvia Ann Hewlett, *A Lesser Life: The Myth of Women's Liberation in America* (New York: William Morrow and Co., 1986), chs. 10 and 11.

[23] Winifred H. Holland, "Is the Ontario Municipal Property Legislation in Need of Reform?" in Pask, Mahoney and Brown (eds.), *Women, the Law and the Economy* (Toronto: Butterworths, 1985), 251-252.

[24] Charter of Rights Educational Fund, *Report on the Statute Audit Project* (Toronto: 1985), 4.2.

[25] Hewlett, *A Lesser Life*, 65; *Report on the Statute Audit Project*, 4.4. Freda M. Steel, "The Role of the State in the Enforcement of Maintenance," in Pask, Mahoney and Brown (eds.), *Women, the Law and the Economy*, 203.

[26] See generally, *ibid.*, ch. 3; *Report on the Statute Audit Project*, ch. 4.

[27] See generally, Hewlett, *A Lesser Life*, and Betty Friedan, *The Second Stage* (New York: Summit Books, 1981).

[28] Carol Gilligan, *In a Different Voice: Psychological Theory and Women's Development* (Cambridge, Mass.: Harvard University Press, 1982).

[29] Shulamith Firestone, *The Dialectic of Sex*, 205-206. Betty Friedan, *The Second Stage*.

[30] Angela R. Miles "Ideological Hegemony in Political Discourse: Women's Specificity and Equality," in Angela R. Miles and Geraldine Finn (eds.), *Feminism In Canada: From Pressure to Politics* (Montreal: Black Rose, 1982), 218.

[31] *Ibid.*, 226.

[32] *Report on the Statute Audit Project*, 1.28-1.32. I have reversed the terminology used in this report more accurately to convey the meaning. "Gender" refers to the classification of words rather than of beings.

[33] *Report on the Statute Audit Project*, 1.27.

[34] Julie White, "Part-time Work: Ideal or No Deal?" in Pask, Mahoney and Brown (eds.), *Women, the Law and the Economy*, 22.

[35] Winifred H. Holland, "Is the Ontario Municipal Property Legislation in Need of Reform?" 251-252.

[36] See Wojciech Sadurski, "Equality Before the Law: A Conceptual Analysis," *The Australian Law Journal* 60:3 (March, 1986), 136, commenting on *Schlesinger* v. *Ballard*, 419 U.S. 498 (1975).

[37] Friedan, *The Second Stage*, 11. Emphasis added.

[38] *Ibid.*, chs. 4 and 8.

[39] *Ibid.*, 113, 116, 121, 277.

[40] *Ibid.*, 121 and ch. 4.

VI

SYSTEMIC DISCRIMINATION

The legal prohibition of systemic barriers is an important weapon in the new war on discrimination. It is a sword, moreover, that cuts two ways. It can serve both as a useful ally in the battle for individual treatment and as a way of promoting equal results for a short list of preferred minorities. Nor does this exhaust its protean character; depending on how it is interpreted and applied, it may promote equal results either by accommodating group differences or by encouraging conformity. However it is understood, the prohibition of systemic discrimination is an instrument of constructivist social technology and serves to augment the power of the guardian elite.

This chapter is divided into four main parts. The first examines the various ways in which the systemic approach may be understood to serve the cause of individual treatment; the second explores its more important role in promoting equality of results for specified groups; the third briefly shows how the systemic approach contributes to the power of the "guardian elite"; and the fourth argues against further extending guardian democracy by interpreting section 15 of the *Charter* to cover systemic discrimination.

Systemic Barriers and Direct Discrimination

The Prophylatic Function. The prohibition of systemic discrimination can be seen as a useful ally in the battle against intentional discrimination. Neutral rules may be adopted not only for truly neutral reasons but also as a subterfuge for intentional discrimination. For example, an employer who had in the past refused to hire blacks or natives might respond to the prohibition of intentional discrimination by adopting educational requirements that are unnecessary to the adequate performance of the job, but that are disproportionately lacked by the target groups. One reason for prohibiting systemic discrimination is to ensure that the attack on intentional discrimination reaches such subterfuge. This might be called the "prophylactic" rationale for the prohibition of systemic discrimination.

The leading U.S. case on systemic discrimination, *Griggs* v. *Duke Power Co.*, may have been decided on the basis of this prophylactic rationale. The reader will recall that in this case the Supreme Court invalidated otherwise neutral aptitude tests that had a discriminatory effect on minority (chiefly black) applicants.[1] As Donald Horowitz notes, however,

> The Court faced this question…in a case involving a company with a history of racial discrimination in employment, a company that had added the aptitude test requirement on the very date the law against employment discrimination became effective. The validity of aptitude testing for all employers was thus decided on a factual record evoking suspicion about the motives of the particular employer before the Court. Could the Court allow the employer to "get away with" its machinations?[2]

This rationale was clearly expressed by the tribunal that originally decided *Bhinder*:

> The issue as to whether intent is an element of discrimination consistently arises where an apparently neutral specification results in adverse consequences for a member of a class of persons protected under human rights legislation. In such cases, it will be rare that the requirement is enacted to maliciously or purposely exclude persons on a prohibited ground. However, to protect against such an eventuality, it is necessary that complaints be found to be valid, notwithstanding that respondents have not acted with intent. Malicious intent is difficult or impossible to prove where an apparently neutral specification results in adverse consequences. If proof of intent were required, a most confounding subversion of the principles enshrined in human rights legislation might well occur.[3]

Ironically, the prophylactic rationale violates the very canons of equal treatment that prohibitions of intentional discrimination are designed to uphold. Anti-discrimination legislation outlaws the use of group membership as a proxy for other relevant qualities because it contravenes the principle that like cases should be treated alike. Thus using sex as a proxy for strength favours men who would have failed an objective strength test and excludes women who would have passed it. Such a rule is either over- or underinclusive (and often both) in selecting the group actually desired—in this case the group of the strong. The result is that individuals who are similarly situated with respect to the purpose of the rule are in fact not equally treated. A prohibition of systemic discrimination based on the prophylactic rationale necessarily falls prey to the same criticism because it is inherently overinclusive: the mischief at which it is aimed is direct discrimination hiding under the cover of neutral rules, but it reaches genuinely neutral rules as well. With respect to its prophylactic purpose, therefore, a prohibition of systemic discrimination cannot treat like cases alike; it is a discriminatory prohibition.

The Compensatory Function. A prohibition of systemic discrimination may also serve in the battle against direct discrimination by overcoming the present effects of past intentional discrimination. For example, if an employer has intentionally discriminated against a group in the past, the exclusion of the group may be continued in the present through the effect of an otherwise neutral rule. The classic example of this is the use of seniority as the basis for promotion and other benefits: naturally, those who were intentionally excluded in the past will be more recent recruits to an employer's labour force and will thus lack seniority. Nepotism rules, which restrict employment to relatives of current employees, would have a similar effect. The abolition or relaxation of such rules can be seen as a way of compensating those who were intentionally discriminated against in the past.

Prohibitions of systemic discrimination serve this "compensatory" function only when the uneven distribution of the trait required by the rule (e.g., seniority or employee relatives) is caused by the past intentional discrimination of the employer. The disparate impact of many systemic barriers cannot be attributed to such past discrimination. For example, the average size difference between men and women, which causes the disparate impact of height and weight requirements, is not caused by past discrimination.[4] Similarly, the religious beliefs that give rise to the disparate impact of some employment requirements are often caused by theological conviction or community adherence and not past discrimination by the employer. The same is true for tests that some groups fail at disproportionately high rates. This lack of success cannot be attributed to the employer unless the employer had discriminated against the group in the provision of pre-test preparation courses.[5] In brief, even where an employer had previously discriminated against a group, the compensatory rationale does not justify the prohibition of systemic barriers against that group when the cause of the disparate impact is something other than the past discrimination. As Martha Chamallas says, "When there is no causal connection between the employer's prior discriminatory acts and the current discriminatory effects, the significance of the employer's prior discriminatory intent greatly diminishes."[6] One cannot justify a general prohibition of systemic discrimination in terms of the compensatory rationale.

The Indirect Incorporation of New Grounds. The systemic approach may also be understood as a way of indirectly promoting the finer sorting of groups implied by the individual-treatment model. What is systemic discrimination against one group is always direct discrimination against another. Thus height and weight requirements not only constitute a systemic barrier against women but also discriminate directly against small people; they can be attacked either because of their disparate impact on women or because, being unreasonable, they fail to treat small people (male or female) as individuals. In practical terms it does not much matter which way the challenge to height and weight requirements is formulated. If they are struck down because of their disproportionate impact on women, small men, who were not being treated as individuals, will also benefit. Similarly, if they are abolished because of their unfairness to small individuals of either sex, the benefit will disproportionately accrue to women.

Because of this practical overlap between the two models, a systemic interpretation of anti-discrimination provisions may be valued as an indirect way of pursuing the aims of individual treatment where the list of prohibited grounds is closed. We have seen that the logic of individual treatment inclines to a steady expansion of explicitly enumerated grounds and reaches its apotheosis in an open-ended anti-discrimination formulation. A prohibition of systemic discrimination indirectly adds new grounds to a closed list to the extent that these new, unlisted grounds significantly overlap the explicitly enumerated grounds. For example, intentional discrimination based on pregnancy or size may be indirectly added to the list of prohibited grounds by showing that such discrimination disproportionately burdens women.[7]

It is not self-evident, however, that legislation which goes to the trouble of enumerating prohibited grounds of discrimination should be interpreted to include other grounds as well. Such an interpretation might well be thought to usurp the legislative function. Human rights activists themselves lend credence to this objection by their constant efforts to expand the list of specified prohibited grounds. Such explicit reform would be unnecessary if unenumerated grounds were already included.

Pregnancy is a good example. The addition of sex as a prohibited ground of discrimination to anti-discrimination legislation soon gave rise to complaints of discrimination because of pregnancy. This raised the legal issue of whether pregnancy was included in the term "sex." As it turns out, it is not easy to conflate the two. Although pregnancy is something that can happen only to women, it is not simply identical to sex. Not all women become pregnant, nor is pregnancy a permanent condition for those who do. Thus an employer who refuses to hire pregnant women is not necessarily discriminating against women *per se*. For example, it is difficult to accuse an employer of discrimination on the basis of sex if, when faced with a choice between, say, a man, a non-pregnant woman, and a pregnant woman, he chooses to hire the non-pregnant woman—even if he rejects the pregnant woman precisely because of her pregnancy.[8] Intentional discrimination because of pregnancy cannot readily be included in a prohibition of intentional discrimination because of sex. Its inclusion in a legislative prohibition of direct discrimination seems to require the addition of a new and different ground.[9]

Because the interpretive addition of new grounds to a statutory enumeration smacks of judicial legislation, Canadian courts and tribunals have often refused to apply prohibitions of sex discrimination to discrimination because of pregnancy. For example, the adjudicators of a Saskatchewan sex discrimination case reluctantly concluded that "If discrimination on the basis of pregnancy, or some related condition, is to be said to be sex discrimination, it will be because the Legislature has so decreed."[10] However, this refusal makes sense only if the legislation does not prohibit systemic discrimination. For discrimination because of pregnancy affects only women, and thus, like height and weight requirements or hard-hat rules, disproportionately excludes

149

members of one of the specifically protected groups; it would thus be reached by a prohibition of systemic discrimination.[11] If the judicial addition of new prohibited grounds of direct discrimination is illegitimate, it follows that, to the extent that it is understood to bring new kinds of direct discrimination within the reach of the legislation, the judicial addition of a prohibition of systemic discrimination is equally illegitimate. If only the legislature can add pregnancy to the list of prohibited grounds, then only the legislature can take the more radical step of adding a virtually unlimited list of new grounds through the prohibition of systemic discrimination.

Raising the Scrutiny Level of Unlisted Grounds. If the advantage in a prohibition of systemic discrimination lay primarily in permitting challenges to discrimination not included in a closed list of prohibited grounds, it would be redundant where the list of grounds is open-ended, as in section 15 of the *Charter* or B.C.'s former "reasonable cause" provisions. This was illustrated in *Foster* v. *British Columbia Forest Products Ltd.,* a 1979 employment discrimination case arising under the reasonable cause provisions of the *British Columbia Human Rights Code*. The company refused to hire Janet Foster as a labourer at one of its mills because she did not meet its preferred height and weight requirements (at least 5' 6" and 140 lbs.). Foster claimed that this requirement violated the Human Rights Code. The board of inquiry agreed, finding the requirement to be discriminatory, but was faced with the question whether to invalidate it because it constituted systemic discrimination against women, a group identified by an enumerated characteristic, or because it constituted discrimination against small people, an unlisted group. The board concluded that the open-endedness of the "reasonable cause" wording rendered the systemic approach superfluous. It compared this open-ended formulation with "closed" lists of prohibited grounds in the legislation of other jurisdictions:

> In Ontario and the United States the courts have been forced to deal with height and weight standards in "sex discrimination" terms. They have concluded that "unreasonable" standards constitute sex discrimination. In British Columbia it is not necessary for boards of inquiry or courts to make this equation in order to invalidate these size standards. In British Columbia, if a standard is "unreasonable" it is discriminatory under s.8(1) of the Code. There is no need to attach the unreasonability to a specific ground of discrimination such as sex.[12]

Interestingly, this argument, despite its logical force, seems to be insufficient to oust the systemic approach in cases where the list of prohibited grounds is open-ended. This has been especially true of the early discussions of section 15 of the *Charter*, in which many commentators both underline the open-endedness of the section *and* urge that it should be interpreted to cover systemic discrimination. This emphasis on the systemic effect on enumerated groups of unlisted forms of discrimination, even when that does not seem necessary to achieve finer sorting, brings us to the third understanding of prohibitions of systemic discrimination. In this view the systemic approach minimizes the prevalent tendency in the case of open-ended lists of prohibited grounds to subject the unnamed grounds to lower levels of judicial scrutiny than the listed grounds. By emphasizing the indirect effect on a listed ground rather than direct discrimination on the basis of an unlisted ground, the systemic approach may be able to take advantage of the higher scrutiny accorded to listed grounds. The prospects of a challenge to height and weight requirements, for example, may be improved by formulating it not in terms of discrimination against small people but in terms of its disparate effect on women.[13]

The subjection of various kinds of discrimination to different levels of scrutiny is a well-established technique in American jurisprudence under the "equal protection" clause of the Fourteenth Amendment. During the period of judicial restraint that followed the "court packing" crisis of 1937, the American Supreme Court upheld all classifications that had *"some* reasonable basis in terms of *some* rational view of the public interest."[14] This came to be known as "minimal scrutiny." In the 1954 case of *Brown* v. *Board of Education*, however, the Court struck down school segregation, a policy that would have passed this minimal scrutiny test. As Archibald Cox has pointed out, "Honest men not only could, but many do, conclude after serious study that the academic progress of children is greater when the races are segregated."[15] *Brown* established race as a "suspect" classification subject to "strict scrutiny." Strict scrutiny required a classification to be justified not only by *some* rational view of the public interest, but by a "compelling governmental objective," and sought not just *some* reasonable connection between this objective and the classification as a means of attaining it, but a very tight fit. Just as virtually all laws subject to minimal scrutiny passed constitutional muster, so strict scrutiny has been said to be "strict in theory and fatal in fact."[16] Since *Brown* certain other grounds of discrimination, such as alienage, have joined race as grounds entitled to "strict scrutiny." Strict scrutiny has also been applied, irrespective of ground of discrimination, when certain fundamental rights, such as the right to vote, were at stake.

In Canada some commentators have suggested that a similar distinction will need to be made between prohibited grounds of discrimination, and that an obvious line of demarcation lies between the enumerated and unenumerated grounds, with the former enjoying stricter scrutiny simply by virtue of being enumerated. In *Lavell and Bedard* the late chief justice, Bora Laskin, pointed out that the prohibition of discrimination in the *Canadian Bill of Rights* differed from the equal protection clause of the American Fourteenth Amendment insofar as it enumerated the prohibited grounds of discrimination. This, he thought, obviated the need for Canadian courts to follow their American counterparts in distinguishing between reasonable and unreasonable classifications. The legislature had forestalled this kind of judicial policy making by enumerating certain grounds, which must therefore be subject to strict scrutiny.[17]

A similar interpretation of the enumeration in section 15 of the *Charter* is burdened by the fact that age and mental and physical handicap are included among the enumerated grounds. These new grounds are almost certain not to receive a level of scrutiny as strict as the rest of the list. Peter Hogg concludes "that the express inclusion of a ground of discrimination in s.15 is not sufficient to qualify that ground for special protection."[18] On the other hand, Hogg believes that all of the enumerated grounds, except for age and handicap, should receive strict scrutiny, and this appears to be due, at least in part, to the fact that they are explicitly enumerated. Sex, for example, "which has not yet made its way into the suspect category in the United States, should in Canada be accorded similar protection to race, national or ethnic origin, colour and religion," not only because it is enumerated along with them, but also because it is explicitly mentioned elsewhere in the *Charter*—namely, section 28, which guarantees Charter rights equally to male and female persons.[19] While explicit mention in the *Charter* does not entirely settle the question of scrutiny, it does appear to make some difference. It is thus not implausible to contend that inclusion in the enumerated list implies a higher level of scrutiny than would be enjoyed by unlisted grounds, even if further distinctions must be made among grounds thus entitled to higher scrutiny. This is the position taken by Mary Eberts, who suggests both that enumerated grounds enjoy a privileged position and that these grounds are themselves "arranged in [a] sort of hierarchy."[20] Like Hogg, Eberts looks to other explicit provisions concerning these grounds to perceive this hierarchy. Thus, just as the position of sex within the category of suspect grounds is buttressed by section 28, so the claim of age to similar status is weakened by other constitutional provisions explicitly establishing age limitations for public office.[21]

The higher status of the enumerated grounds of discrimination was accepted by the Federal Court (Trial Division) late in 1985. In *Smith, Kline and French Laboratories Ltd.* v. *A.-G. Canada* Justice Strayer noted that once a *prima facie* violation of section 15 had been found, it could only be saved under section 1, which "guarantees the rights and freedoms set out in [the *Charter*] subject only to such reasonable limits prescribed by law as can be demonstrably justified in a free and democratic society."[22] It is generally thought that the words "demonstrably justified" place the onus of proof on the defender of the classification.[23] Because the difficulty of discharging this onus approaches strict scrutiny, Strayer considered it of "critical importance to know whether the impugned legislation *prima facie* conflicts with s-s.15(1)." He argued that with respect to the enumerated grounds of discrimination any distinction constituted a *prima facie* violation that had to be defended under section 1. He conceded that with respect to such grounds as age, distinctions "may be more readily justified under s.1," but he insisted that "the onus must be on the defender of such a distinction even then." On the other hand, with respect to distinctions based on unenumerated grounds "no such presumption arises of discrimination and…it is necessary to analyse such distinctions more closely to determine whether they can be regarded as in conflict with s-s.15(1)."[24] Strayer's twofold test for determining this question amounts to minimal scrutiny: "the ends must be among those broadly legitimate for a government, and the means must be rationally related to the achievement of those ends." With respect to ends the proper test may be "no higher than that the essential purpose of the legislation must not be to disadvantage any particular person or group of persons, even if it may have that consequence." Further, "the choice among various possible means is and should remain a political choice: all the court should do is to see whether the means chosen are patently unsuited or inappropriate for the purpose, and if not then the choice of the Legislature should be respected."[25]

The preferred position of the enumerated grounds has seemed problematic even to some of its supporters. For example, although Mary Eberts supports the general claim that enumerated grounds should enjoy higher scrutiny than unnamed grounds, she contends that this cannot be an "iron-clad" rule, especially when a challenged law or policy involves not only discrimination but also the infringement of other constitutional rights. She provides the example of a denial of the right to vote on the basis of region of residence. This is both discrimination on the basis of an unlisted ground (region of residence) and the denial of the section 3 right to vote.[26] Still, if the level of scrutiny is raised in such a case, it is because another right is involved, not because the unlisted ground of discrimination has suddenly acquired a more privileged position. In any case, whatever difficulties may beset the claim that enumerated grounds of discrimination enjoy a privileged position, it appears to be necessary to save the prohibition of systemic discrimination from the charge of redundancy. If enumerated grounds are indeed entitled to stricter scrutiny simply by virtue of their enumeration, then by attacking a classification as systemic discrimination against one of the enumerated groups, rather than attacking it directly as discrimination based on an unenumerated ground, one might be able to bring it within the stricter scrutiny enjoyed by the former.

Such an extension of strict scrutiny to systemic discrimination against an enumerated group is problematic. If one is to subject systemic barriers to the same level of scrutiny accorded to intentional discrimination, then the number of laws and programs open to strict scrutiny challenges will expand without obvious limit. This is especially true if religion is included among the grounds entitled to strict scrutiny—and most commentators agree that it is. There are many secondary differences associated with race and sex that can cause the disparate impact of otherwise neutral policies on these groups, but religious differences are endless, so that almost any policy will disproportionately burden some religious group. Similarly, there are countless differences among groups of differing national and ethnic origin[27]—another enumerated ground usually included in the suspect category. Again, these will inevitably lead to the unequal effect of policies that are ethnically neutral on their face.

Expanding the range of policies open to strict-scrutiny challenges makes them by definition difficult to withstand. As indicated above, what is "strict in theory" is often "fatal in fact." This appears to have been why the American Supreme Court refused to extend the prohibition of the equal protection clause to systemic discrimination. Noting that many policies imposed disproportionate burdens on the poor, and that blacks were disproportionately poor, the Court worried that all such laws might be invalidated if the Fourteenth Amendment was interpreted to prohibit systemic discrimination:

> A rule that a statute designed to serve neutral ends is nevertheless invalid, absent compelling justification, if in practice it benefits or burdens one race more than another would be far-reaching and would raise serious questions about, and perhaps invalidate, a whole range of tax, welfare, public service, regulatory, and licensing statutes that may be more burdensome to the poor and to the average black than to the more affluent white.[28]

Some Canadian authors seek to avoid this conclusion, and thus to buttress an argument for the inclusion of systemic discrimination in section 15, by denying that unintentional discrimination should be as strictly scrutinized as intentional discrimination.[29] However, this cannot mean that systemic barriers ought to be subject to the minimal scrutiny they would receive if they were challenged as intentional discrimination on the basis of an unlisted ground. If that were true we would be faced once again with the redundancy of a prohibition of systemic discrimination. Rather, the contention is that systemic barriers should be scrutinized more strictly than intentional discrimination on the basis of unnamed grounds but not as strictly as intentional discrimination against the disproportionately burdened enumerated group—in brief, that systemic barriers should be subject to "intermediate scrutiny."

In recent years the American Supreme Court has sporadically decided cases on the basis of an analysis that falls somewhere between strict and minimal scrutiny. It has used this approach especially in sex discrimination cases. There has even been some suggestion that this three-tiered approach is too rigid and that the Court ought to adopt a "sliding-scale" or nuanced "spectrum" of levels of scrutiny. This sliding-scale approach has found support in Canada as the appropriate interpretation of section 15 of the *Charter*.[30] In fact, given the nature of some of the prohibited grounds of discrimination in section 15, it is difficult to sustain the claim that enumerated grounds are entitled to stricter scrutiny than unlisted grounds without implying intermediate scrutiny. As noted previously, classifications based on age or mental and physical handicap are not likely to be as strictly scrutinized as are classifications based on race. If they are nevertheless to occupy a more privileged position than unlisted grounds, it must be because they occupy an intermediate position on the scale of levels of scrutiny, below such enumerated grounds as race and above the unnamed grounds.

The adoption of intermediate levels of scrutiny saves the prohibition of systemic discrimination from the twin charges of redundancy or overkill. It is not redundant because association with an enumerated ground, as opposed to a charge of direct discrimination based on an unlisted ground, can raise the level of scrutiny.[31] On the other hand, that higher level of scrutiny need not be as strict as it would be if the classification were based directly on the enumerated ground, thus moderating the fear of wholesale invalidation of laws expressed by the American Court. In effect, discrimination based on an unlisted ground, and thus normally subject to a low level of scrutiny, could be raised on the scale of scrutiny because of its disproportionate impact on an enumerated ground without being promoted to the same level of scrutiny enjoyed by that ground in its own right. Raj Anand summarizes the case for the application of intermediate scrutiny to systemic barriers:

> The fear of invalidating virtually every piece of "social purpose" legislation because of its differential effects on ethnic minorities can be accommodated by applying a less exacting standard in the case of statutes which are facially neutral. A test which approximates an intermediate level of judicial review in the U.S. ("substantial relation to important governmental objectives") would still require the proponent of a classification which adversely affects a particular ethnic group to justify the criterion on non-discriminatory grounds. Yet it would avoid the spectre, for example, of striking down every provision of the *Income Tax Act* whose result is to grant exemptions disproportionately to different ethnic groups because of their disparate income levels and sources of income.[32]

On the other hand, Anand is not willing to accord the same

degree of deference to administrative action as he is to formal legislation. Systemic barriers that arise from administrative discretion, he contends, should be subject to the same, higher level of scrutiny that would be applied to intentional discrimination against the enumerated group.[33]

In sum, the apparently redundant extension of open-ended anti-discrimination provisions to cover systemic discrimination is best understood as a way of increasing the level of scrutiny (and hence the prospects of a successful challenge) for policies that would be subject to minimal scrutiny if challenged as direct discrimination based on an unlisted ground. Often, the level of scrutiny will be increased not all the way to strict scrutiny but to some intermediate level on the "sliding scale."

Systemic Barriers and Equal Results

A Hierarchy of Groups. Although the prohibition of systemic discrimination may be valued as a tactical device in the pursuit of individual treatment—not as something that is sought for its own sake but as a way of reaching more intentional but unjustified categorization or of improving the prospects of defeating such categorization—it remains fundamentally in tension with the individual-treatment model.

This is particularly evident when the systemic approach is used to promote unlisted grounds on the scale of scrutiny in the context of an open-ended anti-discrimination provision. The assumption on which this strategy is based—that enumerated grounds are more important and thus entitled to stricter scrutiny—is difficult to reconcile with the individual-treatment model. That model views discrimination as the unjust effect of categorization as such upon the individual exception, regardless of the group characteristic used to define the category. From this point of view it makes little difference whether the categorization reflects bigotry or not, or even whether or not it is a statistically accurate predictor. It is worth repeating Dale Gibson's claim that discrimination is abhorrent

> whether the stereotype is statistically false or accurate. The unfairness is obvious in the case of inaccurate generalizations...But even stereotypes based on statistically valid generalizations...may be fallacious when applied to any individual member of the groups iden-

> tified...Statistically sound stereotypes are the more dangerous ones
> in fact, because they are more likely to be given wide credence, and
> to be acted upon when decisions are being made.[34]

This reasoning logically implies that all grounds of discrimination should be equally suspect.

Such a conclusion was reached in *Oram and McLaren v. Pho*, a B.C. reasonable cause case. The complainants were refused service in a restaurant because of their long, unkempt hair and apparent dirtiness. They had in fact taken baths just prior to going to the restaurant and service was thus refused because of perceived, rather than actual dirtiness. The tribunal found the discrimination to be unreasonable, thereby adding physical appearance to the list of prohibited grounds. It did so because although the listed grounds contain the "most notorious examples" of grounds of discrimination—for example, race, and religion—"these more common forms of prejudice...by no means exhaust the types of prejudicial conduct directed by the many against the few." There is a plethora of other grounds on which discriminatory conduct is based. The tribunal continued:

> Often these forms of discrimination are as far reaching and devastating in their consequences as those forms more widely publicized. In a sense they are more insidious because they are often more difficult to detect and the victims are less organized and more passive than those whose minority causes have attracted wide attention and support. [I]t is clear [from the wording of section 3(2)] that the very heart and purpose of that section is to protect those persons who for one reason or another find themselves possessed of some differentiating characteristic which attracts to them prejudicial discriminatory conduct.[35]

Oram represents the exception in the interpretation of "reasonable cause"—most tribunals have taken the differential scrutiny approach suggested by Justice Dickson in his Supreme Court opinion in *Gay Alliance* v. *Vancouver Sun*. This case involved the claim that discrimination on the basis of sexual orientation, which was not explicitly listed as a prohibited ground of discrimination, was nevertheless discrimination without "reasonable cause." In considering the relationship between the listed and unlisted prohibited grounds of discrimination, Dickson thought that classifications based on the listed grounds were "automatically deemed 'unreasonable'," whereas "once one moves beyond [these explicitly] proscribed forms of discrimination...the test of 'reasonable cause' indicates a more restrained standard of review and a means of balancing the competing interests involved."[36]

Although Dickson's comments in *Gay Alliance* represent the dominant approach, *Oram* is a more faithful expression of the individual-treatment model of anti-discrimination policy. Taken seriously, that model not only requires an open-ended list of prohibited grounds but is hostile to a hierarchy of grounds in which some are entitled to higher scrutiny than others. The use of the systemic approach to promote unlisted grounds on a scale of scrutiny must thus be understood as something more than a tactic for the better achievement of individual treatment. Implying that some groups occupy a privileged position as regards protection against discrimination, it subordinates the logic of individual treatment (which challenges unreasonable categorization as such) to the special protection of these privileged groups. The degree of challenge to objectively unreasonable categorizations varies with their effect on the preferred groups. A categorization based directly on the major, group-defining trait will attract the most stringent kind of challenge. If the categorization excludes not the preferred group as such but another group that overlaps substantially with the preferred group, the challenge will perhaps be less intense but still significant. Unreasonable discrimination against a group that does not overlap a preferred group will attract only a token challenge, however much it violates the norms of individual treatment. The prohibition of systemic discrimination is thus best understood as a way of promoting equality of result for specified target groups, not as an indirect way of pursuing individual treatment.

Trait Distribution vs. *Bottom Lines.* Under the systemic approach a challenge to discrimination against a secondary group is conditional upon disadvantage to a preferred minority. There is some debate, however, about what kind of disadvantage must be suffered by the minority to trigger a systemic challenge. Does disadvantage exist merely because of a substantial overlap between the two groups, or must one show actual underrepresentation of the minority at the end of a selection process? For example, does a height requirement disadvantage women merely because fewer of them can meet it, or only if women are actually hired in disproportionately low numbers. The one does not necessarily imply the other, for it might be possible to hire enough tall women to achieve an overall sexual balance in the workforce. The first view may be called the "trait-distribution" approach to systemic discrimination because it would sustain a *prima facie* case simply on the basis of an uneven distribution of secondary traits between a target group and the majority; the second is appropriately known as the "bottom-line" approach.

Not all systemic barriers lead to the underrepresentation of groups who are disproportionately burdened by them. If the *qualified* members of such a group apply in disproportionately large numbers, and if no direct discrimination is practiced by the employer, underrepresentation may not occur. Similarly, a voluntary affirmative action program by an employer may achieve statistical balance in the workforce despite the presence of a systemic barrier. Such a program was at issue in the American case *Connecticut v. Teal*.[37] As part of its promotion procedures, a Connecticut state agency had required candidates to pass a written test before they were considered for permanent supervisory positions. This test disproportionately excluded black employees; on the other hand, of those who had passed the test, the agency promoted almost twenty-three percent of the blacks as opposed to about fourteen percent of the whites. In the event, blacks were not underrepresented in supervisory positions.

If systemic barriers are prohibited because they cause group underrepresentation, it follows that they should escape the prohibition when underrepresentation does not occur. As Peter Robertson puts it: "If discrimination exists when there is unjustified...adverse impact then you can avoid a discrimination finding by eliminating impact..."[38] In the United States this is known as the "bottom-line" defence. Under this defence "an employer who eliminates the adverse impact of his practices will not be questioned about the details of his systems or—in the case of tests—be required to validate them."[39]

This bottom-line approach rests on the premise that the mischief at which anti-discrimination legislation is directed is not the discriminatory policy or act in itself but the unequal results it generates. Indeed, we recall that for Robertson this is precisely why the definition of legally prohibited discrimination had to be expanded to include not only direct discrimination but also systemic barriers. It is worth repeating his remarks in this regard:

> ...when we in the U.S. initially confronted the different unemployment rates, occupational distribution, and disparate income levels of minorities and women we attempted to change the situation by

> making it illegal to discriminate. When we discovered that eliminating discrimination (as it was then defined) was having no impact on the problem we began to talk about affirmative action and to perceive that action as something above and beyond eliminating discrimination. [However] that failure to change the underlying facts which had confronted Congress was not a failure of the anti-discrimination legislation but was, instead, a failure to understand the real nature of discrimination. It was only when we began to perceive discrimination in a totally different fashion that we began to have a real impact on the problem…on the facts.[40]

In other words, the concept of discrimination has no independent content and integrity but is defined as whatever causes the unequal results that constitute the real problem. The bottom-line defence implies this reasoning: by protecting systemic barriers that do not cause underrepresentation, it suggests that legally prohibited discrimination does not exist unless it produces such underrepresentation.

The nature of the tension between the systemic and individual-treatment models varies depending on whether the former is given a bottom-line or trait-distribution interpretation. The tension is most pronounced when the bottom-line defence saves barriers that may nevertheless be unnecessary and hence discriminatory categorization from the individual-treatment point of view. The conflict is less obvious if systemic challenges may be sustained simply on the basis of statistical overlap between primary and secondary groups without showing that the primary group is actually underrepresented. In this case the question whether to sustain the barrier or to strike it down would turn not on group representation but on the objective necessity of the requirement. Just as bottom-line analysis reflects the importance of group representation, so "necessity" analysis emphasizes the principle of fairness to individuals. Part of what is objectionable about barriers that cannot be defended as business necessities is that they give unfair advantage to those who can meet the requirements. In effect they violate a central principle of fairness: that like cases be treated alike. Because the requirement is not really necessary it causes the unequal treatment of *individuals*, regardless of their group affiliation, who are similarly situated with respect to objective ability to do the job.

A prohibition of systemic discrimination that emphasized unfairness to individuals would have to reject a bottom-line defence, which saves unfair rules that do not produce under-representation. As Schwartz and Sklover point out, one problem

> with the "bottom line" approach is that its application allows an employer to hire minorities and women from preferred subclasses. For example, an employer may have a high school requirement for the position of window washer or a college requirement for a typist's job. [Under the bottom-line approach] the employer could have immunized and preserved these arbitrary and irrational standards by having met a "bottom line" comprised of overqualified minorities and women.[41]

On the basis of such arguments the American Supreme Court struck down the bottom-line defence in *Teal*. Said Justice Brennan, writing for the majority,

> Title VII strives to achieve equality of opportunity by rooting out "artificial, arbitrary and unnecessary" employer-created barriers to professional development that have a discriminatory impact upon individuals.[42]

The *Teal* approach necessarily de-emphasizes group affiliation. If the entire package of recruitment procedures in *Teal*, including the voluntary affirmative action program, was unjust to blacks, it was not unjust to blacks as a group but to less qualified blacks as individuals. If a *group* of blacks was being discriminated against, it was not blacks *per se* but the sub-class of "unqualified" blacks. The emphasis thus shifted from group identity to qualification. The "group" that was being discriminated against was really the group of "unqualified" individuals, whatever their other characteristics.

Abandoning the bottom-line defence implies that the emphasis of anti-discrimination policy, insofar as it reaches systemic discrimination, is not to guarantee proportional representation of all groups in the work force but to rationalize personnel selection and management processes.

Teal arose because the *Civil Rights Act* was unclear on this point. Ontario's section 10 is less ambiguous. It speaks of requirements "that *would* result in the exclusion, qualification or preference of a group of persons...," and as Judith Keene remarks, the effect of the word "would" is that "...the complainant may successfully challenge the requirement, etc., under section 10 without proving that an exclusion, qualification or preference has occurred."[43] In other words, the bottom-line defence is not available. It follows that the section emphasizes fairness to individuals rather than group representation.

This trait-distribution interpretation of the systemic approach incorporates but does not fulfill the logic of individual treatment. An anti-discrimination provision that emphasizes unfairness to individuals should, logically, extend to all barriers that are unfair in this way. However, prohibitions of systemic discrimination seriously attack unfair barriers only when the unfairness is unevenly distributed—only, that is, when a disproportionate number of the members of a primary group are also found in the group directly subject to the unfair discrimination. Thus Ontario's section 10, like most legislation of this sort, prohibits only unfair classifications whose victims are members of groups identified by a closed list of prohibited grounds. Moreover, it applies only if it is not just the individual but the "group" that "would" be excluded, qualified or preferred by the requirement. As we have seen, a systemic interpretation of open-ended anti-discrimination provisions also implies a similar set of primary groups, which must be particularly burdened by a requirement in order to sustain a serious challenge.

In fact, if fairness to individuals is the object, so-called systemic barriers ought to be attacked not indirectly because of their effect on enumerated groups but directly as intentional discrimination against unlisted groups. As indicated earlier, the logical way to do this is through an open-ended list of prohibited grounds, such as British Columbia's "reasonable cause" formulation or section 15 of the Charter.

Accommodation or Conformity? The group representation approach to systemic discrimination subordinates fairness to representation. When it defends barriers that do not cause the under-representation of a primary group, it implicitly favours those members of a primary group who can live up to prevailing standards and expectations, even if they are a minority of the group. To this extent it promotes conformity. It encourages the selection of "assimilated" group members, who thus become "role models" for other members of the group who, if they wish to succeed, must also conform. The trait-distribution interpretation of the systemic approach, on the other hand, would strike down systemic barriers even when underrepresentation does not result; it thus emphasizes accommodating the existing system to characteristics possessed by a majority of the group. It makes success possible for those who do not conform, thus undermining conformist pressures. Of course this difference in orientation between the two approaches becomes a practical difference only when a systemic barrier is not associated with actual underrepresentation of the primary group and is thus saved by the bottom-line defence. When underrepresentation does occur both approaches lead to the same accommodationist policy outcome.

To illustrate the conformist and accommodationist tendencies of the two approaches, consider the example of an employment policy that excludes all those over the age of thirty from applying for certain positions.[44] Such a policy disproportionately affects women because the period of eligibility coincides with the prime childbearing years. Because women not only bear children but tend to take the dominant responsibility for rearing them, more women than men will be unavailable for full-time work under the age of thirty. If the rule could be struck down on the basis of these facts alone—assuming it is not a "business necessity"—new opportunities would become available to traditional women who assume the primary role in childrearing. Abolition of the rule accommodates existing sex-role differentiation within the traditional family and in itself does nothing to overcome this differentiation. Indeed, it may perpetuate or strengthen existing sex roles, although, being sex-neutral in form, it could also accommodate the androgynous personhood aspired to by many feminists.

By contrast, if actual underrepresentation of women among successful applicants had to be shown in order to sustain a systemic challenge, the under-thirty rule might be saved in spite of the barrier it poses to the majority of women. An employer who felt strongly about keeping such a rule could institute an affirmative action program designed to recruit enough women to satisfy bottom-line requirements. Because the rule disproportionately burdens women in traditional families, the employer will end up recruiting chiefly single women or those who have entered non-traditional family arrangements. Indeed, he may prefer women in the latter category because single women may enter traditional marriages and leave full-time employment sooner. By rewarding non-traditional women, such a program contributes an incentive structure and provides role models for sex-role reform. It thus contributes to conformity.

Systemic Discrimination and Guardian Democracy

Overcoming systemic discrimination entails the growth of guardian democracy. Like individual treatment, the concept of systemic discrimination increases the power of agencies of secondary review. It emphasizes unintended consequences, which frequently do not come to light until the direct preoccupations of the primary decision-maker are set aside and the policy is re-examined in light of its impact on designated target groups. Again, this implies a second look by a reviewing agency that can bring such unintended consequences to centre stage in a way that primary decision-makers are unlikely to do.

Prohibitions of systemic discrimination also promote guardian democracy by subjecting to "intermediate scrutiny" grounds of discrimination that would otherwise not be covered at all (in a closed list of prohibited grounds) or that would be subject to minimal scrutiny (in an open-ended list). Intermediate scrutiny is a recipe for judicial or quasi-judicial second-guessing of primary decision-makers. The extremes of strict and minimal scrutiny both reduce the discretion of supervisory agencies. Being "fatal in fact," strict scrutiny is largely self-applying. Discrimination on the basis of a ground deserving this level of scrutiny is subject to an almost complete prohibition, with few and narrowly defined exceptions, leaving little scope for subordinate policy making at the point of judicial enforcement. Strict scrutiny reflects the view that discrimination on the relevant grounds is almost always unreasonable and thus worthy of relatively unqualified prohibition. Minimal scrutiny, on the other hand, assumes that discrimination based on certain grounds will often be reasonable and leaves it to the primary decision-maker to judge. Intermediate scrutiny is neither fish nor fowl; it establishes a kind of permissive prohibition under which discrimination is permitted if a reviewing agency can be satisfied that it is "objectively reasonable."

Generalized exemptions in anti-discrimination law are the vehicle through which intermediate scrutiny is applied. As regards employment, for example, human rights legislation conjoins the prohibition of discrimination with a broadly worded exemption permitting the discrimination if it is a *bona fide* occupational qualification. *"Bona fide"* requires not only that the qualification be adopted in "good faith" but that it be objectively necessary to the safe and efficient operation of the business. The employer's good faith judgment on the latter question is allowed to stand only if it meets standards of objective proof acceptable to the guardian agencies.

There have always been exemptions in anti-discrimination legislation, of course. When this legislation prohibited only intentional discrimination on stigmatic grounds, it exempted special interest organizations, such as religious bodies, who were allowed to limit hiring to co-religionists. Typically the legislation also exempted situations entailing close personal contact between employer and employee or landlord and tenant, such as domestic labour or rental of accommodation in a "small" residence occupied by the landlord. Although such exemptions were open to interpretation, they were comparatively narrow and well-defined and were thus compatible with a more general orientation to strict scrutiny. As life-cycle and life-style traits were added to the list of prohibited grounds, the number and kinds of "reasonable" exemptions seemed much wider and thus more difficult to enumerate and specify in advance. The result was the generalized BFOQ exemption, which permits "reasonable" discrimination but leaves reasonableness largely undefined, to be determined on a case-by-case basis by reviewing agencies.[45] At the constitutional level the same kind of intermediate scrutiny is achieved by section 1 of the *Charter*, which permits such limits on the section 15 equality rights as the judiciary determines are "reasonable" and "demonstrably justified in a free and democratic society." In both cases the deck is stacked against the discretion of the primary decision-maker and in favour of judicial second guessing because the exemption is formulated as a limit on a *right*. Since rights generally trump countervailing considerations, they may be limited in turn only when it is "objectively necessary" or "demonstrably justified." A balance of mere convenience will not suffice because convenience must not be allowed to undermine rights. Furthermore, if the balance of convenience were the appropriate standard, the primary decision-maker would probably be considered the best judge (as long as he acted in "good faith") and minimal scrutiny would result.

Guardian Democracy and Constitutional Equality Rights

In Canada human rights codes now prohibit systemic discrimination and thus transfer power from private to public authorities. A systemic interpretation of section 15 would further promote guardian democracy by shifting power within the public sector from legislatures to courts. If we wish to avoid this, we should follow the lead of the United States Supreme Court, which has drawn a clear line between the *Civil Rights Act* and the Fourteenth Amendment to the Constitution: the former covers systemic barriers; the latter does not.

If the effects-oriented interpretation of section 15 prevails, the number of laws and programs open to successful constitutional challenge will be dramatically expanded. The emphasis here is on the word "successful," for all laws classify and all classifications are in principle open to a section 15 challenge. Nevertheless, there are many challenges—to progressive income taxes, for example— that most people, including those opposed to the law or program on policy grounds, would consider frivolous, and that would not be seriously entertained by the courts. As we have seen, an effects-oriented interpretation of section 15 must be understood as a way of improving the prospects of certain challenges that would otherwise fall into the frivolous category. If this were not so, the open-ended character of section 15 would make an effects-oriented interpretation redundant.

That systemic discrimination would only be promoted from minimal to intermediate scrutiny is a recognition of the fact that most systemic barriers will be inherently less objectionable among reasonable people than direct discrimination against the enumerated group. This also means that although the prospects of a successful challenge are improved, they are not ensured; intermediate scrutiny is hardly likely to be "fatal in fact." Prohibiting systemic discrimination under section 15, then, will dramatically enlarge the area of inherently contestable policy making subject to judicial second-guessing. To appreciate the significance of this consequence, we must turn to some more general reflections on the judicial enforcement of constitutional rights in general and "equality rights" in particular.

Any constitutional prohibition of discriminatory legislation must confront the reality that all legislation classifies and treats groups differently. The question is how to draw the line between constitutionally permissible and impermissible classifications. Ultimately this is a matter of distinguishing between reasonable and unreasonable classifications. As we have seen, this judgment is likely to be made when the courts turn to the question of whether a *prima facie* violation of section 15 can be justified under section 1.[46] However, judgments of "reasonableness" under section 1 are not inherently legal or judicial in nature. They are not questions that can be disposed of through the application of pre-existing legal standards or principles but are themselves standard-setting or policy questions. Typically such determinations involve the consideration of the kind of "social fact" evidence traditionally excluded from the courtroom but quite familiar to legislators. In its early *Charter* opinions the Supreme Court has several times voiced its concern about the paucity of evidence relevant to a section 1 determination presented to them by counsel. Recognizing that Canadian lawyers were unfamiliar with the preparation of sophisticated "Brandeis briefs," the Court emphasized that section 1 would require frequent departures from more traditional modes of legal analysis.[47]

Some judgments of reasonableness may become so universal that they acquire the aura of legal principles beyond the limits of legitimate partisanship,[48] but most judgments of this sort are simply too contestable to appear in this light. As Peter Russell has argued, there is a difference between the core of certain rights, about which reasonable liberal democrats agree, and the more debatable, secondary questions concerning the outer limits and boundaries of these rights, about which reasonable liberal democrats can and do disagree.[49] Few in contemporary liberal democracies, for example, argue for the establishment of a particular religion and the criminal prohibition of all others. Nor is there a serious argument for the abolition of free speech as such. On the other hand, there are reasonable disagreements about whether freedom of religion requires exemptions from otherwise valid laws on the basis of religious conscience, or whether freedom of expression ought to be interpreted so broadly as to protect not only political speech but also obscene entertainments.

The Supreme Court recognized the difference between these two kinds of questions in one of its early *Charter* cases. The question was whether all violations of the *Charter* could avail themselves of the section 1 defence. In the case at hand Quebec tried to use section 1 to defend its policy of providing a right to English-language education in the province only to those children whose parents were educated in English *in Quebec*. The Court refused even to consider Quebec's section 1 arguments because the very purpose of section 23 of the *Charter* was to overrule precisely this education policy:

> If, as is apparent, Chapter VIII of Bill 101 is the prototype of the regime which the framers of the Constitution wished to remedy by adopting s.23 of the *Charter*, the limitations which this regime imposes on rights involving the language of instruction, so far as they are inconsistent with s.23 of the *Charter*, cannot possibly have been regarded by the framers of the Constitution as coming within "such reasonable limits prescribed by law as can be demonstrably justified in a free and democratic society."[50]

Now the language rights entrenched in section 23 are hardly the fundamental or core rights of a liberal democracy, about which all reasonable liberal democrats agree. As the Court itself recognized, section 23, unlike much of the rest of the *Charter*, "is not a codification of essential, pre-existing and more or less universal rights" but is "a unique set of constitutional provisions, quite peculiar to Canada."[51] Moreover, it is partly because it is a peculiarly Canadian right, referable to specific Canadian controversies, that one can know without question that certain violations of it are so direct and obvious as to be beyond the scope of a section 1 defence. Nevertheless, the Court thought that certain violations of the more general or universal rights could be similarly direct and dramatic, so much so that they too would be indefensible under section 1: "An Act of Parliament or a legislature which, for example, purported to impose the beliefs of a state religion would be in direct conflict with s.2(a) of the *Charter*, which guarantees the freedom of conscience and religion, and would have to be ruled of no force or effect without even considering whether such legislation could be legitimized by s.1."[52] As in the case of Bill 101, such an establishment of religion would be so obvious a violation of the *Charter* that it would be absurd even to consider a section 1 defence. In this case, however, the absurdity arises not from intimate knowledge of recent Canadian history but from the universal agreement among liberal democrats that the establishment of a particular religion clearly violates one of the rights section 2 is intended to protect. In other words, the section 1 "reasonable limit" defence applies only in situations where reasonable liberal democrats can differ. Where that is not the case, as in the establishment of a religion (or a similar violation of the core of any fundamental right), the possibility of a section 1 defence cannot even be entertained.

The core questions must be settled in order for the more peripheral, boundary-setting questions even to arise. Where there is a serious dispute about the inherent value of religious freedom or free speech, questions about whether certain religions should be exempt from hunting[53] or drug laws,[54] or whether obscenity should be censored, will recede into the background. On the other hand, if the core questions do arise they can hardly be settled through judicial enforcement of an entrenched charter. In this sense the Supreme Court's insistence that a state religion would have to be rejected out of hand, without any recourse to section 1, is somewhat naïve. Did the Court really believe that if the liberal democratic consensus disintegrated to the extent that establishment became a viable political possibility, an institution possessed of neither sword nor purse could stand against it? Such an issue would indicate a regime crisis that could not be contained by judicial process, or by the "parchment barriers" on which that process depends.[55]

The questions most likely to be settled by judges under a constitutional charter are the secondary, intra-regime questions about which reasonable liberal democrats can differ. Yet precisely because reasonable differences are possible about such questions, judicial decisions about them are less likely to appear as principled legal decisions than as policy determinations in which judges substitute their view of reasonableness for that of the legislature. The entrenchment of a charter of rights is thus really a way of subjecting inherently contestable policy questions to constitutional adjudication.[56] Furthermore, giving such questions a constitutional dimension does not mean settling them by transmuting one of the answers into a legal standard available for judicial enforcement. The only legal standard embodied in such vague phrases as freedom of expression or freedom of religion is the incontestable core meaning of the right, which does not need to be legalized. Giving a constitutional dimension to contestable policy questions means transferring authority to decide them from a democratic institution that is supposed to make policy to an undemocratic one whose policy-making credentials are controversial.

It is too late in the day to continue debating the question whether this transfer of policy-making power is desirable. The real question for us now, as it has been for the Americans for some time, is one of degree: how much of our political life should be judicialized in this way? In addressing this question it needs to be understood that the promotion of unlisted grounds of discrimination under section 15 from minimal to at least intermediate scrutiny vastly expands the scope of judicial oversight of policy making in inherently contestable areas.

The virtue of a simple division between classifications subject to strict and minimal scrutiny is that it makes certain classifications virtually impossible to sustain while leaving judgments about the rest to the political branches. This is a relatively principled and hence legal approach precisely because it minimizes judicial discretion in the matter of judging reasonableness. The United States Supreme Court has been unable or unwilling to sustain this approach and it is probably impossible in Canada under section 15. As noted above, if enumerated grounds are entitled to stricter scrutiny than unenumerated grounds, and if some of the enumerated grounds are unlikely to be accorded the full measure of "strict scrutiny," some form of "intermediate scrutiny" seems inevitable. In other words, even if section 15 covers only intentional discrimination, there will be an intermediate area in which judges will neither enforce clear prohibitions nor defer to legislative judgment, but will second-guess political judgments of reasonableness. The expansion of the area of intermediate scrutiny necessarily entails the expansion of this kind of judicial second-guessing,[57] and such expansion is the primary effect of the prohibition of systemic discrimination. The problematic nature of this institutional transfer of power can be better appreciated by looking more closely at the kinds of policies that might be subjected to intermediate scrutiny if systemic discrimination were included in section 15.

Proponents of interpreting section 15 so as to prohibit systemic discrimination seem to assume that systemic analysis inevitably serves "progressive" or "liberal" policy interests. This is by no means self-evident. Just as women are on average shorter and lighter than men—and are thus disproportionately disadvantaged by height and weight requirements—so some racial and ethnic groups are on average much younger than others[58]—and are thus disproportionately disadvantaged by laws whose costs are borne mainly by the young. Minimum wage laws may well fall into that category. Some economists argue that minimum wage laws, except when they are temporarily "repealed" by inflation, contribute to youth unemployment by pricing inexperienced and "underqualified" labour out of the market.[59] Under a prohibition of systemic discrimination this argument could be used to attack such laws either as discrimination against the young or as systemic discrimination against those racial or ethnic groups that are disproportionately young. Presumably the latter would be the better choice because systemic barriers will generally be accorded a level of scrutiny below intentional discrimination against the enumerated group. Since age is likely to be lower on the scale of scrutiny than race or ethnicity, systemic barriers against groups defined by the latter characteristics will enjoy a higher level of scrutiny than systemic barriers against age-based groups. Minimum wage laws may also constitute systemic barriers against any protected groups whose membership is disproportionately characterized by low levels of skill or education. This "systemic" effect is especially likely to burden recent arrivals from some Third World countries. Again, this would implicate an enumerated ground ("national or ethnic origin") that is usually thought to be entitled to strict scrutiny, and thus would substantially elevate the level of scrutiny applicable to the law.

Similarly, it is arguable that rent control policies lead to a declining level of building maintenance. If true, this will disproportionately affect older buildings, which require more maintenance and deteriorate faster without it. Older areas might thus degenerate into slums more quickly.[60] Since such older buildings are occupied by those in particular income categories (usually lower), and since particular racial, ethnic, and religious groups are clustered at different points on the income scale, rent control might be considered to be systemic discrimination against the protected groups most affected.

As these examples show, systemic analysis is perfectly congenial to both ends of the ideological spectrum. It is thus especially revealing that those who wish to bring systemic discrimination within the scope of anti-discrimination legislation or constitutional equality provisions never imagine that such things as minimum wage laws might thereby be open to human rights challenge. In fact, of course, in the United States such laws have been subject to successful constitutional challenges in the past under the interstate commerce clause of the Constitution and the due process clause of the Fourteenth Amendment. An interpretation of constitutional equality provisions to include systemic discrimination would open the legislation to renewed constitutional challenge by non-"liberal" or non-"progressive" interests.

One can be certain that if minimum wage laws were successfully attacked as systemic discrimination under a constitutional equality clause, progressive critics would decry this as a return to the bad old days of "economic substantive due process"—and they would be right! According to its liberal critics, "substantive due process" involved the courts in the non-judicial, hence illegitimate function of second-guessing legislatures about the substantive reasonableness of economic policies. When the Supreme Court struck down New York legislation that imposed maximum hours for work in bakeries, it explicitly said that a state could balance costs in health against the benefits of economic liberty and that the former might sometimes outweigh the latter, but it then refused to let New York's balancing stand.[61] Instead, the Court considered the "social fact" evidence concerning the health dangers of prolonged hours in bakeries and concluded that it did not establish a danger sufficient to outweigh economic liberty. Re-doing what the legislature had already done, on the basis of evidentiary considerations much more congenial to legislators than to judges, the Court simply came to a different conclusion. It was never able to explain to the satisfaction of the liberals why, if the Constitution permitted legislatures to balance health against economic liberty, such legislative balances should be superseded by judicial ones. On this institutional question the liberals were clearly right, and in the face of mounting public outrage the Court ultimately backed down.

It is important to untangle the substantive and institutional questions involved in this controversy. The substantive due process decisions of the United States Supreme Court were clearly motivated by conservative policy orientations and liberals criticized the decisions because they opposed the policy embedded in them. The liberal criticism was also institutional, however. Liberals criticized the Court not only because it had made the wrong decisions, but also because it had presumed to make any decision at all on questions that were legislative in nature. For many liberals this institutional criticism was obviously opportunistic, as shown by the fact that they have no similar reservations about substantive due process when the Court uses it to pursue a liberal policy agenda in defiance of more conservative legislatures. When the due process clause was used to protect economic privacy, liberals cried foul; now that procedural due process has once again been abandoned, this time in the name of a penumbral right of social privacy,[62] liberals seem to have forgotten their former institutional reservations. Conservatives who made no institutional criticism of the economic substantive due process decisions, but who now level such a criticism against the new social substantive due process decisions, may be accused of a similar opportunism. Nevertheless, the institutional criticism of substantive due process is, in principle at least, quite independent of partisan affiliation. The question of the correct policy is conceptually distinct from the question of who should have the determining say in choosing the "correct" policy.

In fact, it is unlikely that conservative challenges to liberal economic policies will be seriously entertained by the courts under a prohibition of systemic discrimination. The lessons of the "economic substantive due process" debacle have been too well learned for that. But far from shielding a prohibition of systemic discrimination from criticism, this would only reveal even more clearly that such a prohibition is not a legal principle appropriate for judicial application but a partisan instrument of policy change. Only if systemic challenges of every partisan stripe are taken equally seriously could a prohibition of systemic discrimination escape this charge. If such a prohibition takes seriously only liberal challenges, it will entrench not incontestable human rights but modern liberal ideology. Even if it provides equal time (or "equal opportunity") to all partisan positions, it will still not entrench incontestable human rights; its true effect will be to subject to judicial determination much more of our public life than is generally acknowledged by supporters of the *Charter*.

In truth, it is not the substantive question of whether a systemic barrier should be permitted or not but the institutional question of who ought to make that determination that is crucial in the debate over section 15. In terms of substantive policy debate there is nothing wrong with systemic analysis. With respect to minimum wages, for example, it is perfectly legitimate to oppose them because one believes that despite their laudable intention they have unintended negative effects on the young and the unskilled. Similarly, there is nothing wrong with opposing an "affirmative action" policy on behalf of military veterans because it disproportionately excludes women.[63] Indeed, analysis that focuses only on the intention of the policy-maker is often impoverished and misleading.[64] But such systemic analysis is the investigation of "unintended consequences," a notoriously slippery and debatable realm. Reasonable people can and do differ in making such judgments, not only because the cause-and-effect relationship between the policy and the unintended consequence may be obscure, but also because there may be many unintended consequences, not all of which are equally bad. Moreover, the intended consequences of a policy may be achieved and these may be quite laudable. How to get accurate and reliable information about all of the relevant considerations, and how to weigh and balance these considerations after one has gathered the information (assuming its accuracy), are not easy questions. They are all the more problematic if the information-gathering and the weighing and balancing are done in court rather than in the legislature. Others have analysed at length the comparative advantages and disadvantages of courts and legislatures in the formulation of public policy.[65] For present purposes it is sufficient to point out that courts are institutionally less inclined to make non-categorical decisions that attempt to achieve an optimal balance of the competing values. Furthermore, they are in principle poorly equipped to make incremental adjustments on the basis of ongoing feedback.[66]

This does not mean that policy making by the more political institutions will always be better. In an executive-dominated parliamentary system such as Canada's, policy is often made with less-than-adequate public discussion and balancing of the affected interests. Nevertheless, the political policy-making process can be improved without undermining its political nature. Courts, on the other hand, can become better policy-makers only at the cost of becoming less judicial.[67] Such politicization of the courts is inevitable under the *Charter*, but the question is whether it should be carried farther than necessary. If good policy making is the goal, the wiser course is surely to reform the political policy-making process.[68]

Section 15 clearly protects us against intentional discrimination on the basis of explicitly enumerated grounds. Since the list of enumerated grounds includes those generally thought to require high levels of scrutiny, intentional discrimination on the basis of unenumerated grounds is likely to receive only minimal scrutiny, which is to say that it will usually pass constitutional muster. Thus section 15 is likely to offer less protection against discrimination based on unenumerated grounds. This is as it should be. Section 15 should *not* elevate unenumerated classifications on the scale of scrutiny by prohibiting unintentional discrimination against the enumerated groups.

The prohibition of intentional discrimination against enumerated groups already injects constitutional considerations into a wide range of debatable policy questions. We have laws, for example, that restrict "maternity benefits" to women, not only for the period of disability immediately surrounding the birth, but also for a subsequent period to ensure adequate post-natal care by a parent. Should the latter benefits become "parental" benefits? If so, should they be available only to one parent, thus depriving some women of a benefit they would otherwise have enjoyed, or should they be made simultaneously available to both parents, at considerable extra public expense?[69]

What of the approximately thirty federal statutes and regulations that establish fixed-age retirement policies for various categories of public employment?[70] Should all of these policies be invalidated, or are they "reasonable limits" under section 1? Are some reasonable and others not, and if so, how does one tell the difference?[71]

The *Pension Benefits Standards Act* presently permits sex-based mortality tables.[72] Does section 15 require these to be replaced by unisex mortality tables, or can the latter be considered discrimination against men, who, contributing equally, will collect less in total than their longer-lived wives?

At present the War Veterans Allowance Act and the *Civilian War Pensions and Allowance Act* discriminate in favour of women in the age at which benefits are made payable. Women are entitled to payments at age fifty-five while men must wait until age sixty.[73] Is this policy saved either by section 1 or by section 15(2), which permits affirmative action? If not, must the same age be applied to both men and women, or must age "be disregarded entirely, with eligibility based on service"?[74]

To what extent should women continue to be excluded from combat positions in the armed forces?[75] Are the medical standards used to screen prospective immigrants too stringent?[76] Must other Canadian jurisdictions follow Ontario's lead in giving the mentally disabled the same right to vote as all other Canadians?[77] May the *Unemployment Insurance Act* continue to require longer contribution periods before one is eligible to claim sickness benefits for periods of mental illness?[78] The examples could be multiplied. The point is that these are all policies that intentionally discriminate on the basis of one of the enumerated grounds. They are also questions about which reasonable liberal democrats often disagree. They are important and perplexing policy issues, which raise numerous questions of justice, fairness, efficiency, etc., but they are *not* questions concerning the core rights of a liberal democracy. Nevertheless, these questions have been judicialized by section 15 of the *Charter*.

Should we move even further in subjecting our public life to adjudication by interpreting section 15 to cover systemic discrimination? The issues raised would be no less contestable than those posed by direct discrimination against an enumerated group, and their social fact dimensions are likely to be even more complex and hence more likely to elude the judicial grasp. No doubt the policy questions posed by systemic barriers are important ones, but surely constitutionalism does not require us to give all important policy questions a constitutional dimension. Our political life is not well served by translating every important policy issue into the language of constitutional rights. That language often distorts even those policy issues that we can no longer avoid casting in its terms; we should beware of unnecessarily extending it. Justice McIntyre's remarks regarding the interpretation of the *Charter's* right to freedom of association are equally applicable here:

> It has been said that the courts, because of the *Charter*, will have to enter the legislative sphere. Where rights are specifically guaranteed in the *Charter*, this may on occasion be true. But where no specific right is found in the *Charter* and the only support for its constitutional guarantee is an implication, the courts should refrain from intrusion into the field of legislation. That is the function of the freely elected Legislatures and Parliament.[79]

Should section 15 be interpreted to extend to systemic discrimination, we will have special reason to be grateful for the section 33 legislative override.

Notes

[1] 401 U.S. 424 (1971).

[2] Donald L. Horowitz, *The Courts and Social Policy* (Washington: Brookings, 1977), 42.

[3] *Bhinder v. Canadian National Railways* (1981), 2 C.H.R.R. D/546 at D/599. See also *Morely Rand v. Sealy Eastern Ltd.* (1982), 3 C.H.R.R. D/938 at D/944; and *O'Malley v. Simpsons-Sears* (1986), 7 C.H.R.R. D/3102 at D/3106.

[4] William Black, "Intent or Effects: Section 15 of the Charter of Rights and Freedoms," in Joseph M. Weiler and Robin M. Elliot, eds., *Litigating the Values of a Nation: The Canadian Charter of Rights and Freedoms* (Toronto: Carswell, 1986), 140.

[5] Martha Chamallas, "Evolving Conception of Equality Under Title VII: Disparate Import Theory and the Demise of the Bottom Line Principle," 31 U.C.L.A. L. Rev., 340.

[6] *Ibid.*

[7] The reverse is also true: the addition of new grounds or the enactment of open-ended provisions can be understood not only as a way of protecting members of the newly covered groups from violations of individual treatment, but as a way of accommodating the secondary differences of political minorities.

[8] *Brooks v. Canada Safeway Ltd.* (1985), 6 C.H.R.R. D/2560, at 2564, quoting *Turley v. Allders Department Stores Ltd.*

[9] See Manitoba Human Rights Commission, *Annual Report* 1985, 13, 20-21.

[10] Quoted in Tarnopolsky, *Discrimination and the Law*, 265.

[11] See *ibid.*, 262-263. Where tribunals have conflated pregnancy with sex, they have done so on the basis of an implicit systemic analysis. It is argued that since the "effect" of discrimination on the basis of pregnancy burdens only women, it constitutes sex discrimination, even if not all women become pregnant. See *Affirmation* 5:2(June 1984), 1.

[12] *Foster v. British Columbia Forest Products Ltd.*, April 17, 1979, unreported, 29.

[13] Black, "Intent or Effects: Section 15 of the Charter of Rights and Freedoms," 122, 141-42.

[14] Archibald Cox, *The Role of the Supreme Court in American Government* (London: Oxford University Press, 1976), 59.

[15] *Ibid.*, 60

[16] G. Gunther, "Foreword: In Search of Evolving Doctrine on a Changing Court: A Model for a Newer Equal Protection," *Harvard Law Review* 86(1972), 8.

[17] *Attorney General of Canada v. Lavell and Bedard*, [1974] S.C.R. 1349 at 1386-87.

[18] Peter W. Hogg, *Constitutional Law of Canada*, 2nd ed. (Toronto: Carswell, 1985), 799.

[19] *Ibid.*

[20] Mary Eberts, "The Equality Provisions of the Canadian Charter of Rights and Freedoms and Government Institutions," in Claire Beckton and A. Wayne Mackay, eds., *The Courts and the Charter* (Toronto: University of Toronto Press, 1985), 160.

[21] *Ibid.*, 161.

[22] *Smith, Kline and French Laboratories v. A.-G. Canada* (1985), 24 D.L.R. (4th) 321 at 367.

[23] Hogg, *Constitutional Law of Canada*, 681.

[24] *Smith, Kline* at 367.

[25] *Ibid.* at 369. For a rejection of Strayer's interpretation, see *Kask* v. *Shimizu* (1986), 44 Alta. L.R. (2d) 293 at 304-307 (Court of Queens Bench).

[26] Eberts, "The Equality Provisions of the Canadian Charter of Rights and Freedoms and Government Institutions," 160.

[27] Thomas Sowell, *The Economics and Politics of Race: An International Perspective* (New York: William Morrow and Co., 1983).

[28] *Washington* v. *Davis,* 426 U.S. 229 at 248 (1976).

[29] Anne Bayefsky, "Defining Equality Rights," 34-35; Eberts, "The Equality Provisions of the Canadian Charter," 167.

[30] Bayefsky, "Defining Equality Rights," 58-59.

[31] An example of how racially neutral educational classifications were subjected to a stricter level of scrutiny because of their systemic effect on a racial group may be found in *Hobson* v. *Hansen* 265 F.Supp. 401 (D.D.C. 1967). See the discussion of this case in Horowitz, *The Courts and Social Policy,* 111.

[32] Raj Anand, "Ethnic Equality," in Bayefsky and Eberts, eds., *Equality Rights and the Charter,* 116.

[33] *Ibid.*

[34] D. Gibson, "Stereotypes, Statistics and Slippery Slopes," in N. Nevitte and A. Kornberg, eds., *Minorities and the Canadian State* (Oakville: Mosaic Press, 1985), 126.

[35] *Oram and McLaren* v. *Pho,* unreported, June 8, 1975.

[36] *Gay Alliance Toward Equality* v. *Vancouver Sun,* [1979] 2 S.C.R. 435 at 460-461.

[37] 102 S.Ct. 2525(1982).

[38] Robertson, "Some Thoughts About Affirmative Action," 28. Emphasis in original.

[39] *Ibid.*

[40] Robertson, "Some Thoughts About Affirmative Action," 4-5.

[41] Beverly Jacks Schwartz and Philip B. Sklover, "Connecticut v. Teal: The Final Word on the 'Bottom Line' Problem?" *Columbia Human Rights Law Review* 14(1982), 72.

[42] 102 S.Ct. 2525 at 2533 (1982). Emphasis added.

[43] Judith Keene, *Human Rights in Ontario* (Toronto: Carswell, 1983), 108.

[44] Air Canada had such a maximum hiring age for pilots. See *Carson* v. *Air Canada* (1982), 3 C.H.R.R. D/818. The age limit in this case was twenty-seven.

[45] In Ontario, for example, the introduction of the BFOQ exemption in the employment area coincided with the addition of sex and marital status to the original list of stigmatic grounds (race, creed, colour, nationality, ancestry or place of origin). See S.O. 1972 c.119, s.5, which enacts a new s.4(6) in the Act: "The provisions of this section relating to any discrimination, limitation, specification or preference for a position or employment based on sex or marital status do not apply where sex or marital status is a *bona fide* occupational requirement for the position or employment." Before this, the only employment exemptions, in s.4(4), were the exemptions for domestic employment and special interest organizations. Cf. Thomas Flanagan, "The Manufacture of Minorities," in Neil Nevitte and Allan Kornberg, eds., *Minorities and the Canadian State* (Oakville: Mosaic, 1985), 118.

[46] Hogg, *Constitutional Law of Canada,* 799-801.

[47] For example, *Law Society of Upper Canada* v. *Skapinker* [1984] 1 S.C.R. 357 at 383-384; *Singh* v. *Minister of Employment and Immigration*, [1985] 1 S.C.R. 177 at 217.

[48] See Rainer Knopff, "Parliament vs. the Courts: Making Sense of the Bill of Rights Debate," *Legislative Studies* (Journal of the Australasian Study of Parliament Group) 3:2(1988).

[49] Peter H. Russell, "The Political Purposes of the *Canadian Charter of Rights and Freedoms*," *Canadian Bar Review* 61 (1983), 43-45.

[50] *A.G. Quebec* v. *Quebec Association of Protestant School Boards*, [1984] 2 S.C.R. 66 at 84.

[51] *Ibid.*, at 79.

[52] *Ibid.*, at 88.

[53] *Jack and Charlie* v. *The Queen*, [1985] 2 S.C.R. 332.

[54] *The People* v. *Woody* (1964), 394 p.2d 813 (Supreme Court of California).

[55] Cases that have raised such "regime" issues include the infamous *Dred Scott* case in the United States and the *Guibord* case in Canada. For a discussion of the latter see Rainer Knopff, "Quebec's 'Holy War' as Regime Politics: Reflections on the Guibord Case," *Canadian Journal of Political Science* 12 (1979), 314-331.

[56] Paul C. Weiler, "Rights and Judges in a Democracy: A New Canadian Version," *Journal of Law Reform* 18 (1984), 54.

[57] Cf. F.L. Morton, "The Supreme Court's Promotion of Sexual Equality: A Case Study of Institutional Capacity," *Polity*, 16:3 (1984).

[58] Thomas Sowell, *Knowledge and Decisions* (New York: Basic Books, 1980), 250-251.

[59] *Ibid.*, 168-176; Edwin West and Michael McKee, *Minimum Wages: The New Issues in Theory, Evidence, Policy and Politics* (Hull, Quebec: Economic Council of Canada and the Institute for Research on Public Policy, 1980).

[60] Sowell, *Knowledge and Decisions*, 179-180; F.A. Hayek et. al., *Rent Control: A Popular Paradox* (Vancouver: Fraser Institute, 1975).

[61] *Lochner* v. *New York*, 198 U.S. 45 (1905).

[62] *Griswold* v. *Connecticut, 381 U.S. 479 (1965); Roe* v. *Wade*, 410 U.S. 113 (1973).

[63] Such a "veteran's preference" exists in the *Public Service Employment Act* R.S.C., 1970 Ch. P32. See Russell Juriansz, "Systemic Discrimination and Special Programs," in *Human Rights* (Toronto: Law Society of Upper Canada, 1983), 13. For an American case bearing on this question see *Personnel Administrators of Massachusetts* v. *Feeney*, 442 U.S. 256 (1979).

[64] Sowell, *Knowledge and Decisions*, 97-100.

[65] Horowitz, *The Courts and Social Policy*; Sowell, *Knowledge and Decisions. Cf. F.L. Morton* and Leslie A. Pal, "The Impact of the Charter of Rights on Canadian Public Administration," *Canadian Public Administration* 28:2 (1985).

[66] Horowitz, *The Courts and Social Policy.*

[67] Paul Weiler, "Two Models of Judicial Decision-Making," *Canadian Bar Review* (1968).

[68] Cf. John Hart Ely, *Democracy and Distrust: A Theory of Judicial Review* (Cambridge, Mass.: Harvard University Press, 1980), 53, 67.

[69] *Equality for All*, 9-13. As of February, 1988, the law had not been changed, despite recommendations for reform in *Equality for All*. See William Sheridan, "Equality For All! Report, Response, and Results" (Library of Parliament, Research Branch, February 5, 1988), hereafter cited as "Results."

[70] *Equality for All.*, 18.

[71] Sheridan reports at page 3 of "Results" that "Labour Canada began consultations with the private sector regarding mandatory retirement provisions, and these are still in progress. On 2 July 1986, the section of the Public Service Superannuation Regulations concerning mandatory retirement was repealed. The other Recommendations [of *Equality for All*] are being studied as part of the Justice Department's review of the *Canadian Human Rights Act.*"

[72] *Equality for All.*, 45-46.

[73] *Ibid.*, 47.

[74] *Ibid.*

[75] *Ibid.*, 49-57. *Equality for All* recommended that all trades and occupations in the armed forces be open to women. Sheridan reports that "In the fall of 1987, the Department of National Defence's Charter Task Force Report recommended expanded role opportunities for women in the Armed Forces. Subsequently, 22 additional units and sub-units were open to both sexes, and 12 military occupations that were previously designated as "men only" were opened to mixed recruitment. As a result, gender-free positions open to women increased by 3,500, to a total of 35,440, which means that 73% of Armed Forces roles are now open to both sexes." "Results," 8.

[76] *Equality for All.*, 61-62.

[77] *Ibid.*, 90-91.

[78] *Ibid.*, 91.

[79] *Reference Re Public Service Employee Relations Act (Alta.),* [1987] 1 S.C.R. 313 at 420.

VII

AFFIRMATIVE ACTION

Affirmative action seeks to promote greater equality of result for specified target groups. As its name implies, it is "positive" action in addition to the "negative" prohibition of direct discrimination against the target groups. Affirmative action is thus concerned mainly with the secondary group differences that cause inequality and that are not touched by the decline of direct discrimination. Indeed, the literature frequently emphasizes that affirmative action is primarily a response to "systemic discrimination."

Affirmative action is a necessary supplement to the prohibition of systemic discrimination because the latter cannot ensure equality of result. As we saw in the previous chapter, equality of result in employment may be achieved even in the presence of a systemic barrier if enough qualified members of the target group apply. By the same token, dismantling a systemic barrier will not lead to equal results if a group's application rate remains low.

The kinds of positive measures associated with affirmative action programs include the dismantling of systemic barriers to accommodate group differences, the provision of remedial, pre-employment upgrading programs, and the use of ameliorative preferences and timetables to achieve pre-determined numerical targets. Although affirmative action programs resort to all of these devices, the use of targets and preferences has come to be their distinguishing feature. This has clouded public debate on the subject because some people who support more limited positive measures, such as upgrading programs, now count themselves among the opponents of "affirmative action." If one uses the term in its generic sense, rather than as a term of art for targets and ameliorative preferences, it is clear that there is an important debate not about the desirability of positive measures as such but about the kind and extent of positive measures that should be taken. It was to rescue this debate from rhetorical obfuscation that the Abella commission substituted the term "employment equity" for affirmative action.[1] This new term is not really satisfactory, however, because the issues involved transcend the employment sphere. We could perhaps use "educational equity" to refer to affirmative action programs in higher education, but a single term to describe the same policy thrust in different areas seems desirable. Furthermore, the term "equity" does not so clearly suggest the positive nature of the measures involved. I will therefore continue to refer to affirmative action.

In this chapter I am mainly concerned with what has been called "hard" affirmative action. "Soft" affirmative action embraces such measures as pre-employment upgrading but stops short of numerical targets; it promotes equal results without insisting that they be achieved. "Hard" affirmative action, on the other hand, uses ameliorative preferences and timetables to reach an escalating series of pre-determined goals, culminating ultimately in the random distribution of groups. It emphasizes the achievement (rather than merely the promotion) of equal results and defines equal results in the most all-encompassing way.[2] "Hard" affirmative action is a prime example of constructivist social technology.

The Reconstruction of Merit

One of the questions facing every affirmative action program is whether it should take a conformist or accommodationist approach to secondary target-group variation from prevailing standards. A conformist orientation is apparent in such remedial measures as educational upgrading, which enables target-group members to acquire qualifications they presently lack. Similarly, when affirmative action resorts to preferential selection in education or employment, it frequently purports to prefer target-group members only when they are otherwise equal to competing candidates, never when they are less qualified. By expanding the number of qualified target-group role models in the relevant spheres of activity, such preferential hiring promotes conformity to existing qualifications rather than undermining them. Indeed, this conformist tendency of affirmative action has attracted the criticism of more radical egalitarians. Some feminists, for example, "have queried the value of affirmative action within existing patriarchal and/or class structures and have been particularly hostile to the managerialist perspectives promoted by 'targeting for the top' seminars." In this view, "affirmative action is seen as turning women into corporate clones adapted for success within existing structures."[3]

Many proponents of conformist upgrading balk at preferential selection and are particularly suspicious of numerical targets. They often charge that targets are really quotas that will be filled at the cost of selecting the unqualified, thus diluting standards rather than promoting conformity to them. This fear lies behind the common claim that affirmative action conflicts with the "merit principle."

Some proponents of affirmative action defend the preferential selection of less qualified minority candidates under a quota system.[4] In the absence of discrimination, they contend, such candidates would have had equal or better qualifications than their competitors; selecting them is thus simply restoring them to what they would have enjoyed had they not been victimized by discrimination.[5] Justified in this way, quota selection would lead to a practical dilution of standards but would not represent an accommodationist challenge to the validity of those standards. The "unqualified" are selected, in this account, not because the qualifications are suspect, but because in a just world they would have had those qualifications. Furthermore, the selection of the "unqualified" is usually presented as a temporary measure, which can be disposed of as the group differences in qualifications diminish.

Other proponents of affirmative action reject even a temporary dilution of "merit" and take great pains to distinguish goals from quotas. This has been especially true in Canada, where quotas are associated with a crude and insensitive American approach to equality.[6] This aversion to quotas is well expressed by the Ontario Human Rights Commission:

> Some jurisdictions, particularly in the United States, have attempted to remedy long-established patterns of discrimination against various groups by requiring employers to hire quotas of people belonging to those groups. The Commission believes that this is a crude

> and simplistic approach to a complex problem. Such an approach casts doubt on the legitimacy of minority group achievements. Moreover, it betrays the basic principle of equality of opportunity if people are given jobs or promoted not because they are competent, but because they belong to a minority group. Such reverse discrimination, though well-intentioned, is discrimination none the less. It still spells condescension and, in the long run, it may do far more harm than good. At bottom, it is the antithesis of human rights legislation.[7]

Goals allegedly escape this criticism because, unlike quotas, they do not constitute "an absolute preference based on [group affiliation] without regard to qualifications." They are flexible, temporary reasonable, and "they never require hiring the unqualified."[8]

Goals do not require hiring the unqualified because they are never set so high as to make it difficult for an employer to find enough qualified target-group members to achieve them. They are based on the target group's representation in the "available qualified" population rather than on its representation in the national population as a whole.[9] In other words, goals are set to overcome only the discrepancy between the number of *qualified* members of the target group in the population and the number in an employer's workforce. For example, although women constitute a little over fifty percent of the population, in 1982 they were only about twenty percent of B.A. graduates in Forestry.[10] Affirmative action goals in this area would thus be set closer to twenty percent than to fifty percent. Similarly, in 1981 women received twenty-four percent of the Ph.D. degrees awarded in Canada.[11] Again, this makes it unrealistic to impose an affirmative action target of fifty percent in academia.

However, not all qualified target-group members in the total population are "available." Employers do not always draw their workforce from the national labour pool, nor can they reasonably be expected to. If a target group is generally underrepresented in the employer's recruitment area, then goals based on the number of qualified target-group members nationally would be unrealistic. The geographic distribution of target groups is thus considered in establishing "availability."[12]

The true "availability" of qualified target-group members is also affected by interest in the relevant jobs. The concentration of ethnic groups and women in particular occupations is well known, and this may reflect special affinities. If otherwise qualified members of a minority are not interested in a position, they are not truly available, and goals set as if they were will again be unrealistically high. Recognizing this, the Treasury Board of Canada stated that the objective of the affirmative action programs it introduced in 1983 was "to ensure that target groups participate and are represented equitably in the Public Service, based on their representation within the available, qualified and *interested* workforce."[13]

Goals based on availability require the preferential treatment of target-group members only within a pool of otherwise equally qualified and interested candidates and are thus said not to violate the merit principle. Furthermore, if availability has been overestimated and an employer has real difficulty in hiring enough qualified target-group members, the situation can be reassessed and the goals lowered. By contrast, quotas are inflexible and are too high to accommodate merit because they are derived not from true "availability" but from wider population statistics. Thus the Treasury Board emphasized that the use of numerical goals does not "countenance any infringement upon the merit principle or the imposition of quotas or targets based simply on demographics."[14]

The careful tailoring of goals to avoid a conflict with merit suggests a conformist orientation to group differences. However, this is true only if existing qualifications are used in determining availability, and it is clear that this will rarely be the case. First, existing qualifications often include the less formal (and generally inarticulate) standards of empirical experience, which are unlikely to be considered in availability analysis. Second, the "equal opportunity" component of affirmative action programs may well entail abandoning explicit qualifications that constitute "unnecessary" systemic barriers. In Saskatchewan, for example, employers who "reported some difficulty in finding qualified target-group applicants" were advised "to review job qualifications to determine if they are necessary to the performance of the job."[15] Finally, even where a requirement is deemed to be reasonable with respect to the majority, "reasonable accommodation" may have to be made for groups or individuals who cannot meet them because of traits related to a prohibited ground of discrimination.[16]

In a formal sense a systemic challenge to existing qualifications does not affect the contention that affirmative action is compatible with the merit principle. If existing qualifications are too high, they do not define the "merit" truly required for the job. Numerical targets set on the basis of lower but more reasonable qualifications may be larger than those based on existing qualifications, but they will not infringe merit properly understood. Needless to say, to those who believe that existing standards represent "merit properly understood," numerical "goals" based on lower standards will exhibit all the characteristics of quotas.

Even without an explicit challenge to systemic barriers, it is doubtful whether affirmative action can really avoid diluting existing standards of merit. We saw in chapter four that the demand for individual treatment reflects the rationalist belief that information is readily and cheaply available and that human tasks can be minutely specified. This perspective also animates the attempt to control for the "available qualified" population. Availability analysis assumes that it is possible rationally to determine and articulate all of the requirements for a job and that individuals who possess an articulated set of requirements are interchangeable. From the rival empiricist perspective, this approach inevitably misses qualifications and differences between individuals that are difficult to articulate in advance but that are important in the development of a high-quality workforce. It ignores the fact that employers often do not hire randomly from a number of minimally qualified candidates but attempt to find the "*best*" available" person. Formal "availability" will thus be established on the basis of the lowest common denominator of qualifications, not on actual existing qualifications, and higher qualifications will no longer be permitted whenever they work to exclude protected minorities. The goals established on the basis of this distorted vision of availability will be too large to permit the selection of those who are *best* qualified and will thus undermine excellence.[17] This empiricist critique of availability analysis is beautifully expressed by Antonin Scalia:

> Affirmative action requirements...are said repeatedly "not to require the hiring of any unqualified individuals." That gives one a great feeling of equal justice until it is analysed. Unfortunately, the world of employment applicants does not divide itself merely into "qualified" and "unqualified" individuals. There is a whole range of ability—from unqualified, through minimally qualified, qualified, well-qualified, to outstanding. If I can't get Leontyne Price to sing a concert I have scheduled, I may have to settle for Erma Glatt. La Glatt has a pretty good voice, but not as good as Price. Is she unqualified? Not really—she has sung other concerts with modest

> success. But she is not as good as Price. Any system that coerces me
> to hire her in preference to Price, because of her race, degrades the
> quality of my product and discriminates on racial grounds against
> Price. And it is no answer to either of these charges that Glatt is
> "qualified." To seek to assuage either the employer's demand for
> quality or the disfavored applicant's demand for equal treatment by
> saying there is no need to hire any unqualified individuals is a sort
> of intellectual shell game, which diverts attention from the major
> issue by firmly responding to a minor one. [18]

It is worth repeating that the empiricist model of decision making, which permits the search for the best rather than the merely
"qualified" (even though some of the criteria determining the
best are inevitably experiential and inarticulate), more clearly
approximates the ideal of individual treatment than the rationalistic model of decision making favoured by human rights activists.

The issue is further complicated by the fact that employment
situations are not often like the hiring of a concert singer for a single event. The better analogy in many cases is building and maintaining a winning sports team. As in the above example, the
coach or manager is concerned not only with minimal technical
proficiency but with degrees of virtuosity. However, even the fine
distinctions of technical ability do not exhaust the relevant considerations. A winning team requires a blend of characteristics,
including experience, youthful enthusiasm, leadership, mental
toughness, humour, etc.—all of which can sometimes outweigh
pure technical skill. When an opening arises, the manager must
reflect on which components of a "winning combination" the
team already possesses and which "gaps" most urgently need to
be filled. The person "best qualified" at one point in a team's
development may be quite unsuitable at another. This highly var-
iegated and "individualized" process cannot be captured by a
system of articulated "qualifications" for the purpose of availability analysis. It is counter-intuitive to suggest that quasi-judicial
mandarins armed with such a system can do a better job of player
recruitment than coaches and managers, that the aloof rationalism of the former is an adequate replacement for the powerful
self-interest and ongoing empirical experience of the latter. The
same can be said of many of the "teams" built by employers in
the non-sporting world.

The multiple criteria of excellence for many positions, and the
fact that their relative importance varies with time and circumstances, make it difficult to maintain the fiction that goals, unlike

quotas, are compatible with the merit principle. This difficulty becomes even more acute when one considers that standards of excellence are often open-ended, with no obvious ceiling at which all of the "best" are equally good.[19] Taken together these facts undermine the claim that the ameliorative preferences of affirmative action come into effect only when all other things are equal. The fact is that other things are hardly ever equal. Such considerations have led even staunch proponents of numerical goals to admit that they cannot be distinguished from quotas, that the alleged distinction is "a distinction without a difference."[20] Both rigid quotas and flexible goals limit the discretion of primary decision-makers to pursue excellence or merit as traditionally understood.

Of course, there is always the possibility that discretion in the hands of such primary decision-makers as coaches or employers will be misused and abused—in particular, that it will be used to give vent to irrational prejudice. Entire sports, for example, have in the past excluded certain racial groups. However, such discrimination against the truly qualified on the basis irrelevant group traits persists on a massive scale only when it is common to an entire sphere of activity. Once blacks "broke into" baseball, the constraints of competition overcame the resistance of even the most prejudiced owners, managers, and coaches. And when competition does not work perfectly to overcome discrimination, the answer lies in anti-discrimination legislation, not in affirmative goals and timetables based on an insensitive, rule-bound "availability analysis." The latter solve the problems inherent in discretion by undermining the discretion itself. This may appear quite appropriate to the rationalistic and legalistic mind, which assumes that the "rule of law" can and should replace the rule of men in all spheres of activity, but it is in fact a recipe for the undermining of excellence. As Thomas R. Kearns argues, there are "matters that are not easily or wisely subjected to rules," and discretion "is most valuable in connection with [these] matters."[21] In fact, it is impossible to do away with discretion. In an important sense the "rule of law" is the rule of law makers and interpreters. In subjecting the employment sphere to the rationalistic formulae of affirmative action, discretionary rule is not so much destroyed as shifted from those who are qualified by interest and experience to exercise it to those who are not.

Animism and Inequality

Constructivism is the attempt to remake society according to rationally preconceived criteria, such as "individual treatment" or "equality of results." It is a rationalistic orientation, deploring unguided and inarticulate processes that lead to unpredictable results. It thus tends to replace spontaneous processes with formal rules and procedures based on articulated and generalized criteria. We have seen this tendency at work in both the pursuit of individual treatment and the formulation of "qualified availability."

The faith that such constructivist projects can succeed is often fed by the assumption that the patterns and structures to be transformed were themselves intentionally created, that what was once constructed can now be reconstructed. Hayek and those he has influenced reject this intentionalist explanation of societal patterns in favour of a more "evolutionary" account of their development. This latter perspective, though not denying that deliberate design plays an important role in human affairs, insists that overall societal patterns or results cannot be explained simply in terms of a corresponding overall design. In this view individuals certainly have their particular designs or purposes, and consciously constructed organizations often reflect a "founding intention," but societal patterns as a whole arise in a more amorphous and mysterious way. They emerge out of the interaction of innumerable individuals, groups and organizations, all pursuing their own particular designs or purposes, and all continually adjusting their actions in light of the changing environment produced by the uncontrollable and thus unpredictable action of others. Out of this constant jostling and mutual adjustment of particular purposes emerge orders and patterns that are the "result of human action but not of human design."[22] From this perspective "some events are in fact the result of purposeful activity toward the goal achieved, but the general presumption that this *must* be the case can be classified as 'the animistic fallacy.'"[23]

Proponents of affirmative action commit the animistic fallacy most obviously when they establish the "random distribution" of groups as the standard of constructivist transformation and then attribute almost all current departures from that standard to discrimination.[24] More modest versions of the equal-results orientation are possible, but this ambitious approach is common in the literature of "hard" affirmative action. For example, CEIC's Affirmative Action Training Manual states:

> The basic premise of affirmative action is that the operation of discriminatory social, educational and employment practices is the force which causes disproportionate representation of groups of people in the labour force. In the absence of such discrimination, which is interwoven throughout the fabric of our society, women, Natives and disabled people would be randomly distributed throughout the labour force in approximately the same proportion as they are distributed in the population—with rare exceptions reflecting genuine preferences of some women and Native people and actual limitations of some disabled individuals.[25]

The animism of this line of thought is most apparent when *intentional* discrimination is seen as the main cause of inequality. When discrimination is defined more broadly to include systemic barriers the charge of animism seems, at least at first glance, to be less compelling. After all, the idea of systemic discrimination emphasizes unintentional consequences and thus appears to concede that patterns of inequality cannot be explained in terms of deliberate design. Furthermore, I shall shortly argue that when discrimination is defined as whatever causes group inequality, it eventually encompasses not just neutral rules with disparate impact but much more extensive and amorphous social forces, such as socialization patterns within the disadvantaged groups. This wider, "societal" definition of discrimination is seemingly even less open to the charge of animism; indeed, it might almost be taken as an admission that societal patterns of inequality are the "result of human action but not of human design." Despite this appearance, I shall argue that explaining variance from random distribution in terms of discrimination (however broadly defined) remains an example of the animistic fallacy.

As with so many other aspects of affirmative action, the "random distribution" hypothesis is borrowed from the United States. According to Thomas Sowell it arose out of the original civil rights movement, which was dedicated almost exclusively to bettering the condition of American blacks. One of the traditional justifications of the inferior position of blacks in American society had been their alleged lack of innate ability. Against this, reformers argued it was due to discrimination. These eventually became the only explanations of black underrepresentation. With time this explanatory dichotomy was extended (wrongly in Sowell's view) to the disadvantage or underrepresentation of other racial and ethnic groups and women. Although it was not always recognized by those who accepted this analysis, Sowell argues that it leads inevitably to the "result-oriented" emphasis on random distribution typical of affirmative action rhetoric. "If the causes of intergroup differences can be dichotomized into discrimination and innate ability, then non-racists and non-sexists must expect equal results from non-discrimination. Conversely, the persistence of highly disparate results must indicate that discrimination continues to be pervasive...."[26]

If this is true, the uneven distribution of qualifications for which availability analysis controls is itself caused by discrimination. For example, if a group disproportionately lacks a desirable qualification, it might be because its members have been denied equal educational opportunities. In the constructivist view even differences of interest are ultimately attributable to discrimination. While the CEIC manual mentions variations in preferences, it dismisses "genuine" differences of this kind as being rare—too rare, certainly, to significantly affect the ultimate goal of random distribution. To the extent that inequality is due to different group preferences, they must be non-genuine, that is, caused by discrimination. Thus a group's lack of interest in pursuing certain educational qualifications might be due to having been excluded from occupations requiring those qualifications. Furthermore, in addition to affecting a group's direct opportunity to pursue particular qualifications and its interest in doing so, discrimination may more generally affect attitudes to education, work, etc. Enslaved American blacks, for example, were unlikely to develop the positive attitudes to hard work that are such an important component of success.

This means that the moderate goals based on availability analysis, which controls for qualifications and interest, must be understood as "medium-term" objectives, which fall short of random distribution not because of non-discriminatory determinants of underrepresentation but because of concessions to practical considerations:

> Clearly, this long-term objective, which represents an ideal standard, is not useful to the individual company in establishing its immediate and medium-term goals. However, a comparison of the company's current workforce status with the ideal of random distribution does provide a measure of the magnitude of the problem to be overcome.

> The comparison of workforce data with availability data, on the other hand, provides a practical measure of current status and achievable goals, given the present, imperfect state of the labour market.[27]

In addition to long- and medium-term goals, there are also "immediate" or "short-term" goals, which are even more modest. These are arrived at by modifying medium-term goals in light of "attrition rates, availability of target-group members and the particular situation of the company at the time." Nevertheless, "It should be remembered that the long-term quantitative objective is representativeness of target-group participation in the workforce."[28] Thus the much vaunted flexibility of goals turns out to lie in their inevitable upward revision whenever they are achieved. Failure to reach these modest goals would almost always indicate insufficient diligence, or bad faith, on the part of affirmative action managers in designing and implementing their programs, and would justify the negative career evaluations contemplated in the affirmative action literature.

It should be noted that the use of numerical targets need not necessarily be conceived as part of an escalating strategy to overcome all group differences (including existing job affinities) that impede random distribution. More modestly, targets could be used to ensure that a group is not prevented by ongoing intentional discrimination from attaining the degree of representation warranted by its actual interest, without assuming that job affinities or qualifications will ever be randomly distributed. For example, a group that is underrepresented in a certain occupation because of lack of interest may be even more dramatically underrepresented in a particular firm because of demonstrated, ongoing intentional discrimination. In the absence of such discrimination one could plausibly assume that the group's representation would more closely approximate the occupational average, though it would be no more likely to rise to the level of random distribution in that firm than in the general occupational category. If the firm is large and complex, with influence over hiring being widely distributed, it might be inefficient to attempt to monitor, prove, and redress all cases of intentional discrimination, and one might choose to impose an affirmative action program using the group's average representation in the occupation as the numerical target. Since the object is to prevent continuing intentional discrimination, however, there would be no need to push on toward random distribution after this initial target had been met.

An example may clarify the point. In 1982 thirteen percent of blue collar workers in Canada were women, while women constituted less than one percent of the blue collar workforce at Canadian National Railways.[29] The discrepancy appeared to be caused by intentional discrimination. A study of male personnel at CN showed the widespread presence of such opinions as "railroading is a man's sport—there's no room for women."[30] This attitude extended to supervisors who made remarks such as "unless I'm forced, I won't take a woman."[31] To overcome the ongoing intentional discrimination evident at CN, a human rights tribunal ordered the company to fill one of every four vacancies in specified positions with a woman until the Canadian average of thirteen percent was achieved.[32] In the modest view of affirmative action being proposed, thirteen percent would be an ultimate (not a short- or medium-term) target because it is intended to remedy only the effect of ongoing intentional discrimination in the particular firm, not the additional causes of the general underrepresentation evident in the group's occupational average. In the more radical understanding of affirmative action described above, meeting the (low) occupational average would be only the first step in a continuing effort to achieve random distribution. This radical view is the main subject of this chapter.

As indicated, the radical approach to affirmative action understands the group differences that prevent random distribution as the result of past discrimination. Assuming for the moment that only intentional discrimination is at stake, it is certainly true that it *can* affect the development or entrenchment of group differences, including differences of qualifications or interest. On the other hand, critics of the constructivist interpretation of inequality deny that intentional discrimination is the sole, or even the primary, cause of inequality-generating group differences. It is difficult, they suggest, to explain group traits in terms of discrimination when those traits remain constant for long periods of time and do not vary markedly from one society to another, especially when they predominate in the country of origin, where the group constitutes the majority. Thus the Chinese are everywhere overrepresented in the scientific and technological fields, as are the Germans in industry and family farming.[33] Similarly, the Jews are well represented in commercial endeavours virtually everywhere.[34] True, these groups are hardly disadvantaged by virtue of their overrepresentation in these fields, but the point is that these statistical imbalances, and the differences that generate them, seem to arise independently of intentional discrimination; indeed, some of these groups routinely achieve overrepresentation in high status or financially lucrative occupations *despite* overt discrimination against them.[35] This has certainly been true in Canada. As Conrad Winn observes,

> ...the present incomes of Japanese and Jewish Canadians are remarkable considering the discrimination in college admissions, housing, and employment which prevailed against these groups until after World War II and which persists in some sectors of the economy today.[36]

Indeed, many "low-prestige" ethnic groups, including most of the "visible minorities," have shown dramatic upward mobility relative to the dominant "high-prestige" groups. "Not one Protestant ethnic group," says Winn, reporting 1971 and 1981 census figures, "increased its relative position [from one generation to the next] in a land where the most prestigious faiths are Protestant and where the work ethic is considered to be Protestant."[37] Winn even goes so far as to suggest that moderate discrimination against some groups may stimulate achievement rather than retard it, that a group might react to discrimination by becoming more ambitious than it otherwise would have been.[38] This upward mobility of low-status groups in the face of discrimination makes it even more difficult to believe that statistically unequal groups are disadvantaged solely because of discrimination, though discrimination may play a part.

The fact that group success or failure is significantly independent of discrimination not only supports the evolutionist claim that deliberate design cannot explain societal patterns but also buttresses the corollary that society cannot easily be reconstructed through deliberate design. If intentional discrimination against groups is often unsuccessful, why should one be so confident that affirmative action in favour of groups will more readily achieve its ends? In both cases powerful cultural forces are at work that may confound deliberate action. The constructivist view assumes that if group differences are not natural they must reflect a rational construction that can be deliberately changed. Critics of this view, such as Thomas Sowell, contend that cultural traits can in fact be as difficult and perhaps even more difficult to change than natural traits:

> ...far more dramatic changes have been achieved in genetically determined plant and animal characteristics by selective breeding than have been achieved in environmentally determined characteristics such as regional or national differences in automobile driving habits, attitudes toward education, or respect for the rights of others. Genetically determined nearsightedness may be readily correctable by eyeglasses, while environmentally determined habits of overeating may resist numerous efforts to change. The very survival of the Jewish culture and religion is evidence of the extreme difficulty of changing environmental characteristics, despite centuries of efforts at absorption of the Jews by church and state across the continent of Europe.[39]

For such critics the near impossibility of deliberately changing the cultural traits of groups bespeaks the futility of social engineering.

Constructivism and Societal Discrimination

The foregoing arguments serve mainly to counter the claim that inequality-generating differences are caused by *intentional* discrimination. But, as I have said, proponents of affirmative action are often perfectly willing to admit this, emphasizing that inequality of result can be traced to discrimination only if the term is broadened to include unintentional or "systemic" barriers. Thus a group's lack of interest in an occupation may be influenced not only by past direct exclusion from the job or appropriate job training but also by indirect exclusion in the form of systemic barriers. If women's lack of interest in police work is due to the absence of appropriate female role models, it matters little if that absence flows from direct discrimination against women or from height and weight requirements that few women can meet.

If affirmative action is oriented to random distribution, and if existing departures from that goal are to be understood as the products of discrimination, then the definition of discrimination must be expanded even further. Unequal results are caused not only by direct and systemic discrimination but also by more amorphous causes of group differences. The fact that there are fewer female than male police officers, for example, is no doubt due in part to past discrimination in the form of intentional exclu-

sion or systemic barriers (such as height and weight requirements), but it is surely also due to patterns of socialization in appropriate sex roles and to the structure of such social institutions
as the family. Certainly direct and systemic discrimination can
contribute to and strengthen such patterns of socialization, but
these patterns probably have other causes. Whatever their cause,
they have an independent force and vitality that exerts its influence even after the abolition of direct or systemic discrimination.
Even as direct discrimination ends and systemic barriers fall,
women continue to congregate in traditional, lower-paying (often
part-time) occupations.

According to one school of thought imbalance of this kind is
not the result of discrimination at all. In this view the distinction
may be stated as one between "forced" and "unforced" segregation, with only the former qualifying as discrimination. Thus
women who would have been forcibly excluded from police work
had they applied when a height and weight requirement was in
effect, or when direct discrimination was being practiced, are not
being discriminated against if they do not apply when these conditions no longer obtain; they are voluntarily excluding
themselves.

From another perspective there is no such thing as "unforced"
segregation. The women who are allegedly excluding themselves
are not doing so voluntarily; they have been subject to a long
process of socialization in the dominant assumptions concerning
the kinds of work appropriate to men and women.[40] These assumptions reflect prevailing power structures, and although their
transmission may be subtle and unconscious, it is not "unforced." Their alleged self-segregation having been forced upon
them, it is as much the result of unjust discrimination as are the
other forms of segregation.

A similar argument can be made about the persistent racial
segregation in certain southern American school districts after
the 1954 desegregation decision, *Brown v. Board of Education*.[41] The
school boards in question administered school systems in rural
districts where the black and white populations were not residen-
tially segregated, but where the schools had been legally segregated in the past. When the latter policy was found unconstitutional by the Supreme Court, a typical reaction was to institute a
policy of "free choice" under which each child would be free to
attend the school of his choosing. The predictable outcome of this

policy was that very few black children elected the formerly all-white schools and no white children chose the formerly all-black schools.[42] This might be interpreted as voluntary self-segregation, but it is more plausible to suggest that, given the predictable social pressures, indeed the intimidation, brought to bear on the so-called "free choice" of school children in the rural American South, the choices were free only in the most formal and abstract sense. Moreover, the state can be understood to have anticipated this result and to have encouraged it by doing nothing about it, in effect by not providing "equal protection" of the laws to blacks who wished to attend formerly all-white schools. This was the view of the American Supreme Court. Since the administration of the "free choice" plans was more complicated and more expensive than the familiar neighbourhood attendance plan would have been, and since the latter plan would inevitably, in the context of unsegregated neighbourhoods, have led to greater integration, the Court inferred that the "free choice" plans were a subterfuge on the part of the boards to maintain the old dual school system.[43]

While it is possible to view sexual self-stereotyping, or the "self-segregation" of southern school children under free choice plans, as the negative effect of invidious social forces, there are other kinds of self-segregation that are more difficult to describe in this way. There is, for example, an observable desire on the part of certain ethnic and racial groups to maintain identifiable geographic communities. Almost every major North American city, for example, has its "Chinatown." No doubt direct and systemic discrimination may also contribute to the phenomenon of ethnic and racial neighbourhoods, but the influence of the less blameworthy trait of group identification cannot be discounted. People may simply want to be among their own. Indeed, in the U.S. it has been recognized that even the black ghetto, which is now largely responsible for the segregated school, is in part maintained by the pull of racial identification. Similarly, studies in the 1970s indicated that black academics in the U.S. showed a strong preference for working in black colleges and universities—so much so that the financial inducement required to persuade a black professor to move to a non-black institution, even if it was much more prestigious, was significantly higher than what was needed to persuade a white professor to move to a better university. This was surely one of the causes of the underrepresentation of black academics at leading research universities.[44] Adherence to the position that all imbalance is due to discrimination is difficult to maintain in the face of such phenomena unless one claims that there is no innate preference for "one's own," and that such preferences are themselves forms of discrimination. Precisely this conclusion seems to have animated the judicial opinion in a Detroit school desegregation case:

> In the most realistic sense, if fault or blame is to be found it is that of the community as a whole, including of course the black components. We need not minimize the effect of the actions of federal, state, and local governmental officers and agencies...to observe that blacks, like ethnic groups in the past, have tended to separate from the larger group and associate together. The ghetto is a place of confinement and a place of refuge. There is enough blame for everyone to share.[45]

In this view statistical imbalance is transformed from a symptom of direct or systemic discrimination to an alternative definition of discrimination, and nothing more than its presence need be shown. Alternatively, imbalance itself is seen as an unjustifiable inequity, whatever its cause. To put it still differently, the term "systemic" in the phrase "systemic discrimination" comes to refer to the whole "system" of forces contributing to imbalance. These forces include direct and "adverse effect" discrimination, of course, but they also include the more subtle influences that underlie allegedly private self-segregation, such as group consciousness, patterns of socialization in what was traditionally considered to be the private sphere, and such social institutions as the family. Thus critics of affirmative action who argue that much of the underutilization of women has to do not with employer discrimination but with the disproportionate share of domestic responsibilities assumed by women upon marriage can be said to be missing the point: they are using too narrow a conception of discrimination, which in this case inheres in the traditional family structure itself.[46] According to a Labour Canada report,

> The broadest definition [of discrimination] would include differences in productive attributes resulting from such factors as the traditionally unequal division of household responsibilities between married couples, and conditioning to sex roles in the family and educational institutions. Under this definition, virtually all the observed female-male wage differential would be labelled sex discrimination.[47]

For those who take this broad definition of discrimination seriously, individual interests are not really voluntary but socially or "systemically" produced, which helps to explain the depreciation of the interest factor in the more radical formulations of affirmative action. In order to avoid terminological confusion, I have chosen to call the broader form of discrimination "societal discrimination," retaining the term "systemic discrimination" as the label for neutral rules having an unequal impact.

As noted above, when discrimination is defined this broadly, and when its unintentional dimension is explicitly acknowledged, its use as a causal explanation for unequal results no longer fits a simple model of constructivism. To say that a group's inferior status is caused by discrimination no longer implies that a dominant group has deliberately willed and effected the inequality. Indeed, defined in this way discrimination could be understood simply as a convenient code word for the complex and undesigned societal process of evolutionist thinking.

Such an understanding is undermined, however, by the very fact that "discrimination" is the word used to designate this process. In common parlance the word inevitably conveys the sense of deliberate design, and the rhetorical effect of its new use is not at all to dispense with intentionality but subtly to attribute intentionality to "society" as a whole. Changing the meaning of a word so that it can cover new and quite different phenomena almost always serves rhetorical need, hardly ever scientific clarity. In this case it rhetorically preserves the constructivist notion that there is a coherent and unified plan that can be reconstructed. The word discrimination also designates existing patterns as evil and in need of reconstruction. One might well wonder, of course, at the hubris of opposing a particular contemporary design to that of society as a whole. This is surely a more presumptuous project than the reconstruction of the designs of particular groups or individuals. As I shall argue below, the idea that such grand-scale reconstruction is possible is fed by a faith that the principles of modern technology are applicable to the social sphere. Certainly the terms "systemic" and "societal" discrimination are calls to social transformation, not symbolic representations of the wisdom of unplanned social evolution. They make it clear that the unintentional forces that contribute to inequality of result are "discrimination," and thus evils to be overcome.

Constructivist affirmative action benefits from the rhetoric of discrimination in other ways as well. The equality of result at which it aims requires the overcoming of causes—such as group consciousness and group occupational affinities—that are not generally viewed as intrinsically blameworthy phenomena, or as identical to negative prejudice. On the other hand, there does seem to be widespread disapproval of blatant discrimination and a willingness to contemplate its legal prohibition. By describing itself as a remedy for discrimination, affirmative action cashes in on the latter sentiment while hiding its disagreement with the former. For this strategy to work, of course, the most radical expansion of the definition of discrimination on which it depends— the inclusion of what I have called "societal discrimination"— must remain largely implicit. It is blatant discrimination and to a lesser extent systemic barriers that are generally considered to be unjust, and the rhetorical success of affirmative action depends on the association of its enemy with these forms of discrimination.

Affirmative action needs the enemy of traditional discrimination in yet another, deeper sense. The central claim of affirmative action programs is that an "equal opportunity response" is not enough and must be supplemented by special measures, including remedial programs and numerical goals. Remedial programs and goals are necessary because their beneficiaries cannot be expected to succeed without them. But this suggests that these beneficiaries are in some sense less capable than those who can do well without affirmative action. The typical response is that this "inferiority" is not natural but the result of historically produced social disadvantage. This response is inadequate, however, because disadvantaged individuals both within and without the target group can and do overcome social disadvantage on their own.[48] Expecting disadvantaged non-target-group individuals to do so while giving special help to similarly situated target-group members implies that the latter are inferior to the former. To avoid this unpalatable conclusion, affirmative action needs the fall-back claim of continuing present discrimination against target-group members. This extra burden, not inferiority, allegedly justifies the extra help given to target-group members. As Harvey Mansfield puts it, "The unprotected must admit their guilt so that the protected do not have to admit their incapacity."[49] The unprotected, of course, are white males, at least those who do not support affirmative action. "Not that those guilty white males *do* anything discriminatory," continues Mansfield, for

> any overt action to discriminate would be illegal without affirmative action. Rather, it is their bad attitudes. Those white males glare balefully at the protected groups, wounding and disabling them with negative vibrations and looking out for any chance to do them in by wishing them ill.

It cannot be overtly discriminatory acts that justify preferential treatment, because such actions would close off opportunities, and "If opportunities were not open, we could not know that affirmative action beyond opening opportunities was needed."[50] The present discrimination that justifies affirmative action thus amounts to the wishful thinking of white males that they could release the door of opportunity they so resolutely hold open. The absurdity of this position underlines both the fact that affirmative action has little to do with traditional discrimination and its desperate need of this sort of discrimination as a rhetorical cover.

It is worth pausing at this point to note that the case for affirmative action, at least in its conformist version, is not undermined if one declines to explain the differences it seeks to overcome in constructivist terms as the products of discrimination. As Conrad Winn observes, "Special efforts to upgrade the skills of a minority group can be justified by a society's desire for equality without having to assume that the inequality in question was caused by discrimination."[51] It is always a matter of regret when a group disproportionately fails to measure up to legitimate standards, whatever the cause of that failure. Furthermore, self-conscious minorities that cluster at the bottom of prevailing hierarchies are likely to challenge the standards of excellence on which those hierarchies are based. Thus liberal democrats who support existing standards have a practical stake in promoting a more nearly random distribution of groups throughout society's hierarchies.[52] Substantial inequality among groups may also cause other political problems that any decent liberal democracy would prefer to avoid. These considerations suffice to support the conformist inclination to help a group overcome its failings, not just negatively by eliminating discrimination against the group, but "affirmatively" by engaging in remedial measures. However, if one abandons the constructivist notion that social patterns flow from human design and can readily be reconstructed in the same manner, it is more difficult to justify the "hard" result orientation reflected in the use of goals and ameliorative preferences, and the tendency is to prefer "soft" means of promoting the desired result. The latter perspective relies on education and exhortation, which cannot, of course, guarantee results. It is the way of the statesman, who seeks to achieve as much of the good as possible without ever forgetting that the "art of the possible" cannot expect to attain perfection. The constructivist version of affirmative action substitutes a perfectionist social technology for such political statesmanship.

The more moderate approach to affirmative action finds support in Hayek's evolutionist alternative to constructivism. From this perspective deliberate intervention to reform society is not powerless and should not be rejected *tout court*, but unless it becomes totalitarian in scope it can do no more than affect the ongoing evolutionary process; it cannot control it because in an atmosphere of freedom it is impossible to know and predict the innumerable particular actions and reactions that contribute to the development of societal patterns. It is thus vain to proceed with a view to *achieving* rather than *promoting* an overall societal result, however desirable it may seem. Indeed, the guaranteed achievement of societal results is possible only if spontaneous and unpredictable human action is *made* predictable and controllable (i.e., turned into "behaviour") by destroying the freedom on which it depends.

Affirmative Action as Social Technology

The human psychology implicit in constructivist affirmative action completes the depreciation of human action begun in the attack on systemic barriers. Proponents of the most radically result-oriented affirmative action do not see the self-segregation of groups as voluntary in any meaningful sense. From their point of view those who manifest such behaviour are forced to do so by discrimination just as surely as if they were being actively and directly segregated by the intentional action of others. The discrimination is "societal" and its chains are often internalized, but they remain chains nonetheless. Affirmative action thus rests on a behavioural view of man, one in which people do not "act affirmatively" but respond in predictable ways to stimuli coming from the social environment. Affirmative action's own response to the "societal" stimuli it designates as discriminatory is not to recommend to the "victims" that they refuse to be determined—that they begin to "act affirmatively"—but to substitute a new "non-discriminatory" set of stimuli. For example, one of the ways in which society allegedly produces the group occupational affinities that affirmative action wishes to overcome is through role modelling. Far from rejecting the formative power of such role modelling, however, affirmative action proposes to harness it for its own purposes. Indeed, the stated objective of many affirmative action programs is to provide non-traditional role models in order to re-socialize the groups to which the models belong. Inasmuch as affirmative action aims to overcome the results of group socialization, it operates by replacing one kind of role modelling with another: the unregulated role modelling of "society" (which seems inevitably to lead to imbalance and which is therefore defined as discriminatory) with state-supervised role modelling designed to break down the occupational affinities of various groups.

This kind of affirmative action represents an application to the social sphere of the modern technological impulse. Just as physical technology subdues non-human nature, turning it to humanly willed purposes, so this social technology seeks to modify human behaviour to produce pre-determined societal patterns. One may speak of both projects as technological not only because of the control each attempts to exercise over its domain but, more importantly, because of the way in which control is connected to knowledge. The term "technology" comes from the Greek words *techne* and *logos* and embodies a peculiarly modern combination of making and knowing in which the latter serves the former. In this account science is oriented not to the contemplation of a teleological order of nature (because such an order is not thought to exist) but to understanding the forces of a non-teleological nature with a view to predicting, and thus controlling, the formerly unpredictable, thereby overcoming chance. Such a science is possible with respect to social as well as physical matters to the extent that human beings do not *act* freely and spontaneously but *behave* predictably. If this is true, behaviour and the societal patterns it generates can be altered by appropriate manipulations of the systemic and societal environment. Thus affirmative action may be understood as an exercise in applied behavioural science—in

205

short, as social technology. Furthermore, the concern that such technological manipulations might interfere with freedom cannot properly arise because the manipulees, who behave rather than act, are not free in any case. In the old conflict between equality and freedom, the former wins by default.

Notes

[1] Judge Rosalie Abella, Commissioner, *Equality in Employment: A Royal Commission Report* (Ottawa: Supply and Services, 1984), 6-7.

[2] See Gabriel Moens, *Affirmative Action: The New Discrimination* (Australia: Centre for Independent Studies, 1985), 10-13.

[3] Marian Sawer, ed., *Program for Change: Affirmative Action in Australia* (Sydney: Allen & Unwin, 1985), xxi.

[4] L.J.M. Cooray, ed., *Human Rights in Australia* (Epping NSW: ACFR, 1985), 116.

[5] Ralph A. Rossum, *Reverse Discrimination: The Constitutional Debate* (New York: Dekker, 1980), 16, 26.

[6] Cf. Conrad Winn, "Affirmative Action for Women: More than a Case of Simple Justice," *Canadian Public Administration* 28:1(1985), 28-29.

[7] Ontario Human Rights Commission. *Life Together: A Report on Human Rights in Ontario* (1977), 35.

[8] Peter Robertson, "Some Thoughts About Affirmative Action in Canada in the 1980s" (CEIC, 1980), 21-22.

[9] Section 53(b)(iii) of the regulations used by the Saskatchewan Human Rights Commission for approving affirmative action programs states: "Goals shall be based on the extent of underrepresentation identified and on the availability of members of the target or protected groups who are qualified, or who can become qualified through reasonable efforts on the part of the sponsor organization, or who are eligible through reasonable efforts on the part of the sponsor organization, for positions or places within the sponsor organization." See Saskatchewan Human Rights Commission, "Affirmative Action: A Case Book of Legislation and Affirmative Action Programs in Saskatchewan" (March 1983). See also (1980), 1 C.H.R.R. D/135. The Canadian Human Rights Commission has a similar understanding of "availability": "The term 'labour pool'...will refer to those persons with the requisite skills or potential to acquire the skills necessary to perform the functions of given occupations, within the geographical area from which an employer might reasonably be expected to acquire workers." See Canadian Human Rights Commission, "Special Programs in Employment: Criteria For Compliance" (Minister of Supply and Services Canada, 1981), 12, fn. 1.

[10] This is up from 1.5 percent in 1972-73. See Abella, *Equality in Employment*, 140.

[11] Up from 9 percent in 1971. *Ibid.*, 139.

[12] Section 50(e) of the Saskatchewan Affirmative Action regulations state that "'underrepresentation' means having fewer members of the target or protected groups in a particular sector, unit, grouping, classification, or level within the sponsor organization than would reasonably be expected by their representation in the population, or in those subclasses of the population defined by qualification, eligibility, or *geography*, from which the sponsor organization may reasonably be expected to draw its employees, students, tenants, clients, customers or members." Emphasis added. See (1980), 1 C.H.R.R. D/135

[13] News Release, Annex A, 1. Emphasis added.

[14] *Ibid.*, 1.

[15] Saskatchewan Human Rights Commission, *Newsletter*, 16:2 (Fall, 1987), 5.

[16] *Employment Equity Act, S.C. 1984-85-86, c.31, s.4(a).*

[17] See Cooray, ed., *Human Rights in Australia,* 114-120.

[18] Quoted in Richard E. Morgan, *Disabling America: The 'Rights Industry' in Our Time* (New York: Basic Books, 1984), 156-157.

[19] Moens, *Affirmative Action,* 65.

[20] John C. Livingston, *Fair Game: Inequality and Affirmative Action* (San Francisco: W.H. Freeman, 1979), ch. 2.

[21] Quoted in Morgan, *Disabling America,* 158.

[22] Friedrich Hayek, *Law, Legislation and Liberty, Volume 1, Rules and Order* (Chicago: University of Chicago Press, 1973), 20. Hayek is quoting Adam Ferguson.

[23] Thomas Sowell, *Knowledge and Decisions* (New York: Basic Books, 1980), 97. Cf. Thomas Flanagan, "Equal Pay for Work of Equal Value: Some Theoretical Criticisms," *Canadian Public Policy* 13:4(1987), 438: "What Sowell calls *animism* is also often called 'anthropomorphism,' which originally meant the attribution of human characteristics to the Deity, but now also refers to any attribution of human traits to natural, impersonal, or social processes."

[24] Geoffrey Partington points out that such claims are made selectively: "We are told often enough that more boys than girls study mathematics and sciences in years 11 and 12 and that this proves that girls suffer from unfair discrimination in education; it is not suggested that because more girls than boys study in years 11 and 12 a language other than their own, an educational attainment also prized, the boys suffer from unfair educational discrimination. We are told that a far larger number of Aborigines than non-Aborigines proportionally are arrested on crimes of violence each year and that this is evidence of discrimination against Aborigines; nobody has been silly enough so far to claim that because the proportion of men arrested each year for crimes of violence is much greater than that for women, this shows that the law or the police are prejudiced against men." "Education for Citizenship," *Quadrant* 32:8(August 1988), 29-30.

[25] CEIC, *Affirmative Action Technical Training Manual* (1982), 60-61. Often quoted is the following statement from the American case, *International Brotherhood of Teamsters v. The United States* 97 S. Ct. 1843, 57 n. 20 (1977): "...such imbalance is often a tell tale sign of purposeful discrimination; absent explanation, it is ordinarily to be expected that non-discriminatory hiring practices will in time result in a workforce more or less representative of the racial and ethnic composition of the population in the community from which employees are hired." See Saskatchewan Human Rights Commission, *Affirmative Action News* (January, 1982), 2, and *Affirmative Action in the 1980s: Dismantling the Process of Discrimination* (A Statement of the United States Commission on Civil Rights, Clearinghouse Publication 70, November 1981), 2.

[26] Thomas Sowell, *Civil Rights: Rhetoric or Reality?* (New York: William Morrow, 1984), 37-38.

[27] CEIC, *Affirmative Action Technical Training Manual* (1982) 60-61.

[28] *Ibid.,* 102.

[29] *Action Travail des Femmes v. Canadian National Railway Co.* (1987), 8 C.H.R.R. D/4210 at D/4216 (S.C.C.).

[30] *Ibid.,* D/4213.

[31] *Ibid.*

[32] *Ibid.*, D/4218-D/4219. To permit some flexibility, the one-in-four requirement had to be met not within each set of four new positions but in the aggregate over the course of each trimester.

[33] Thomas Sowell, *The Economics and Politics of Race* (New York: William Morrow & Co.), ch. 2 and 53-56.

[34] *Ibid.*, 80-84.

[35] *Ibid.*, chs. 2 and 3.

[36] Conrad Winn, "Affirmative Action and Visible Minorities: Eight Premises in Quest of Evidence," *Canadian Public Policy* 11:4 (1985), 688.

[37] *Ibid.*

[38] *Ibid.*, 693. See also Conrad Winn, "Affirmative Action for Women," 32.

[39] Thomas Sowell, *The Economics and Politics of Race*, 145.

[40] *Offierski v. Board of Education*, 1 C.H.R.R. D/33 at D/38 (1980).

[41] 347 U.S. 483 (1954).

[42] *Green v. County School Board*, 391 U.S. 430 (1968).

[43] *Ibid.*

[44] Thomas Sowell, *Affirmative Action Reconsidered: Was It Necessary in Academia?* (Washington, D.C.: American Enterprise Institute, 1975).

[45] Quoted in Nathan Glazer, *Affirmative Discrimination: Ethnic Inequality and Public Policy* (New York: Basic Books, 1975), 106.

[46] Carl Hoffman and John Reed, "When Is Imbalance Not Discrimination," in W.E. Block and M.A. Walker (eds.), *Discrimination, Affirmative Action and Equal Opportunity* (Vancouver: The Fraser Institute, 1981); Thomas Sowell, *Civil Rights: Rhetoric or Reality?* (New York: William Morrow, 1984), ch. 5.

[47] Morley Gunderson and Frank Reid, "Sex Discrimination in the Canadian Labour Market: Theories, Data and Evidence," Labour Canada, Women's Bureau, Discussion Series A: No. 3, 1981, 31.

[48] Cf. Partington, "Education for Citizenship," 32.

[49] Harvey C. Mansfield Jr., "The Underhandedness of Affirmative Action," *National Review* (May 4, 1984), 28.

[50] *Ibid.*

[51] Winn, "Affirmative Action for Women," 27.

[52] See Marian Sawer, "The Pursuit of Social Justice in Employment: Australia and the United States," in Christine Jennett and Randal G. Stewart, eds., *Three Worlds of Inequality: Race, Class and Gender* (Melbourne: MacMillan, 1987), 298-299.

VIII

CONCLUSION

The new war on discrimination is both a war of words and a war about words. In the latter sense it is a battle about the ownership of the traditional language of liberal democracy, especially the language of rights.[1] This language is being successfully appropriated by the foes of liberal democracy.

Originally the language of rights defined and secured a sphere of private liberty. Private freedom had to be limited in order better to secure it, but these limits were modest in scope and intent. In particular, they did not seek to remodel human nature to do away with its less attractive side. Indeed, the whole point of classical liberalism was to allow men to be what they actually are, to free them from traditional attempts to make them be their better selves. The idea of political equality lay at the foundation of this project and this idea needed to be publicly defended against the kind of prejudice that leads groups to claim a right to rule—it sometimes needed to be defended even against private manifestations of such prejudice lest it infect public policy. This is one of the justifiable limitations on individual freedom.

However, the traditional and legitimate battle *against* this kind of inegalitarian prejudice is not the same as the current battle *for* "individual treatment." Nor is it a battle for the social equality of targeted minorities. Under the influence of the latter notions, the language of rights has become the instrument of societal transformation; it no longer limits freedom in order better to secure its exercise by imperfect men, but destroys private freedom in order to perfect "human nature"—albeit in the name of a more perfect and unlimited (though untested) future freedom. Perfect men, like the gods, can be perfectly free.

211

Animism and Behaviourism

The new war on discrimination is an exercise in constructivist social technology. Deploring unplanned and inarticulate processes that lead to unpredictable results, it coercively subjects social processes to rationalist rules designed to achieve the intellectually derived criteria of "individual treatment" or "equality of result." This adventure in social reconstruction is justified by imputing the "deficiencies" of existing society to discrimination. The logic of individual treatment does this by calling "discriminatory" all predictive generalizations that are not accepted as objectively "necessary" by the egalitarian "guardians." The equal-results orientation claims that discrimination explains existing inequality among groups. The latter perspective also requires generalizations to defend themselves as "necessary" whenever they disproportionately burden one of the target groups. Often the same practices can be challenged both as violations of individual treatment and as systemic discrimination against a specified group.

Constructivist projects often find rhetorical support in the animistic fallacy. If the prevailing state of affairs was itself deliberately constructed, it seems more plausible to think that it can now be reconstructed. The claim that group inequality is caused by discrimination is an example of this fallacy. The rhetorical advantage of this claim is maintained by continuing to use the animistic term "discrimination" even as that term is redefined to include the unplanned systemic and societal processes that actually account for much existing inequality. Society as a whole is thus rhetorically transformed into an anthropomorphic being with an evil, discriminatory plan that must be opposed and overcome by the counter-plan of the guardians.

As it deifies society, the social technology of equal results denigrates the power of individual action. Societal structures and patterns do not flow from the free choices of innumerable individuals; to the contrary, individual choices are the socially determined products of existing societal structures. If individuals are left "free," they will perpetuate existing patterns by continuing to make the choices induced by those patterns. Precisely because they are not really free, however, their "behaviour," and the patterns it generates, can be altered through social engineering.

Social structures can be coercively changed, and after a period of time individuals molded by the new structures will "freely" choose to maintain them.

The confidence that societal patterns can be so easily or massively rearranged seems to be at odds with the animistic attribution of intent to "society." Can one really believe that "societal intent" could be successfully opposed by the particular intent of concrete human beings? Surely if society is to be thought of in anthropomorphic terms, it must be an infinitely more powerful being than the particular individuals and groups who compose it. Would it not be folly to think that the intent and will of such a being could successfully be opposed? Can Leviathan be tamed by pygmies?

In fact, although the constructivist pursuit of equal results makes rhetorical use of the animistic fallacy, it does not depend on it and is certainly not committed to its more subtle implications. Explaining group inequality in terms of discrimination implicitly deifies society, but egalitarian constructivism relies more fundamentally on the modern technological view that there are no deities whose intent can properly limit human making. Technology views both the physical and social worlds as governed by purposeless but predictable forces that can be understood and controlled by human intelligence and will. In the case of social technology this assumption takes the form of a behaviourist social science that sees men as the products of their social environments and thus as appropriate objects of social engineering.

Human Rights and Social Technology

It is more than a little ironic that the doctrine of human rights, in its origin a bulwark of individual freedom, should have become the vehicle for a perspective that denies the reality of such freedom and thus has no hesitation in suppressing it. This can itself be attributed to the complete unfolding and ultimate victory of the technological viewpoint. Technology and liberalism flow from the same account of the nature of things and were originally understood to be allies. The alliance was never a theoretically stable one, however, and it has come unstuck. It turns out that the view of nature that supports technology really doesn't support liberalism after all.

Technology, as the conquest of nature, requires the assumption that nature is bereft of its own meaningful order and is thus material fit to be ordered by man. In an important sense the founders of this view understood it to apply to human nature as well. In opposition to the ancients, they denied that human nature directed man to ends above and beyond the almost universal fear of death and desire for comfortable self-preservation. Indeed, it was the primacy of the passions associated with mere life that impelled and justified the technological conquest of non-human nature. Alleged standards of the "good life" were not only vain but pernicious because they caused self-deception about the true human situation, and because the inevitable quarrels between contending (and deluded) versions of the good actually caused men to sacrifice their dearest and only real interests for chimerical fantasies.

In this early formulation the same passions that justified, and were served by, the technological "relief of man's estate" were also the foundation of the doctrine of individual rights. The primacy of bodily self-preservation entailed the primacy of the individual because bodies are necessarily individual and because the individual is constituted *qua* individual most obviously by his body. The primacy of individuals, moreover, meant that social and political life, and the duties and virtues required by it, were secondary and derivative phenomena, expressing not the fulfillment of human nature but the consent of basically asocial, even anti-social, individuals, based on their common calculation of what best served their security and comfortable self-preservation. One of the things that served security was liberty, for among essentially selfish individuals, no one, no matter how superior in intellect or other distinctions, could be expected to care enough about another's security to be considered a better judge of its requirements. A *summum bonum* might justify the rule of those best able to incarnate the way of life it decreed, but with respect to avoiding the *summum malum* each individual was the best judge. All were therefore politically equal, and being equal they were equally free. Without some limitation, however, this absolute freedom among anti-social individuals gave rise to the war of each against all in which the life of man was "solitary, poor, nasty, brutish, and short," and thus undermined the very interest

214

whose primacy justifies that freedom. In view of this, individuals in their freedom consented to limit that freedom somewhat by establishing government, but that consent was given only better to secure what remained of their freedom, not to promote particular visions of the good life. Government existed not to promote particular visions of human excellence or happiness but to secure the individual rights to "life, liberty, and the *pursuit* of happiness."

Not only were the technological conquest of nature and the liberal doctrine of individual rights developed from the same non-teleological account of nature, but they were originally seen to be mutually supporting. Liberalism provided an unprecedented freedom to science (which in this case meant a science oriented to the conquest of nature) and technological science benefited liberalism by satisfying the passions it considered primary, demonstrating that the ancients were wrong in thinking that because "mere life" could not be reliably secured against chance it was vain to prefer it to the "good life." Among other things, it was anticipated that this satisfaction of the fundamental and universal passions would wean men away from their destructive delusions of grandeur.

As it turned out, however, this founding alliance between liberalism and technology rested on ground that was theoretically weak. It was based on the attempt to save one part of nature from the ambit of technological conquest in order to provide a purpose for (and thus a limit upon) that conquest. Human nature was no longer conceived teleologically, as something that provided positive standards for human endeavour, but there was still a human nature of sorts, as manifested in the state of nature, which provided negative standards—the avoidance of death and discomfort. Technology was not intended to conquer "this last refuge of nature"[2] but to serve it and the liberal rights based upon it. These rights were not themselves matters of technological will but were solidly rooted in nature. Once the enterprise of reading standards out of nature was begun, however, it proved impossible to limit it to positive standards. As Rousseau pointed out, if man was truly not social and political by nature, then he could not really be anti-social either, for the anti-social passions Hobbes and Locke saw in the state of nature presupposed social life.[3] If teleology was to be excluded, it would not do to fall back on crypto-teleology, reading passions generated by social life back into the state of nature and

215

then, in a circular fashion, deriving social and political principles from them.[4] In a non-teleological world there could be nothing *natural* that would necessarily drive men into society. Thus the passions that for Hobbes and Locke were the natural (and permanent) foundation of rights were reconceived as socially produced. This meant that the rights grounded on these passions could not be "natural" rights. As this insight was progressively unfolded by Rousseau's successors, it eventually became impossible to conceive of any ground for moral categories more solid than simple human will.

This is reflected in the word "values," perhaps the central moral category of our time. Originally an economic term expressing the relativity of supply and demand, "value" was transformed by Nietzsche and Weber into a term that now signifies a more general moral relativity.[5] The only rival to the language of values nowadays is the language of rights. Indeed, when push comes to shove, the rhetoric of rights is preferred; the term "value" seems insubstantial whenever one has something truly important to defend or promote, while the language of rights still carries with it some of the aura of solidity it acquired from its original grounding in nature. This aura is chimerical, however, because it has become difficult to think of rights as anything other than values, or as second order emanations of more fundamental values.[6] In the face of the contemporary inability to provide a more solid foundation for rights, the stubborn attachment to the language of rights may be understood as reflecting the need for a civil religion even among those who, in their constant use of the term "values," unwittingly express the thought that "God is dead." As H.D. Forbes has astutely observed, contemporary liberalism combines "piety about human rights with impiety on every other subject."[7]

The collapse of rights into values means that rights are ultimately whatever we choose or will them to be. This accounts for the unending proliferation of rights and our inability persuasively to deny the label to any claim that wishes to adopt it, thereby robbing the notion of rights of any real significance. As Forbes wittily asks, "if human rights, why not animal rights? And what rights will humans have if they have only the rights of animals?"[8] Modern relativism also helps to explain why "minorities," which are politically more powerful than mere aggregations of individuals, have been able to promote "group rights" at the expense of traditional individual rights, and why the social technology of equal results, which disdains rights as originally conceived, has managed to drape itself in their rhetorical mantle. In a world so conceived, technology cannot be constrained by a particular set of rights (or values);[9] instead, the rhetoric of rights will be used to legitimate whatever technological projects are fashionable. Fashionable, moreover, not among democratic coalitions working through representative institutions—these are by definition tainted by the corrupt system—but among rationalistic, rule-oriented intellectuals and their favoured (i.e., unaccountable) institutions.

Notes

[1] For a discussion of the turning of established "talismanic words" to new purposes, see Thomas Flanagan, "Equal Pay for Work of Equal Value: An Historical Note," *Journal of Canadian Studies*, 22:3 (1987).

[2] Leo Strauss, *Natural Right and History* (Chicago: University of Chicago Press, 1953), 201.

[3] On the question of how Hobbes' state of nature is really a social state see C.B. Macpherson, *Possessive Individualism: Hobbes to Locke* (Oxford: Oxford University Press, 1964), 18-19, 22-29.

[4] See Strauss, *Natural Right and History,* 252-53; Allan Bloom, "Jean-Jacques Rousseau," in Leo Strauss and Joseph Cropsey, eds., *History of Political Philosophy,* 2nd ed. (Chicago: Rand McNally, 1972); Marc F. Plattner, *Rousseau's State of Nature: An Interpretation of the Discourse on Inequality* (DeKalb: Northern Illinois University Press, 1979).

[5] Martin Diamond, "The Dependence of Fact Upon Value," *Interpretation*, 2:3 (1972).

[6] See *R. v. Oakes*, [1986] 1 S.C.R. 103 at 136. This is evident in the leading modern attempts to shore up the liberal doctrine of rights. Ultimately these endeavours are undermined by their inability to transcend cultural and value relativism. See Thomas Pangle's "Rediscovering Rights," *The Public Interest*, (Winter, 1978), 157-60, a review of Ronald Dworkin's *Taking Rights Seriously.* Cf. Fred Baumann, "Affirmative Action: Human Rights at Home," in Marc F. Plattner, ed., *Human Rights in our Time: Essays in Memory of Victor Baras* (Boulder: Westview, 1984), 82-84. This criticism applies to the rights grounded on John Rawl's "original position" rather than on the "state of nature." See George Grant, *English-Speaking Justice* (Toronto: Anansi, 1985), part 2. Cf. Barry Cooper's review of G.B. Madison, *The Logic of Liberty,* in *Canadian Philosophical Reviews* 7:10 (1987), 416-418. See also Jeremy Waldron, ed., *Nonsense Upon Stilts: Bentham, Burke and Marx on the Rights of Man* (New York: Methuen, 1987), 2-3.

[7] H.D. Forbes, "The Doctors of Desire," *The Idler* 13(1987), 22.

[8] *Ibid.*

[9] Cf. George Grant, *Technology and Justice* (Toronto: Anansi, 1987) ch. 1.

A COMMENT ON *ANDREWS* V. *LAW SOCIETY OF BRITISH COLUMBIA*[1]

The Supreme Court handed down its decision in *Andrews*, its first major section 15 case, just as this book went to press. Instead of integrating discussion of the case into the body of the work, therefore, I have had to content myself with this brief appendix.

Andrews wished to practice law in British Columbia and had met all the standards for admission to the bar except for the requirement of Canadian citizenship contained in section 42(a) of the *Barristers and Solicitors Act*. He argued that this legislative discrimination against non-citizens infringed section 15 of the *Charter*. Since "citizenship" is not one of the prohibited grounds of discrimination explicitly enumerated by section 15, the case raised questions about the reach of that section's open-ended wording. The Court unanimously agreed that the citizenship requirement violated section 15 but divided on the question of whether it could be saved as a "reasonable limit" under section 1: five of the six-judge panel[2] concluded that it could not be so defended; Justice McIntyre, who wrote the controlling opinion on most other issues, dissented on this section 1 question.

In terms of the analysis of this book, two facets of the case stand out. First, the Court attempted to reduce the number of potential section 15 challenges by placing some limits on the open-endedness of section 15; second, it applied the systemic definition of discrimination it had adopted in *O'Malley* and *Bhinder* to the constitutional realm. If the argument of chapter six has merit, these two elements of the judgment are contradictory.

In particular, the systemic definition of discrimination indirectly removes the limits the Court has tried to place on the list of prohibited grounds. The point of capping the list of grounds was to restrict the scope of judicial second guessing of inherently debatable legislative policy choices; the systemic definition of discrimination undermines this restriction.

Closing the Front Door on Section 15

The Court was obviously concerned about the potential for the open-ended wording of section 15 to force the judicial evaluation of almost all legislation. This would occur especially if the term "discrimination" were interpreted in a neutral fashion as meaning simply "distinction," and if the open-ended phraseology were taken literally to cover all distinctions. Most laws make distinctions and would, under such an interpretation, violate section 15;[3] they could thus be sustained only as "reasonable limits" under section 1. Although such an interpretation had been suggested by leading commentators, it was too daunting for the Court. Justice La Forest, for example, could not "accept that all legislative classifications must be rationally supportable before the courts" because this would involve the judicial assessment of "much economic and social policy-making [that] is simply beyond the institutional competence of the courts." The proper judicial role, he said, "is to protect against incursions on fundamental values, not to second guess policy decisions."

Writing for a unanimous court on this point, Justice McIntyre reduced the potential for violating section 15 by placing two limitations upon its scope. First, he held that "discrimination" did not mean merely "distinction" but required the showing of some harm or prejudice. Second, he restricted the reach of the open-ended wording to grounds "analogous" to the enumerated grounds. (In the case at hand, all of the judges agreed that "citizenship" was such an analogous ground because of its close ties to national and ethnic origin.) These qualifications on the scope of section 15 were designed to ensure that some legislative distinctions will not violate the Charter's equality rights and will thus not have to defend themselves under section 1 as "reasonable limits...demonstrably justified in a free and democratic society."

Judicial Second Guessing Under a Closed List of Prohibited Grounds

If all legislative discrimination on the enumerated or analogous grounds violated "fundamental values" and was thus properly subject to "strict scrutiny," one might plausibly conclude, with Justice La Forest, that this capping of section 15 precludes judicial "second guessing." This will not be the case, however, to the extent that the included grounds attract some form of intermediate scrutiny, for intermediate scrutiny occurs precisely when reasonable differences of opinion are possible within the framework of "fundamental values."[4]

There was some debate among the judges about the level of scrutiny appropriate to the enumerated and analogous grounds. The question arose in the context of section 1 considerations. The Court, in its nationalism, preferred not to use the "American" terminology of levels of scrutiny, but the substantive concerns underlying the labels really could not be avoided. Indeed, it was partly to restrict section 15 to situations requiring higher levels of scrutiny that the Court limited the section to enumerated and analogous grounds. This was especially evident in the opinion of Justices Dickson, Wilson and L'Heureux-Dubé. Writing for this group, Justice Wilson addressed the question whether the methodology for deciding section 1 questions established in *The Queen* v. *Oakes*[5] was too stringent to apply in the context of section 15. *Oakes* had established a two-stage section 1 inquiry. The first stage required the government to show that the purpose of the legislation was sufficiently "pressing and substantial" to justify the infringement of a *Charter* right. The "pressing and substantial" formulation obviously sets a high standard and, as Justice Wilson recognized, "If every distinction between individuals and groups gave rise to a violation of s. 15, then this standard might well be too stringent for application in all cases and might deny the community at large the benefits associated with sound and desirable social and economic legislation." Justice Wilson argued, however, that the "pressing and substantial" requirement "remains an appropriate standard when it is recognized that not every distinction between individuals and groups will violate s. 15"—when it is recognized, in other words, that the section covers only enumerated and analogous grounds. These grounds deserve to be subject to the strict-scrutiny standard of demonstrating a "pressing and substantial" purpose.

The other three judges, writing through Justice McIntyre, disagreed.[6] Justice McIntyre thought the "pressing and substantial" standard, if applied in all cases, would indeed "frequently deny the community-at-large the benefits associated with sound social and economic legislation." It was sometimes enough, in his view, that the legislation sought to attain "a *desirable* social objective which would warrant overriding constitutionally protected rights."[7] As regards legislative purpose, then, Justice McIntyre clearly thought that some lesser degree of scrutiny should sometimes be substituted for the strict scrutiny implied by the "pressing and substantial" standard. Thus, although Justice McIntyre formulated the "enumerated and analogous grounds" restriction, he must have thought that not all of these grounds deserved strict scrutiny.

Justice McIntyre's conclusion may have been influenced by the perception of significant differences among the grounds covered by section 15. Even if the section were limited to the enumerated grounds, for example, the presence of age and handicap would mean that some prohibited distinctions should not have to meet a strict-scrutiny standard. Some of the "analogous" grounds are bound to raise difficulties similar to those posed by age and handicap. Presumably the grounds that would receive "minimal scrutiny" have been excluded by the "enumerated and analogous" restriction, but the newly capped list is not restricted to grounds always entitled to strict scrutiny; Justice McIntyre's approach seems to recognize that intermediate scrutiny is inevitable in section 15 questions.

In a sense this disagreement about how weighty a legislative purpose must be to meet the criteria of section 1 may be of greater symbolic than practical significance. According to *Oakes*, if the purpose of a challenged law passes muster, the courts then consider whether the legislative means are proportional to that purpose. This proportionality test is used to determine whether the legislature has tailored its means to achieve the end with as little infringement of *Charter* rights as possible. As Patrick Monahan points out, it is highly unlikely that legislation will ever fail the purpose test—even if the test is formulated in terms of the "pressing and substantial" standard—because disagreeing with the legislature over the importance of its policy objectives would make it impossible for the courts to pretend that they were not involved in second guessing political choices. It will be easier for the courts to maintain the façade of legalism, Monahan argues, if, in failing a piece of legislation under section 1, they concede the importance of the legislative objective and restrict themselves to arguing that the legislature should choose more finely tuned policy instruments.[8] Thus far Monahan appears to be right: no legislation has been invalidated because it has failed to meet the compelling purpose test. And even in this case, despite her insistence on maintaining the "pressing and substantial" formulation for section 15 cases, Justice Wilson strikes the legislation down because it fails the proportional means test.[9] Thus the "pressing and substantial" formulation might represent "strict scrutiny" only in theory. Nevertheless, the debate about the appropriateness of even a largely symbolic representation of strict scrutiny testifies to the importance of the underlying issue. The levels-of-scrutiny debate will find its practical outlet somewhere, if not in the application of the purpose test, then in the application of the proportional means test.

The proportional means test requires the balancing of a host of factors. As Justice McIntyre put it:

> The Court must examine the nature of the right, the extent of its infringement, and the degree to which the limitation furthers the attainment of the desirable goal embodied in the legislation. Also involved in the inquiry will be the importance of the right to the individual or group concerned, and the broader social impact of both the inpugned law and its alternatives.

Justice McIntyre also quoted Justice Dickson's remark in *Edwards Books* that "in describing the criteria comprising the proportionality requirement the Court has been careful to avoid rigid and inflexible standards." McIntyre concluded that "There is no single test under s. 1; rather, the Court must carefully engage in the balancing of many factors in determining whether an infringement is reasonable and demonstrably justified." Justice La Forest agreed, although he preferred "to think in terms of a single test for s. 1, but one that is to be applied to vastly differing situations with the flexibility and realism inherent in the word 'reasonable' mandated by the Constitution."[10] Clearly, there is room in these formulations for a "sliding scale" of scrutiny that will enable the courts to save some distinctions on the enumerated and analogous grounds while striking down others. Some degree of inter-mediate scrutiny, and thus judicial second guessing, is inevitable under section 15.

Opening the Back Door

Although the limitation of section 15 to enumerated and anal-ogous grounds cannot solve the problem of second guessing, it can be understood as a way of restricting its scope by placing some kinds of legislative discrimination completely beyond the reach of section 15. The Court's attempt to close the door some-what on the open-endedness of section 15 is vitiated, however, by its "systemic" interpretation of the term "discrimination." Extending its interpretation of human rights legislation to the constitutional realm, the Court finds that the prohibited (i.e., harm-causing) discrimination against those defined by the enu-merated or analogous grounds need not be intentional. In other words, legislative distinctions not based directly on the appar-ently limited list of prohibited grounds may yet be reached because of their disparate impact on groups defined by that list. As I argued at length in chapter six, because indirect discrimina-tion against one group is always direct discrimination against another, the prohibition of systemic discrimination can be under-stood as an indirect way of opening an apparently closed list of prohibited grounds. Moreover, it should not be difficult to find some overlap between almost any legislative distinction and one of the enumerated or yet-to-be-defined analogous grounds and thus to establish a *prima facie* case of systemic discrimination.

In principle, the restriction to enumerated and analogous grounds establishes a "closed" list of prohibited grounds, though the precise contents of that list remain rather indeterminate and depend on what is bound to be a controversial process of estab-lishing an appropriate analogy. The problems of defining the con-tents of this apparently closed list are compounded when even non-analogous grounds are indirectly covered by a systemic interpretation of discrimination. In fact, the Court's attempt to rein in the open-endedness of section 15 is thoroughly under-mined by this interpretation. If the systemic definition of discrim-ination is taken seriously, the vulnerability of the vast majority of legislative distinctions to section 15 challenges will remain unaffected by the ostensible limitation of the section to enumerated and analogous grounds. Instead of being beyond the reach of section 15, many apparently excluded distinctions will not only be indirectly covered but will become subject to a level of scrutiny somewhere in the "intermediate" range. Of the two qualifications to the meaning of section 15, only the stipulation that discrimination (direct or systemic) must have a harmful or prejudicial effect remains to save a legislative distinction from justification under section 1—and the question of whether harm is caused is also likely to be controversial.

Conclusion

We have seen that the attempt to limit the scope of section 15 was, in Justice La Forest's words, to ensure that the courts stick to their role of protecting "fundamental values" rather than second guessing debatable policy decisions. One of the arguments of this book has been that even if section 15 were restricted to the explicitly enumerated grounds it would be impossible to avoid the kind of second guessing that worries Justice La Forest. Legislative distinctions based on the enumerated grounds (and this does not include only distinctions based on age and handicap) often pose issues that, far from being settled by a societal consensus on "fundamental values," are open to legitimate debate among reasonable people.[11] This is bound to be equally true of the "analogous" grounds. The limitation to enumerated and analogous grounds cannot do away with judicial second guessing, as Justice La Forest's rhetoric implies, but it represents a healthy judicial inclination to restrict the scope for such second guessing. Unfortunately, the adoption of a systemic definition of discrimination dissolves this limitation.

Notes

[1] At the time of writing the judgment is unreported. I have worked from an unpaginated preliminary version secured through the "on line" services of *Quick Law.* Hence I have not supplied references to this case.

[2] Justice Le Dain was on the panel but took no part in the judgment.

[3] Justice McIntyre, following the court below, uses the example of laws forbidding children or drunk persons from driving.

[4] Justice McIntyre recognized this when he addressed the question whether the law was saved by section 1. In determining whether a law is a reasonable limit, he said, it is important for the courts to remember that "When making distinctions between groups and individuals to achieve desirable social goals, it will rarely be possible to say of any legislative distinction that it is clearly the right legislative choice or that it is clearly a wrong one."

[5] [1986] 1 S.C.R. 103.

[6] Justice McIntyre wrote for Justice Lamer. Justice La Forest wrote a separate opinion, which concurred in the result arrived at by Justices Dickson, Wilson and L'Heureux-Dubé but agreed with Justice McIntyre's interpretive approach in most other respects, including this one.

[7] Emphasis added.

[8] Patrick Monahan, *Politics and the Constitution: The Charter, Federalism and the Supreme Court* (Toronto: Carswell/Methuen, 1987), 62-68.

[9] Because it "is not carefully tailored" to achieve such legitimate objectives as ensuring "familiarity with Canadian institutions and customs," "a real attachment to Canada," and the proper performance of the important governmental functions carried out by the legal profession.

[10] Disagreement on the proportionality test arose not so much in defining its components as in applying them to the case at hand.

[11] See the concluding discussion of chapter six.

Index

Animism (*See* Constructivism, animistic fallacy)

Anti-Discrimination Law (*See also* Discrimination; Systemic Discrimination—Prohibitions Of; Human Rights Commissions)
  human rights legislation
    administrative model 35-36, 48, 49-50
    areas covered 37, 39
    criminal-law model 36, 46, 49
    exemptions 40, 44, 52, 55, 66n, 68n, 165-166, 179n
    historical development 36-40
    life-cycle grounds 75-76, 79-81, 84, 123
    life-style grounds 75, 76-77, 80, 81-83, 84, 123
    open-ended prohibitions 39, 85-86, 95, 110, 116, 117, 148, 151, 163
    proliferation of prohibited grounds 10, 24-26, 39, 64, 65n, 71, 74-75, 86-89, 116, 148
    reasonable accommodation 54-56, 64, 68n
    stigmatic grounds 75, 76, 77-79, 83, 84, 93, 94, 123
  section 15 of the Charter 35, 42-44
    open-ended prohibition 43, 44, 167, 219, 220, 221, 224

Attorney General of Canada v. *Lavell and Bedard* 42, 43, 152

Attorney-General of Quebec v. *Quebec Association of Protestant School Boards* 180n

Bhinder v. *Canadian National Railways* 51, 54, 55, 67n, 68n, 146, 219

Bigotry (*See* Prejudice)

Bliss v. *Attorney-General of Canada* 42, 43

Board of Education v. *Barnette* 143n

Bona Fide Occupational Qualification (*See* Anti-Discrimination Law, human rights legislation: exemptions

Bone v. *Hamilton Tiger Cats Football Club* 68n

Brooks v. *Canada Safeway Ltd.* 178n

Brown v. *Board of Education* 151, 152, 198

Canadian Bill of Rights 41-42, 43, 152

Carson v. *Air Canada* 179n

Central Alberta Dairy Pool v. *Alberta Human Rights Commission* 68n

Central Okanagan School District No. 23 v. *Renaud* 68n